Composing
in a
Second Language

Sandra McKay
San Francisco State University

NEWBURY HOUSE PUBLISHERS, INC.
ROWLEY, MASSACHUSETTS 01969
ROWLEY • LONDON • TOKYO

1984

Library of Congress Cataloging in Publication Data

McKay, Sandra.
    Composing in a second language.

    1. English language--Study and teaching--Foreign
speakers.   I. Title.
PE1128.A2M39   1984   808'.042   82-22099
ISBN 0-88377-390-2

Cover design by Jean Ploss

NEWBURY HOUSE PUBLISHERS, INC.

Language Science
Language Teaching
Language Learning

ROWLEY, MASSACHUSETTS 01969
ROWLEY • LONDON • TOKYO

Printed in the U.S.A.

First printing: February 1984
5   4   3   2

Acknowledgments

Content and Written Form: A Two-Way Street. By Barry Taylor. 1981. *TESOL Quarterly* 15, 1:5–13. Copyright 1981 by Teachers of English to Speakers of Other Languages. Reprinted by permission of the publisher and the author. Barry Taylor is Director of the English Program for Foreign Students at the University of Pennsylvania.

Writer-Based Prose: A Cognitive Basis for Problems in Writing. By Linda Flower. 1979. *College English* 41, 1:19–37. Reprinted by permission of the publisher and author. Linda Flower is a member of the Department of English at Carnegie-Mellon University.

Cultural Thought Patterns in Inter-cultural Education. By Robert Kaplan. 1966. *Language Learning* 16:1–20. Reprinted by permission of the publisher and author. Robert Kaplan is Professor of Linguistics at the University of Southern California.

Reading Research and the Composition Teacher: The Importance of Plans. By Bonnie Meyer. 1982. *College Composition and Communication* 33, 1:37–49. Reprinted by permission of the publisher and author. Bonnie Meyer is Associate Professor of Educational Psychology at Arizona State University.

Thunder and Lightning. From *African Myths and Legends* retold by Kathleen Arnott, Copyright 1962 by Kathleen Arnott. Reprinted by permission of Oxford University Press.

Anguish As a Second Language? Remedies for Composition Teachers. By Ann Raimes. In A. Freedman, I. Pringle, and J. Yalden (eds.). *Learning to Write: First Language/Second Language*. New York, Longman, 1983, pp. 258–272. Reprinted by permission of the publisher and author. Ann Raimes is the Coordinator of the English for Bilingual Students Program at Hunter College, the City University of New York.

The Use and Abuse of Models in the ESL Writing Class. By Cynthia Watson-Reekie. 1982. *TESOL Quarterly* 16, 1:5–14. Copyright 1982 by Teachers of English to Speakers of Other Languages. Reprinted by permission of the publisher and author. Cynthia Watson-Reekie teaches ESL in Edinburgh, Scotland.

Contents

Introduction

As a composition teacher you will be faced with the challenging task of helping your students learn to write effectively in their second language. The purpose of this text is to explore several important issues related to this task. One issue which will be addressed in the text is the question of what composition is. Composition has been defined in a variety of ways. Included in these definitions are certain recurring terms such as thinking process, style, organization, form, and correctness. The lack of consensus as to what exactly composition is reflects the complexity of the process. Traditionally definitions of composition have clustered around two major poles—one which emphasizes the ideas and thought processes involved in writing and the other which emphasizes the form of the ideas. For a long time research in composition focused on form and investigated the composed product. Current research in composition tends to emphasize the composing process by investigating the strategies writers utilize in attaining the final product. This type of research has been valuable in demonstrating the fact that writing is not a linear process; it is rather a dynamic and recursive process which involves such activities as generating ideas, setting goals, planning, evaluating, and revising. Clearly, the more we can learn about the process of composing and how this process differs in a second-language situation, the more effective we will be as teachers.

Another issue that will be explored in the text is the issue of methodology. Much of the literature in ESL composition has tended to support one of two major approaches to writing: free composition in which quantity is taken as the primary measure of success and controlled composition in which correctness of form is viewed as the major criterion of success. The first approach reflects a concern with the content of writing, while the second demonstrates a concern with form. Unfortunately, some teachers and material developers have viewed these two dimensions of composition as somehow mutually exclusive. Thus, there are materials which deal only with the thought-generating aspect of writing with minimal attention to form, and others which emphasize form to the exclusion of content. One goal of this text will be to help you achieve a balance between these two aspects of writing in your teaching.

Finally, as a composition teacher you will be faced with the difficult task of evaluating compositions. Because of this, another issue that will be explored in the text is the question of what our role as essay evaluators should be. Much of the literature on evaluating has tended to focus on correctness of form. However, since effective writing involves a good deal more than mere accuracy of form, we cannot, in our role as evaluators, limit ourselves to this aspect of composing. Rather, we need to respond to essays in a fashion which will help our students to clarify and elaborate on their ideas, as well as to express these ideas in an appropriate and correct form.

All the articles included in the text deal with one of the major issues discussed above, namely, theories of composition, teaching strategies, or evaluating essays. Each article in the text is followed by a variety of suggested activities. These activities were designed to complement the special emphasis of the particular article rather than to adhere to a set format in the text. Thus, while some of the articles are followed by activities which primarily involve evaluating essays, others are followed by exercises which involve designing teaching materials or discussing and applying the theoretical assumptions of the article. All the exercises, however, begin with a presentation of relevant background material, either from the article itself or from articles which deal with related topics. This background information is followed by an application task which asks you to respond to some theoretical issue or to undertake some limited research or material development. It may be that you will be assigned to do a particular task or given a choice to answer one of the questions following a specific article. In any case, it is important that you share your work with other students in the class and, if possible, use your materials and the correction strategies presented in the text with ESL students.

The articles in Section 1, Theory, address the question of what occurs when a person composes. The focus of all of them is on the process involved in composing rather than on the product. Taylor, in keeping with an emphasis on process, argues for an experiential based writing program, while Flower makes an important distinction between writing written for the author (writer-based prose) and writing written with the reader in mind (reader-based prose). Flower presents a convincing argument that writer-based prose is an important step in the formation of a well-developed text. In the next article, Kaplan sets forth a stimulating hypothesis about second-language composing in which he contends that the writing of nonnative speakers exemplifies a rhetorical pattern which is entirely different from English prose. Finally, Meyer discusses the implications of her research on reading and rhetorical plans for the teaching of composition. In the suggested activities, you will be asked to undertake a number of projects related to a process model of composition such as examining your own strategies for composing, as well as those of nonnative writers, evaluating compositions in light of various theories of composition, and developing teaching materials to help students find topics to write about.

The articles in Section 2, Teaching Strategies, present a variety of perspectives for developing classroom materials. Raimes maintains that a teacher's most important task is to help students find something to say. In her article she describes a series of techniques for providing students with writing topics, among these the use of reading models. Watson-Reekie, in "The Use and Abuse of Models in the ESL Writing Class," discusses the advantages of using models in ESL classes and makes several suggestions as to how to use them. In the next article, Zamel outlines several techniques for dealing with an often-ignored element of composing, namely, the use of linking devices. Finally, Weissberg and Buker discuss specific strategies for teaching composition to students in the field of science and technology. In the suggested activities for this group of readings, you will be encouraged to develop classroom materials which are described in the readings.

The articles in Section 3, Evaluating, address what is perhaps the most troublesome aspect of ESL composition teaching, namely, evaluating essays. Kroll and Schafer describe the implications of the process model of composition for approaching errors. In addition, they point out that the same error can be due to a variety of causes and may thus warrant different solutions. In the suggested activities, you will be asked to analyze a variety of student errors in terms of possible causes and solutions. Hendrickson, in "The Treatment of Error in Written Work," describes several techniques for correcting essays. As a way of applying his strategies, the suggested activities for this article contain several essays which are to be corrected according to his method. Finally, Sommers in her article makes a convincing argument that the primary benefit of teachers' comments is to help students first rethink what they are saying and then evaluate how they are saying it. As a follow-up activity for this article, you will be asked to respond to essays in a way which helps students rethink and evaluate their own work.

While the readings in the text present an introduction to the central issues of what composition is and how to approach it in the classroom, the exercises provide you as a prospective teacher with an equally essential component of your training, namely, the opportunity to explore these topics for yourself.

This collection would not have been possible without the help of several people. I wish to express my special appreciation to John Dennis for his help and encouragement in undertaking this project. I am also grateful to the contributors of this volume for granting me permission to reprint their work; to Barbara Kroll and Elizabeth Lantz for their constructive suggestions; to my graduate students, especially William Rindfleisch, for their careful work and insightful comments in field testing the materials; and finally, to my ESL students for helping me learn something about the process of teaching composition.

Composing
in a
Second Language

1 THEORY

In the past, the field of composition emphasized the composed product rather than the composing process. Thus, the focus of researchers and teachers tended to be on analyzing and classifying written discourse. Presently the focus is on the composing process rather than the product. This shift in paradigms has led to new questions for investigation. In general, the thrust of current research has been to discover what it is that proficient writers do when they compose. A major method for investigating this question has been to get proficient writers to describe what it is they do when they compose. Whether or not individuals can or do give an accurate description of their writing process is not easy to ascertain. In addition, even if individuals can accurately account for their procedure in writing one essay, this process will undoubtedly vary from writing task to writing task and from individual to individual. Furthermore, in terms of ESL composition, it is possible that writers will follow quite a different process in writing an essay in their second language as opposed to their native language.

Nonetheless, current research on the composing process suggests several general conclusions. First, the process of writing rarely proceeds in a linear fashion. Various components of writing such as generating ideas, organizing, and editing are called into play throughout the writing process. In addition, the manner in which each aspect is utilized varies from individual to individual and from task to task. The complexity of the writing process makes it clear that we will not be able to give our students simple formulas for good writing. What we can do is to engender in our students an awareness of the complexity of the writing process and help them better manipulate each component of the process in order to meet their specific writing objectives.

The articles and activities which follow are designed to help you explore several important theoretical questions. First, what processes and strategies do writers tend to follow as they work to achieve a finished product? What special difficulties do writers face in attempting to compose in a second language? Are there certain types of writing, such as narrative or descriptive writing, which are

1

less difficult to master than others? If so, why? And finally, what are the implications of research in reading for composition instruction?

Such questions are not easy to answer, but to the extent that they demonstrate the complexity of the composing process, they will make us hesitant about accepting simple solutions to the teaching of composition. The relationship between theory and practice has always been and will continue to be a difficult one to define. Clearly, the things we need to know about the composing process will not always be directly applicable to the classroom. However, the insights we gain from examining some of these difficult theoretical questions are essential to the selection and design of effective teaching methods.

1

Content and Written Form:
A Two-Way Street

Barry P. Taylor

There is a fairly common practice in language teaching wherein students are taught to outline their essays before they actually write. This activity is based on the presumption that writing is a one-way process of recording, on paper, ideas which are already well thought out and carefully organized. The validity of this premise is brought into question by the following example:

Dear Ann Landers:
I am a boy who is 12 years of age. I did something my parents didn't think was right and as punishment they made me stay home from a ball game I was dying to see. The tickets were bought and everything. They took my cousin instead of me.
I decided they were terrible to treat me so bad and I started to pack my suitcase to run away. I finished packing and I thought maybe I should write a goodbye letter. I wanted my folks to know why I was running away. I got to thinking about lots of things as I was writing and decided I ought to be very fair and apologize for a few things I had done that weren't right.
After I started to write I thought of lots of things that needed apologizing for. I then began to thank them for the nice things they had done for me and there seemed to be an awful lot of them.
By the time I finished writing the letter, I unpacked my suitcase and tore up what I wrote.
I hope all kids who think they want to run away from home will sit down and write a letter to their parents like I did and then they won't go.
—A Rotten Kid
(From *The Philadelphia Inquirer*, September 9, 1978)

As this passage clearly illustrates, writing is not the straightforward *plan-outline-write* process that many of us believe it to be. Quite the contrary. Research on the composing process does not in fact support the claims made by many college composition texts that writing is simply a process of filling in a prepared outline and that rewriting involves only correcting grammar and usage errors (Cooper and Odell 1978). Britton (1978), for example, even suggests that not only does outlining or advance planning not guarantee success but it may also even militate against it. As Flower and Hayes (1977:457) have noted, "a writer's normal task is a thinking task."

Although it is certainly true that advance planning can be valuable in essay writing, the traditional teaching model ignores what research had shown to be a fundamental characteristic of the composing process: The art of writing, in addition to reflecting thought, can itself serve as a facilitator of thought and may in fact even help the writer in the process of writing to shape and refine ideas which are not yet fully formed. One may therefore view essay writing as a simultaneous two-way street—a dynamic, creative process of give and take between content and written form.

Donald Murray (1968, 1978) argues that our profession's traditional, long-standing emphasis of product over process in writing has created serious misconceptions about how writing is produced. He suggests that the act of writing, upon examination, turns out to be a complex process wherein writers use language as a tool to discover and clarify meaning in experience in order to say exactly what they want.

A study by Perl (1979) of the composing processes of five unskilled college writers provides empirical evidence to support these observations. Perl discovered, for example, that frequently her subjects "began writing without any secure sense of where they were heading, acknowledging only that they would 'figure it out' as they went along" (Perl 1979:330–331). She concluded that by seeing their ideas on paper her subjects were able to reflect upon, change, and develop their ideas further. By accumulating discrete bits and then reworking them, Perl's subjects were able to express more fully what they wanted to say.

Writing then is a creative discovery procedure characterized by the dynamic interplay of content and language: the use of language to explore beyond the known content. Although writers do plan, they are obliged to adapt their strategies as they write (Murray 1978, Perl 1979); the process itself frequently results in the creation of an entity which had no shape or configuration prior to the act of composing and may well assume a form which its author has not foreseen. As Perl (1979:331) has pointed out,

> Composing always involves some measure of both construction and discovery. . . . Rereading or backward movements become a way of assessing whether or not the words on the page adequately capture the original sense intended. Constructing simultaneously affords discovery. Writers know more fully what they mean only after having written it. In this way the explicit written form serves as a window on the implicit sense with which one began.

Central to this view of writing as a discovery procedure is revision, a skill all but ignored in the literature on composing and largely unexplored in most writing programs. Unfortunately, many inexperienced writers have a mistaken sense of failure if they cannot produce a polished essay on their first attempt; this negative attitude then leads to the serious misconception that rewriting is a punishment for that failure (Murray 1978). Furthermore, although the process of revision actually gives writers unlimited opportunities to reshape their essays, revision is too often confused with cosmetic editing or proofreading (Beach 1976, 1979; Emig 1971). The extent to which revision can play a role in writing is rarely made explicit to students. It is therefore no small wonder that much of what students submit more closely resembles rough drafts than finished essays. Revision, however, is that crucial point in the process when discovery and organization come together, when writers refine and recast what they have written and shape it into a coherent written statement.

Murray (1978) identifies two distinct kinds of revision: internal and external. Through internal revision writers concentrate on fully exploring what has been discovered on the page and then rework the subject, the information, the arguments, and the structure until they are satisfied that the meaning is successfully communicated. External revision is that briefer final process of preparing the essay for an external audience. It involves concern with style, tone, language, and mechanics.

Inherent in any discussion of composing and revising is the issue of organization: how writers, once they have identified their thoughts, put them together. Recent research designed to investigate the common pedagogical practice of teaching rhetorical patterns and organizational structure through the analysis of well-written models has raised some important questions. Meade and Ellis (1970), for example, found that some of the methods of paragraph development presented and taught in some composition texts did not exist in the actual pieces of writing which they examined. Braddock (1974) discovered that many of our customary assumptions about the use of topic sentences were not supported by his analysis of published expository writing.

While these findings suggest only that the traditionally taught patterns and structures may not accurately reflect actual writing, recent second language acquisition research also suggests that in terms of the actual learning process teaching writing solely by analyzing and studying models may also be questionable.

Kessler et al. (1979), for example, undertook a study designed to describe the interlanguage of Arabic speakers learning English. One of their objectives was to find support for Krashen's (1978) distinction between input and intake, a distinction which suggests that only a subset (intake) of the language to which a learner is exposed (input) is actually utilized in acquiring a second language. The findings from their study "suggest that emergence of grammatical structure does not closely reflect the sequencing followed in the language teaching materials." That is, the work of Kessler et al. supports the view that student learning is governed more by communicative need than by syllabus design, that the need to express meaning is the primary motivating force in language learning, and that form will arise and be acquired out of attempts at communicating.

Although these findings may not be directly applicable to questions concerning the acquisition of organizational patterns in writing, it seems clear at least that we have no more right to assume that analyzing written models with an eye toward teaching the explicit structure of discourse will necessarily improve writing ability any more than to assume that grammar drills will necessarily improve speaking ability (beyond possibly serving a monitoring function). Hatch (1978) claims that the acquisition of syntax may arise out of experiences in oral discourse or experiences in oral communication, and it is possible that the same might be true for written discourse or experiences in communicating in writing.

The view of composing which has emerged from the research we have considered so far is that writing is a discovery procedure which relies heavily on the power of revision to clarify and refine that discovery. This view has raised important questions about three common composition teaching practices: (1) teaching students to fully outline and plan prior to writing rather than using writing as a discovery procedure; (2) teaching revision as a mechanical and formal editing job rather than as a powerful writing tool; and (3) teaching students to fit their ideas into preexisting organizational molds (implying that there is a limited number of supposedly correct ways to organize) rather than teaching them that organization grows out of meaning and ideas. Why, despite research observations and findings which are at variance with these practices, have these pedagogical approaches nevertheless found favor in our classrooms? There are several possible interrelated explanations which we will now consider.

Our central responsibility as teachers of ESL is to teach students to operate effectively in a language which they at best only partially control. The importance which we place on accomplishing this task has naturally determined the attitudes which many of us have adopted regarding the teaching of composition. As long as ESL students continue to have serious written language problems (even though they may be orally proficient), many ESL writing programs will concentrate primarily on teaching language form and correctness, though this practice may well render the student unable to experience the processes of discovery and thorough revision discussed here. For many of us, the formal aspects of writing simply carry more importance, at least for the time being.

We must beware, however, Shaughnessy (1977) among others warns us, about the dangers of adopting these attitudes. She suggests in fact that despite our good intentions many of our teaching practices may actually encourage an "obsession with error" (p. 10). She writes that

so absolute is the importance of error in the minds of many writers that "good writing" to them means "correct writing," nothing more (1977:8). . . . [The student] is aware that he leaves a trail of errors behind him when he writes. He can usually think of little else . . . (1977:7).

And Raimes adds that

we damage that important reader-writer relationship if we pick out in red all the mistakes we can find. . . . We do the writer harm if we are interested solely in the product and not in the process of writing (1979:3–4).

A major result of a writing program which focuses primarily on form is an insufficient emphasis on content which would create the opportunity for students to experience the process of discovering meaning and then of struggling to give it form through revision. Rarely is a writing assignment compelling enough to give students an opportunity to immerse themselves totally in the topic to the extent that they really find that they have something important to say about it. Rarely do writing assignments provide an opportunity for students to communicate ideas of serious interest to them. Writing outside the classroom is motivated by the need of the writer to persuade, or inform, or complain, or express an opinion for any one of a number of purposes. It is goal-oriented (Flower and Hayes 1977) and actively involves the writer. It is purposeful in that it is directed toward a specific audience and is intended to achieve a specific objective or to solve a particular problem or to fulfill a particular function. Classroom writing assignments designed to practice rhetorical form rarely involve the writer so directly. Students rarely experience the struggle of deciding what it is exactly that they want to say and then of making the ideas on paper conform to those in their heads, expressed as clearly and persuasively as possible. Classroom writing rarely requires any commitment on the part of the students. As Flower and Hayes (1977) point out, "when inspiration breaks down, it's a grim picture for both the writer who has to grind something out and for the reader (teacher) who has to pretend it resembles serious thought" (1977:452).

There is no real reason why inspiration should break down if we can accept that language need not be a major stumbling block to successful ESL composition and that an ESL student need not have to be able to generate a perfect, eloquently flowing piece of writing the first time around to be a successful academic writer. And, lest we think that students are the only victims of this mystique about writing, we should consider Murray's (1978) anecdote about a philosophy professor who, after reading one of Murray's writing texts,

confessed that he had been ashamed of the way he wrote, that he didn't know what to say or how to say it when he sat down to write. He had to write and write and write to find out what he had to say. He was embarrassed and didn't want his colleagues to know how dumb he was (1978:87).

This attitude has heavily influenced most writing instruction. One wonders how many composition courses are taught according to our notions of how we think people should write rather than how they actually do.

Thus far we have examined some of the recent insights resulting from research in composing and have related those insights to composition teaching practices. To what extent are these observations, gleaned from work with native speakers of English, applicable to the teaching of composition to ESL students? Although it is clear that ESL students have their own particular language problems which require attention, we must recognize that writing as a process is only partially linguistic. Regardless of language proficiency, a writer also needs to master the essentially nonlinguistic intellectual and cognitive skills which underlie writing (Taylor 1976: 310–311). Since so many ESL students never acquire a proficiency even approaching that of a native speaker, and most only control the language in an incomplete way, we cannot justify indefinitely postponing a pedagogical emphasis on content in favor of form. The reality of the situation suggests that once students are accepted into academic programs they will need to start producing content in writing well before we may feel that their language is ready.

How then can we apply some of these insights to the skill of composing in an ESL writing program? First and foremost, the emphasis in such a program must be on communicating meaning. Simply put, the writer must have something to say. There are several valuable techniques to help writers to identify areas of interest. Root (1979), for example, proposes that students keep daily journals. Although Root's justification for journalkeeping is to provide a nonthreatening, uncorrected, unstructured vehicle for extensive practice in writing, it can also serve writers as a mirror into their interests; that is, what a journalkeeper chooses to personally comment on or react to in a journal undoubtedly identifies a territory of topics of interest. Once that territory has been identified, oral brainstorming and the written brainstorming approach suggested by Flower and Hayes (1977), whereby students write as much as they can without censoring or worrying about how it all fits, might be useful ways for students to immerse themselves in a topic. Writers need to gather more information than they could ever hope to use (Murray 1968), and brainstorming is a way to begin to gather that information.

As students brainstorm in writing, we can expect that they will begin to make generalizations and to see connections and relationships among their observations, thoughts, and facts. And as ideas begin to emerge, the students can begin to narrow down the scope of their topics. The kind of help they will need during this process can be provided through conferences, oral brainstorming, class debates, discussions, and role-playing sessions. In this way the students can come to grips with their topics and learn to identify and test out support for their own arguments.

As the students identify their topics more carefully and specifically, they can then go back through their notes, their journals, and the ideas which they collected during their brainstorming sessions. Once they have found what Britton (1978:21) calls "a way in"—a way of beginning that will both open up the topic and relate it to what the reader anticipates—they can start to write a first draft, not concerning themselves with form but simply with getting ideas down on paper. The written information which has been generated up to this point can serve as data for this manipulation, to be shaped and refined.

What the students will probably not realize at this point is that in these last few steps they have been actively engaged in the processes of discovery and revision. Revision can now begin in earnest as students turn to their teachers and each other for feedback on the content of their writing. Points that are not clear and ideas that are inadequately supported can be pointed out, thought out again, and revised.

It will be necessary for students eventually to learn to be their own critics and to be able to revise without extensive outside input. One of the most crucial skills to acquire in order to make self-revision possible is critical reading. The skills that readers use when they read—judging validity, accuracy, strength of argumentation—are the very skills that writers must acquire in order to be successful at revision (Emig 1978, Petrosky and Brozick 1979, Raimes 1979, White 1978). Writers must read their writing over and over, analyzing it, thinking about it, weighing it as if it were someone else's, with an eye toward testing it objectively. Does it do what it was written to do? Does it work?

Teaching TESL students to acquire writing skills is by no means easy. Learning to write is a complex process that takes long practice and extensive experience (Petrosky and Brozick 1979). Thus there are compelling reasons for starting instruction early and for emphasizing the benefits of continual practice (Taylor 1976). We should also consider the potential advantages of a writing program which is experientially based, one in which the creativity which is basic to writing and the writing process is central and which recognizes that at least at the early stages the act of producing may well be more important than the finished product. In this kind of program the focus is on discovering meaning through various written and oral activities which will lead up to the process of tying those ideas together cohesively in writing.

One significant characteristic of this kind of writing program is its reliance on the writing and revising of original, student-generated material. Although most ESL students who are learning to write in English will actually be called upon to produce more objective/academic writing than writing which is personal, there is evidence (Beach 1979, Perl 1979) to support focusing on personal writing at the early stages of writing instruction, when the skills are first being acquired. In her examination of the composing process of one writer in both objective and personal modes, Perl (1979) found that her subject wrote longer, more correct essays in less time with less planning when he was writing on a personal topic. Rather than offering students assignments which require that they grind out essays on teacher-assigned topics on the spot, or imitate a model, or follow a controlled exercise, it is more effective to teach students to build up from their own written ideas. The notion of revision could hardly be made more explicit than by having students sit down with their own random, isolated sentences and phrases from their journals, debates, and brainstorm sessions and begin to pull them together.

Teaching students how to revise is not easy. Lacking nativelike intuitions about vocabulary, syntax, tone, style, formality, and organizational patterns, students often cannot see problems in their own writing (Beach 1979, Perl 1979) and will need to rely extensively on positive, constructive feedback. While in-class teacher presentations of common grammatical and organizational problems, and analyses of model paragraphs and standard rhetorical devices are practices that undoubtedly have some pedagogical merit, it appears that what will be ultimately more useful for student writers is for them to learn the elements of writing experientially through useful, productive feedback on their own writing. Teacher presentations of standard patterns of organization or discussions on how to support an argument certainly have their place, but there is no guarantee that the necessary skills will be transferred and that the students will be able to draw on the information when they actually need it. Showing students where their own arguments are weak or where their logic breaks down appears to be a more effective approach, according to the research which has been examined.

Once again, extensive daily reading to help students acquire the critical reading skills needed for revision is valuable. This value stems not just from content but also from the exposure it gives students to a variety of culturally appropriate rhetorical and stylistic writing options, organizational patterns, and patterns of logic and support. Extensive reading also fosters vocabulary growth and the acquisition of syntax, all in context. Developing personal intuitions about what good writing looks like through reading, and then practicing and applying those intuitions in writing, is probably the best way for a student to become a self-reliant writer. And that is after all what our goal should be.

EXPLORING THE IDEAS — *Composition evaluation*

ACTIVITY 1

Background   Taylor points out that "many inexperienced writers have a mistaken sense of failure if they cannot produce a polished essay on their first attempt; this negative attitude then leads to the serious misconception that rewriting is a punishment for that failure" (page 4). One technique for encouraging students to revise their papers is to have other students in the class write questions that they would like answered in the essay. Then students revise their papers answering these specific questions. The following essays illustrate this strategy. (The revisions in the second draft are italicized.)

WRITING TOPIC
    Write a paper about something in your life that has changed. It could be an object that you no longer use or that no longer has special meaning for you, a special occasion that you no longer celebrate or that you celebrate in a different way, a hobby or sport that you no longer participate in, a job you no longer work at, or simply an everyday activity that you no longer do or that you do differently. You must comment on how and why this change has affected you. Be sure to use lots of specific details to support your generalizations.

FIRST DRAFT
    One particular thing has changed in my life since I've been in the U.S. is the way I value my education. Before I didn't care about school; I attended school because of my parents' request, and it was required by the Greek government. I didn't realize the importance of my education and how it would help me to make it in our society. Instead of studying I tried to have fun as much as possible because I used to think it is the only way to enjoy life. I did this by spending my allowances uselessly and by buying unimportant and unnecessary things. But now, since I've been in the U.S., I have to budget my money because I get a specific amount of money every month. Therefore, I have to buy only important and useful things. I also realize the importance of my education because without a diploma, in my country, I can't get a good job. The other fact that make me to change my opinion about education is because my father pays for it, so I can't afford not passing my classes. Thus by being in the U.S. I start taking my education seriously by trying to accomplish my goals.

Students' Questions
1. Why don't you find a job for yourself while going to school?
2. What unnecessary things did you buy?
3. What necessary things do you buy?

SECOND DRAFT

One particular thing has changed in my life since I've been in the U.S. is the way I value my education. Before I didn't care about school; I attended school because of my parents' request, and it was required by the Greek government. I didn't realize the importance of my education and how it would help me to make it in our society. Instead of studying I tried to have fun as much as possible because I used to think it is the only way to enjoy life. I did this by spending my allowances uselessly and by buying unimportant and unnecessary things. *For example, I used to buy magazines, clothes that I didn't need, and other things.* But now, since I've been in the U.S., I have to budget my money because I get a specific amount of money every month. *I cannot work because I'm a foreign student, and the immigration does not allow me to work.* Therefore, I have to buy only important and useful things *like books for school, and educational magazines.* I also realize the importance of my education because without a diploma, in my country, I can't get a good job. The other fact that make me to change my opinion about education is because my father pays for it, so I can't afford not passing my classes. Thus by being in the U.S. I start taking my education seriously by trying to accomplish my goals.

Application   Write out several questions that you as a teacher could pose to help the student continue to revise his paper. Be sure to pose questions that would help the student address the issues raised in the writing topic and eliminate irrelevant details. As specified in the assignment, the essay should explain what effect the author's new attitude toward education has had on him.

Applying theoretical concepts

ACTIVITY 1

Background   Taylor points out that Meade and Ellis (1970) found that some of the methods of paragraph development taught in composition texts did not exist in actual pieces of writing. By reviewing virtually all high school texts published in the 1960s, Meade and Ellis determined that the following methods of development are the most commonly discussed: description, comparison, contrast, reasons, examples, definition, and chronology. They then sought to ascertain if writers actually do use these methods of development. They examined three hundred paragraphs from contemporary written material—one hundred from the *Saturday Review,* one hundred from the *Richmond Times-Dispatch,* and one hundred from the *English Journal.*

They discovered that for all three sources, the traditional methods of paragraph development described in textbooks were present less than 50 percent of the time. Based on their investigation, Meade and Ellis concluded that "a paragraph may demand a certain method because it fits the broader context directed . . . by the writer's overall purpose. A method of development may thus enter naturally and without conscious decision" (page 200). However, they point out that teachers often encourage students to choose a method of development and then suit the topic to this method.

Application   Select six intermediate or advanced ESL writing texts and analyze each of them to determine which methods of development are dealt with in each text. Then compare the manner in which one method such as classification or cause-effect is presented in the different textbooks. Finally, point out any examples you find that exemplify Meade and Ellis' criticism of asking students to first select a method of development and then suit the topic to this method rather than vice versa.

ACTIVITY 2

Background   Taylor questions why "many composition courses are taught according to our notion of how we think people should write rather than how they actually do" (page 7). This discrepancy is further illustrated by Emig (1971) in her citing of two accounts of how the writing process proceeds. The first quote is from Warriner's *English Grammar and Composition*, 11, one volume of a widely used series; the second is by Gertrude Stein.

1. A good writer puts words together in correct, smooth sentences, according to the rules of standard usage. He puts sentences together to make paragraphs that are clear and effective, unified, and well developed. Finally, he puts paragraphs together into larger forms of writing—essays, letters, stories, research papers.

In practice, as you know from your own experience, a writer begins with a general plan and ends with details of wording, sentence structure, and grammar. First, he chooses the *subject* of his composition. Second, he tackles the *preparation* of his material, from rough ideas to final outline. Third, he undertakes the *writing* itself, once again beginning with a rough form (the first draft) and ending with a finished form (the final draft) that is as nearly perfect as he can make it.

These three basic stages of composition are almost always the same for any form of writing. Each of the three stages proceeds according to certain definite steps, listed below in order.

a. Choosing and limiting the subject	1. Subject
b. Assembling materials	
c. Organizing materials	2. Preparation
d. Outlining	
e. Writing the first draft	3. Writing
f. Revising	
g. Writing the final draft	

2. You will write . . . if you will write without thinking of the result in terms of a result, but think of the writing in terms of discovery, which is to say the creation must take place between the pen and the paper, not before in a thought or afterwards in a recasting. Yes, before in a thought, but not in careful thinking. It will come if it is there and if you will let it come, and if you have anything you will get a sudden creative recognition. You won't know how it was, even what it is, but it will be creation if it came out of the pen and out of you and not out of an architectural drawing of the thing you are doing. . . . I can tell how important it is to have that creative recognition. You cannot go into the womb to form the child; it is there and makes itself and comes forth whole—and there it is and you have made it and felt it, but it has come itself—and that is creative recognition. Of course you have a little more control over your writing than that; you have to know what you want to get; but when you know that, let it take you and if it seems to take you off the track don't hold back, because that is perhaps where instinctively you want to be and if you hold back and try to be always where you have been before, you will go dry.

Application   When you write, do you follow all the steps set forth by Warriner? Do you address them in that order? Do you agree with Stein that "the creation must take place between the pen and the paper, not before in a thought or afterwards in a recasting"? Write an account of how you typically proceed when you write something. If you find your method of writing differs under different circumstances, be sure to describe what causes it to change and how it changes.

ACTIVITY 3

Background   Taylor argues persuasively for an experientially based writing program. However, as Zamel (1976) points out in her survey of research in ESL composition, there is little evidence to support one method over another. Sommers (1979) makes a similar point in relation to the teaching of composition to native speakers:

> The field of composition is dominated by studies with methodological or pedagogical intentions. For decades, researchers have continued to focus their energies on defending classroom techniques and on trying to solve the proverbial quest—why are students not learning to write and how can we better teach them? The problem with so many of these instructional studies is that they lack a clearly articulated theoretical base and that not only have they yielded very little to development of a theory of the composing process, but also they have restricted our thinking about composition to classroom problems. Researchers have sought to give currency to a discipline without its own theoretical base by grasping on to whatever is culturally or intellectually in vogue—journal-writing, role-playing, bio-feedback; all of these and others have been statistically tested to see what effects these methods might have upon the written product of students. These numerous, and sometimes conflicting, methodological studies have blurred the important distinctions between the teaching of writing and the learning of how to write. We don't really know how a student develops competence in composing, and yet we are inundated with divergent methods of teaching composition.

Application   List two research questions that you believe should be investigated to get at the issue of how students learn to compose in a second language. You might consider questions such as the following: Do proficient ESL writers ever rely on their native language in the composition process? If so, at what stage of the process is it most frequently used? Are there certain types of topics that pose more difficulty for students to write on in their second language? Does a high level of oral proficiency in a second language influence writing proficiency? Then describe how you would design a study to answer your research question.

Teaching strategies

ACTIVITY 1

Background   Taylor maintains that writing outside the classroom is "motivated by the need of the writer to persuade, or inform, or complain, or express an opinion for any one of a number of purposes. It is goal-oriented and actively involves the writer" (page 7). However, writing assignments in the classroom rarely are so compelling.

Application   Describe three different ESL classes. Indicate the cultural background, age, and language proficiency of the students. Then design a writing topic for each situation that you believe would involve the students so they feel they have something important to say. Be sure to explain why you believe it would be a motivating topic.

REFERENCES

Beach, Richard. 1976. Self-Evaluation Strategies of Extensive Revisers and Non-Revisers. *College Composition and Communication* 27, 160–164.

Beach, Richard. 1979. The Effects of Between-Draft Teacher Evaluation versus Student Self-Evaluation on High School Students' Revising of Rough Drafts. *Research in the Teaching of English* 13, 2:111–119.

Braddock, R. 1974. The Frequency and Placement of Topic Sentences in Expository Prose. *Research in the Teaching of English* 8, 287–302.

Britton, James. 1978. The Composing Processes and the Functions of Writing. In C. Cooper and L. Odell (eds.). *Research on Composing*. Urbana, Illinois: National Council of Teachers of English.

Cooper, Charles R., and Lee Odell. 1978. Introduction. In C. Cooper and L. Odell (eds.). *Research on Composing*. Urbana, Illinois: National Council of Teachers of English.

Emig, Janet. 1971. *The Composing Processes of Twelfth Graders*. Urbana, Illinois: National Council of Teachers of English.

Emig, Janet. 1978. Hand, Eye, Brain: Some "Basics" in the Writing Process. In C. Cooper and L. Odell (eds.). *Research on Composing*. Urbana, Illinois: National Council of Teachers of English.

Flower, Linda S., and John R. Hayes. 1977. Problem-Solving Strategies and the Writing Process. *College English* 39, 4:449–461.

Hatch, Evelyn. 1978. Discourse Analysis and Second Language Acquisition. In E. Hatch (ed.). *Second Language Acquisition*. Rowley, Massachusetts: Newbury House Publishers.

Kessler, Carolyn, David C. Harrison, and Curtis W. Hayes. 1979. Teacher Input—Learner Intake: Aspects of Discourse Analysis. Paper presented at the 13th Annual TESOL Convention, Boston, Massachusetts, February 28–March 4, 1979.

Krashen, Stephen. 1978. Individual Variation in the Use of the Monitor. In W. C. Ritchie (ed.). *Second Language Acquisition Research*. New York: Academic Press.

Meade, R., and W. G. Ellis. 1970. Paragraph Development in the Modern Age of Rhetoric. *English Journal* 59, 219–226.

Murray, Donald M. 1968. *A Writer Teaches Writing*. Boston: Houghton Mifflin Company.

Murray, Donald M. 1978. Internal Revision: A Process of Discovery. In C. Cooper and L. Odell (eds.). *Research on Composing*. Urbana, Illinois: National Council of Teachers of English.

Perl, Sondra. 1979. The Composing Processes of Unskilled College Writers. *Research in the Teaching of English* 13, 4:317–336.

Petrosky, Anthony R., and James R. Brozick. 1979. A Model for Teaching Writing Based upon Current Knowledge of the Composing Process. *English Journal* 68, 1:96–101.

Raimes, Ann. 1979. *Problems and Teaching Strategies in ESL Composition*. In *Language in Education: Theory and Practice* 15. Arlington, Virginia: Center for Applied Linguistics.

Root, Christine B. 1979. The Use of Personal Journals in the Teaching of English to Speakers of Other Languages. *TESL Reporter* 12, 2:3.

Shaughnessy, Mina P. 1977. *Errors and Expectations*. New York: Oxford University Press.

Sommers, Nancy. 1979. The Need for Theory in Composition Research. *College Composition and Communication* 30, 1:46.

Taylor, Barry P. 1976. Teaching Composition to Low-Level ESL Students. *TESOL Quarterly* 10, 3:309–319.

White, Ronald V. 1978. Integrating Reading and Writing. *Modern English Teacher* 6, 3:23–26.

Zamel, Vivian. 1976. Teaching Composition in the ESL Classroom: What We Can Learn from Research in the Teaching of English. *TESOL Quarterly* 10, 1:41.

2

Writer-Based Prose: A Cognitive Basis for Problems in Writing

Linda Flower

If writing is simply the act of "expressing what you think" or "saying what you mean," why is writing often such a difficult thing to do? And why do papers that do express what the writer meant (to his or her own satisfaction) often fail to communicate the same meaning to a reader? Although we often equate writing with the straightforward act of "saying what we mean," the mental struggles writers go through and the misinterpretations readers still make suggest that we need a better model of this process. Modern communication theory and practical experience agree; writing prose that actually communicates what we mean to another person demands more than a simple act of self-expression. What communication theory does not tell us is how writers do it.

An alternative to the "think it/say it" model is to say that effective writers do not simply *express* thought but *transform* it in certain complex but describable ways for the needs of a reader. Conversely, we may find that ineffective writers are indeed merely "expressing" themselves by offering up an unretouched and underprocessed version of their own thought. Writer-based prose, the subject of this paper, is a description of this undertransformed mode of verbal expression.

As both a style of writing and a style of thought, writer-based prose is natural and adequate for a writer writing to himself or herself. However, it is the source of some of the most common and pervasive problems in academic and professional writing. The symptoms can range from a mere missing referent or an underdeveloped idea to an unfocused and apparently pointless discussion. The symptoms are diverse, but the source can often be traced to the writer's underlying strategy for composing and to his or her failure to transform private thought into a public, reader-based expression.

In *function*, writer-based prose is a verbal expression written by a writer to himself and for himself. It is the record and the working of his own verbal thought. In its *structure*, writer-based prose reflects the associative, narrative path of the writer's own confrontation with her subject. In its *language*, it reveals her use of privately loaded terms and shifting but unexpressed contexts for her statements.

In contrast, reader-based prose is a deliberate attempt to communicate something to a reader. To do that, it creates a shared language and shared context between writer and reader. It also offers the reader an issue-centered rhetorical structure rather than a replay of the writer's discovery process. In its language and structure, reader-based prose reflects the *purpose* of the writer's thought; writer-based prose tends to reflect its *process*. Good writing, therefore, is often the cognitively demanding transformation of the natural but private expressions of writer-based thought into a structure and style adapted to a reader.

This analysis of writer-based prose style and the transformations that create reader-based prose will explore two hypotheses:

1. Writer-based prose represents a major and familiar mode of expression which we all use from time to time. While no piece of writing is a pure example, writer-based prose can be identified by features of structure, function, and style. Furthermore, it shares many of these features with the modes of inner and egocentric speech described by Vygotsky and Piaget. This paper will explore that relationship and look at newer research in an effort to describe writer-based prose as a verbal style which in turn reflects an underlying cognitive process.

2. Writer-based prose is a workable concept which can help us teach writing. As a way to intervene in the thinking process, it taps intuitive communication strategies writers already have, but are not adequately using. As a teaching technique, the notion of transforming one's own writer-based style has proved to be a powerful idea with a built-in method. It helps writers attack this demanding cognitive task with some of the thoroughness and confidence that comes from an increased and self-conscious control of the process.

My plan for this paper is to explore writer-based prose from a number of perspectives. Therefore, the next section, which considers the psychological theory of egocentrism and inner speech, is followed by a case study of writer-based prose. I will then pull these practical and theoretical issues together to define the critical features of writer-based prose. The final section will look ahead to the implications of this description of writer-based prose for writers and teachers.

Inner Speech and Egocentrism   In studying the developing thought of the child, Jean Piaget and Lev Vygotsky both observed a mode of speech which seemed to have little social or communicative function. Absorbed in play, children would carry on spirited elliptical monologues which they seemed to assume others understood, but which in fact made no concessions to the needs of the listener. According to Piaget, in Vygotsky's synopsis, "In egocentric speech, the child talks only about himself, takes no interest in his interlocutor, does not try to communicate, expects no answers, and often does not even care whether anyone listens to him. It is similar to a monologue in a play: The child is thinking aloud, keeping up a running accompaniment, as it were, to whatever he may be doing."[1] In the seven-year-olds Piaget studied, nearly 50 percent of their recorded talk was egocentric in nature.[2] According to Piaget, the child's "noncommunicative" or egocentric speech is a reflection, not of selfishness, but of the child's limited ability to "assume the point of view of the listener: [the child] talks of himself, to himself, and by himself."[3] In a sense, the child's cognitive capacity has locked her in her own monologue.

When Vygotsky observed a similar phenomenon in children he called it "inner speech" because he saw it as a forerunner of the private verbal thought adults carry on. Furthermore, Vygotsky argued, this speech is not simply a by-product of play; it is the tool children use to plan, organize, and control their activities. He put the case quite strongly: "We have seen that egocentric speech is not suspended in a void but is directly related to the child's practical dealings with the real world . . . it enters as a constituent part into the process of rational activity" (*Thought and Language*, p. 22).

The egocentric talk of the child and the mental, inner speech of the adult share three important features in common. First, they are highly elliptical. In talking to oneself, the psychological subject of discourse (the old information to which we are adding new predicates) is always known. Therefore, explicit subjects and referents disappear. Five people straining to glimpse the bus need only say, "Coming!" Second, inner speech frequently deals in the sense of words, not their more specific or limited public meanings. Words become "saturated with sense" in much the way a key word in a poem can come to represent its entire, complex web of meaning. But unlike the word in the poem, the accrued sense of the word in inner speech may be quite personal, even idiosyncratic; it is, as Vygotsky writes, "the sum of all the psychological events aroused in our consciousness by the word" (*Thought and Language*, p. 146).

Finally, a third feature of egocentric/inner speech is the absence of logical and causal relations. In experiments with children's use of logical-causal connectives such as *because, therefore,* and *although*, Piaget found that children have difficulty managing such relationships and in spontaneous speech will substitute a nonlogical, noncausal connective such as *then*. Piaget described this strategy for relating things as *juxtaposition*: "the cognitive tendency simply to link (juxtapose) one thought element to another, rather than to tie them together by some causal or logical relation."[4]

One way to diagnose this problem with sophisticated relationships is to say, as Vygotsky did, that young children often think in *complexes* instead of concepts.[5] When people think in complexes they unite objects into families that really do share common bonds, but the bonds are concrete and factual rather than abstract or logical. For example, the notion of "college student" would be a complex if it were based, for the thinker, on facts such as college students live in dorms, go to classes, and do homework.

Complexes are very functional formations, and it may be that many people do most of their day-to-day thinking without feeling the need to form more demanding complex concepts. *Complexes* collect related objects; *concepts*, however, must express abstract, logical relations. And it is just this sort of abstract, synthetic thinking that writing typically demands. In a child's early years the ability to form complex concepts may depend mostly on developing cognitive capacity. In adults this ability appears also to be a skill developed by training and a tendency fostered by one's background and intellectual experience. But whatever its source, the ability to move from the complexes of egocentric speech to the more formal relations of conceptual thought is critical to most expository writing.

Piaget and Vygotsky disagreed on the source, exact function, and teleology of egocentric speech, but they did agree on the features of this distinctive phenomenon, which they felt revealed the underlying logic of the child's thought. For our case, that may be enough. The hypothesis on which this paper rests is not a developmental one. Egocentric speech, or rather its adult written analogue, writer-based prose, is not necessarily a stage through which a writer must develop or one at which some writers are arrested. But for adults it does represent an available mode of expression on which to fall back. If Vygotsky is right, it may even be closely related to normal verbal thought. It is clearly a natural, less cognitively demanding mode of thought and one which explains why people who can express themselves in complex and highly intelligible modes are often obscure. Egocentric expression happens to the best of us; it comes naturally.

The work of Piaget and Vygotsky, then, suggests a source for the cognitive patterns that underlie writer-based prose, and it points to some of the major features such a prose style would possess. Let us now turn to a more detailed analysis of such writing as a verbal style inadequately suited for the needs of the reader.

Writer-Based Prose: A Case Study of a Transformation   As an introduction to the main features of writer-based prose and its transformations, let us look at two drafts of a progress report written by students in an organizational psychology class. Working as consulting analysts to a local organization, the writers needed to show progress to their instructor and to present an analysis with causes and conclusions to the client. Both readers—academic and professional—were less concerned with what the students did or saw than with *why* they did it and *what* they made of their observations.

To gauge the reader-based effectiveness of this report, skim quickly over Draft 1 and imagine the response of the instructor of the course, who needed to answer these questions: As analysts, what assumptions and decisions did my students make? Why did they make them? At what stage in the project are they now? Or, play the role of the client-reader who wants to know: How did they define my problem, and what did they conclude? As either reader, can you quickly extract the information the report should be giving you? Next, try the same test on Draft 2.

DRAFT 1: GROUP REPORT

(1) Work began on our project with the initial group decision to evaluate the Oskaloosa Brewing Company. Oskaloosa Brewing Company is a regionally located brewery manufacturing

several different types of beer, notably River City and Brough Cream Ale. This beer is marketed under various names in Pennsylvania and other neighboring states. As a group, we decided to analyze this organization because two of our group members had had frequent customer contact with the sales department. Also, we were aware that Oskaloosa Brewing had been losing money for the past five years and we felt we might be able to find some obvious problems in their organizational structure.

(2) Our first meeting, held February 17th, was with the head of the sales department, Jim Tucker. Generally, he gave us an outline of the organization from president to worker, and discussed the various departments that we might ultimately decide to analyze. The two that seemed the most promising and most applicable to the project were the sales and production departments. After a few group meetings and discussions with the personnel manager, Susan Harris, and our advisor Professor Charns, we felt it best suited our needs and the Oskaloosa Brewing's to evaluate their bottling department.

(3) During the next week we had a discussion with the superintendent of production, Henry Holt, and made plans for interviewing the supervisors and line workers. Also, we had a tour of the bottling department which gave us a first hand look into the production process. Before beginning our interviewing, our group met several times to formulate appropriate questions to use in interviewing, for both the supervisors and workers. We also had a meeting with Professor Charns to discuss this matter.

(3a) The next step was the actual interviewing process. During the weeks of March 14–18 and March 21–25, our group met several times at Oskaloosa Brewing and interviewed ten supervisors and twelve workers. Finally during this past week, we have had several group meetings to discuss our findings and the potential problem areas within the bottling department. Also, we have spent time organizing the writing of our progress report.

(4) The bottling and packaging division is located in a separate building, adjacent to the brewery, where the beer is actually manufactured. From the brewery the beer is piped into one of five lines (four bottling lines and one canning line), in the bottling house where the bottles are filled, crowned, pasteurized, labeled, packaged in cases, and either shipped out or stored in the warehouse. The head of this operation, and others, is production manager, Phil Smith. Next in line under him in direct control of the bottling house is the superintendent of bottling and packaging, Henry Holt. In addition, there are a total of ten supervisors who report directly to Henry Holt and who oversee the daily operations and coordinate and direct the twenty to thirty union workers who operate the lines.

(5) During production, each supervisor fills out a data sheet to explain what was actually produced during each hour. This form also includes the exact time when a breakdown occurred, what it was caused by, and when production was resumed. Some supervisors' positions are production staff oriented. One takes care of supplying the raw material (bottles, caps, labels, and boxes) for production. Another is responsible for the union workers' assignment each day.

These workers are not all permanently assigned to a production line position. Men called "floaters" are used filling in for a sick worker, or helping out after a breakdown.

(6) The union employees are generally older than 35, some in their late fifties. Most have been with the company many years and are accustomed to having more workers per a slower moving line. They are resentful of what they declare "unnecessary" production changes. Oskaloosa Brewery also employs mechanics who normally work on the production line, and assume a mechanics job only when a breakdown occurs. Most of these men are not skilled.

DRAFT 2: MEMORANDUM

TO: Professor Martin Charns
FROM: Nancy Lowenberg, Todd Scott, Rosemary Nisson, Larry Vollen
DATE: March 31, 1977
RE: *Progress Report: The Oskaloosa Brewing Company*

Why Oskaloosa Brewing?

(1) Oskaloosa Brewing Company is a regionally located brewery manufacturing several different types of beer, notably River City and Brough Cream Ale. As a group, we decided to

analyze this organization because two of our group members have frequent contact with the sales department. Also, we were aware that Oskaloosa Brewing had been losing money for the past five years and we felt we might be able to find some obvious problems in their organizational structure.

Initial Steps: Where to Concentrate?

(2) Through several interviews with top management and group discussion, we felt it best suited our needs, and Oskaloosa Brewing's, to evaluate the production department. Our first meeting, held February 17, was with the head of the sales department, Jim Tucker. He gave us an outline of the organization and described the two major departments, sales and production. He indicated that there were more obvious problems in the production department, a belief also implied by Susan Harris, personnel manager.

Next Step

(3) The next step involved a familiarization of the plant and its employees. First, we toured the plant to gain an understanding of the brewing and bottling process. Next, during the weeks of March 14–18 and March 21–25, we interviewed ten supervisors and twelve workers. Finally, during the past week we had group meetings to exchange information and discuss potential problems.

The Production Process

(4) Knowledge of the actual production process is imperative in understanding the effects of various problems on efficient production; therefore, we have included a brief summary of this process.

The bottling and packaging division is located in a separate building, adjacent to the brewery, where the beer is actually manufactured. From the brewery the beer is piped into one of five lines (four bottling lines and one canning line) in the bottling house where the bottles are filled, crowned, pasteurized, labeled, packaged in cases, and either shipped out or stored in the warehouse.

People behind the Process

(5) The head of this operation is production manager, Phil Smith. Next in line under him in direct control of the bottling house is the superintendent of bottling and packaging, Henry Holt. He has authority over ten supervisors who each have two major responsibilities: (1) to fill out production data sheets that show the amount produced/hour, and information about any break-downs—time, cause, etc., and (2) to oversee the daily operations and coordinate and direct the twenty to thirty union workers who operate the lines. These workers are not all permanently assigned to a production line position. Men called "floaters" are used to fill in for a sick worker or to help out after a breakdown.

(6) The union employees are a highly diversified group in both age and experience. They are generally older than 35, some in their late fifties. Most have been with the company many years and are accustomed to having more workers per a slower moving line. They are resentful of what they feel are unnecessary production changes. Oskaloosa Brewing also employs mechanics who normally work on the production line, and assume a mechanics job only when a breakdown occurs. Most of these men are not skilled.

Problems

Through extensive interviews with supervisors and union employees, we have recognized four apparent problems within the bottle house operations. First, the employees' goals do not match those of the company. This is especially apparent in the union employees whose loyalty lies with the union instead of the company. This attitude is well-founded as the union ensures them of job security and benefits. . . .

In its tedious misdirection, Draft 1 is typical of writer-based prose in student papers and professional reports. The reader is forced to do most of the thinking, sorting the wheat from the chaff and drawing ideas out of details. And yet, although this presentation fails to fulfill our needs, it does have an inner logic of its own. The logic which organizes writer-based prose often rests on three principles: its underlying focus is egocentric, and it uses either a narrative framework or a survey form to order ideas.

The *narrative framework* of this discussion is established by the opening announcement: "Work began. . . ." In paragraphs 1 to 3 facts and ideas are presented in terms of when they were discovered, rather than in terms of their implications or logical connections. The writers recount what happened when; the reader, on the other hand, asks, "Why?" and "So what?" Whether he or she likes it or not the reader is in for a blow-by-blow account of the writers' discovery process.

Although a rudimentary chronology is reasonable for a progress report, a narrative framework is often a substitute for analytic thinking. By burying ideas within the events that precipitated them, a narrative obscures the more important logical and hierarchical relations between ideas. Of course, such a narrative could read like an intellectual detective story, because, like other forms of drama, it creates interest by withholding closure. Unfortunately, most academic and professional readers seem unwilling to sit through these home movies of the writer's mind at work. Narratives can also operate as a cognitive "frame" which itself generates ideas.[6] The temporal pattern, once invoked, opens up a series of empty slots waiting to be filled with the details of what happened next, even though those details may be irrelevant. As the revision of Draft 2 shows, our writers' initial narrative framework led them to generate a shaggy project story, instead of a streamlined logical analysis.

The second salient feature of this prose is its focus on the discovery process of the writers: the "I did/I thought/I felt" focus. Of the fourteen sentences in the first three paragraphs, ten are grammatically focused on the writers' thoughts and actions rather than on issues: "Work began," "We decided," "Also we were aware . . . and we felt. . . ."

In the fourth paragraph the writers shift attention from their discovery process to the facts discovered. In doing so they illustrate a third feature of writer-based prose: its idea structure simply copies the structure of the perceived information. A problem arises when the internal structure of the data is not already adapted to the needs of the reader or the intentions of the writer. Paragraph five, for example, appears to be a free-floating description of "What happens during production." Yet the client-reader already knows this and the instructor probably does not care. Lured by the fascination of facts, these writer-based writers recite a litany of perceived information under the illusion they have produced a rhetorical structure. The resulting structure could as well be a neat hierarchy as a list. The point is that the writers' organizing principle is dictated by their information, not by their intention.

The second version of this report is not so much a "rewrite" (i.e., a new report) as it is a transformation of the old one. The writers had to step back from their experience and information in order to turn facts into concepts. Pinpointing the telling details was not enough: they had to articulate the meaning they saw in the data. Second, the writers had to build a rhetorical structure which acknowledged the function these ideas had for their reader. In the second version, the headings, topic sentences, and even some of the subjects and verbs reflect a new functional structure focused on process, people, and problems. The report offers a hierarchical organization of the facts in which the hierarchy itself is based on issues both writer and reader agree are important. I think it likely that such transformations frequently go on in the early stages of the composing process for skilled writers. But for some writers the undertransformed writer-based prose of Draft 1 is also the final product and the starting point for our work as teachers.

In the remainder of this paper I will look at the features of writer-based prose and the ways it functions for the writer. Clearly, we need to know about reader-based prose in order to teach it. But it is also clear that writers already possess a great deal of intuitive knowledge about writing for audiences when they are stimulated to use it. As the case study shows, the concept of trying to transform writer-based prose for a reader is by itself a powerful tool. It helps writers identify the lineaments of a problem many can start to solve once they recognize it as a definable problem.

Writer-Based Prose: Function, Structure, and Style   While writer-based prose may be inadequately structured for a reader, it does possess a logic and structure of its own. Furthermore, that structure serves some important functions for the writer in his or her effort to think about a subject. It represents a practical strategy for dealing with information. If we could see writer-based prose as a *functional system*—not a set of random errors known only to English teachers—we would be better able to teach writing as a part of any discipline that asks people to express complex ideas.

According to Vygotsky, "the inner speech of the adult represents his 'thinking for himself' rather than social adaptation [communication to others]: i.e., it has the same function that egocentric speech has in the child" (*Language and Thought*, p. 18). It helps him solve problems. Vygotsky found that when a child who is trying to draw encounters an obstacle (no pencils) or a problem (what shall I call it?), the incidence of egocentric speech can double.

If we look at an analogous situation—an adult caught up in the complex mental process of composing—we can see that much of the adult's output is not well adapted for public consumption either. In studies of cognitive processes of writers as they composed, J. R. Hayes and I observed much of the writer's verbal output to be an attempt to manipulate stored information into some acceptable pattern of meaning.[7] To do that, the writer generates a variety of alternative relationships and trial formulations of the information she has in mind. Many of these trial networks will be discarded; most will be significantly altered through recombination and elaboration during the composing process. In those cases in which the writer's first pass at articulating knowledge was also the final draft—when she wrote it just as she thought it—the result was often a series of semi-independent, juxtaposed networks, each with its own focus.

Whether such expression occurs in an experimental protocol or a written draft, it reflects the working of the writer's mind upon his material. Because dealing with one's material is a formidable enough task in itself, a writer may allow himself to ignore the additional problem of accommodating a reader. Writer-based prose, then, functions as a medium for thinking. It offers the writer the luxury of one less constraint. As we shall see, its typical structure and style are simply paths left by the movement of the writer's mind.

The *structure* of writer-based prose reflects an economical strategy we have for coping with information. Readers generally expect writers to produce complex concepts—to collect data and details under larger guiding ideas and place those ideas in an integrated network. But as both Vygotsky and Piaget observed, forming such complex concepts is a demanding cognitive task; if no one minds, it is a lot easier to just list the parts. Nor is it surprising that in children two of the hallmarks of egocentric speech are the absence of expressed causal relations and the tendency to express ideas without proof or development. Adults too avoid the task of building complex concepts buttressed by development and proof, by structuring their information in two distinctive ways: as a narrative of their own discovery process or as a survey of the data before them.

As we saw in the Oskaloosa Brewing Case Study, a *narrative* structured around one's own discovery process may seem the most natural way to write. For this reason it can sometimes be the best way as well, if a writer is trying to express a complex network of information but is not yet sure how all the parts are related. For example, my notes show that early fragments of this paper started out with a narrative, listlike structure focused on my own experience: "Writer-based prose is a working hypothesis because it works in the classroom. In fact, when I first started teaching the concept. . . . In fact, it was my students' intuitive recognition of the difference between writer-based and reader-based style in their own thought and writing. . . . It was their ability to use even a sketchy version of the distinction to transform their own writing that led me to pursue the idea more thoroughly."

The final version of this sketch keeps the reference to teaching experience but subordinates it to the more central issue of why the concept works. This transformation illustrates how a writer's major propositions can, on first appearance, emerge embedded in a narrative of the events or thoughts which spawned the proposition. In this example, the writer-based early version recorded the raw material of observations; the final draft formed them into concepts and conclusions.

This transformation process may take place regularly when a writer is trying to express complicated information which is not yet fully conceptualized. Although much of this mental work normally precedes actual writing, a first draft may simply reflect the writer's current place in the process. When this happens rewriting and editing are vital operations. Far from being a simple matter of correcting errors, editing a first draft is often the act of transforming a narrative network of information into a more fully hierarchical set of propositions.

A second source of prefabricated structure for writers is the internal structure of the information itself. Writers use a *survey* strategy to compose because it is a powerful procedure for retrieving and organizing information. Unfortunately, the original organization of the data itself (e.g., the production process at Oskaloosa Brewing) rarely fits the most effective plan for any given piece of focused analytical writing.

The prose that results from such a survey can, of course, take as many forms as the data. It can range from a highly structured piece of discourse (the writer repeats a textbook exposition) to an unfocused printout of the writer's memories and thoughts on the subject. The form is merely a symptom, because the governing force is the writer's mental strategy, namely, to compose by surveying the available contents of memory without adapting them to a current purpose. The internal structure of the data dictates the rhetorical structure of the discourse, much as the proceedings of Congress organize the *Congressional Record*. As an information processor, the writer is performing what computer scientists would call a "memory dump": dutifully printing out memory in exactly the form in which it is stored.

A survey strategy offers the writer a useful way into the composing process in two ways. First, it eliminates many of the constraints normally imposed by a speech act, particularly the contract between reader and writer for mutually useful discourse. Second, a survey of one's own stored knowledge, marching along like a textbook or flowing with the tide of association, is far easier to write than a fresh or refocused conceptualization would be.

But clearly most of the advantages here accrue to the writer. One of the tacit assumptions of the writer-based writer is that, once the relevant information is presented, the reader will then do the work of abstracting the essential features, building a conceptual hierarchy, and transforming the whole discussion into a functional network of ideas.

Although writer-based prose often fails for readers and tends to preclude further concept formation, it may be a useful road into the creative process for some writers. The structures which fail to work for readers may be powerful strategies for retrieving information from memory and for exploring one's own knowledge network. This is illustrated in Linde and Labov's well-known New York apartment tour experiment.[8] Interested in the strategies people use for retrieving information from memory and planning a discourse, Linde and Labov asked one hundred New Yorkers to "tell me the layout of your apartment" as a part of a "sociological survey." Only 3 percent of the subjects responded with a map which gave an overview and then filled in the details; for example, "I'd say it's laid out in a huge square pattern, broken down into 4 units." The overwhelming majority (97 percent) all solved the problem by describing a tour: "You walk in the front door. There was a narrow hallway. To the left, etc." Furthermore, they had a common set of rules for how to conduct the tour (e.g., you don't "walk into" a small room with no outlet, such as a pantry; you just say, "on the left is . . ."). Clearly the tour structure is so widely used because it is a remarkably efficient strategy for recovering all of the relevant information about one's apartment, yet without repeating any of it. For example, one rule for "touring" is that when you dead-end after walking through two rooms, you don't "walk" back but suddenly appear back in the hall.

For us, the revealing sidenote to this experiment is that although the tour strategy was intuitively selected by the overwhelming majority of the speakers, the resulting description was generally very difficult for the listener to follow and almost impossible to reproduce. The tour strategy—like the narrative and textbook structure in prose—is a masterful method for searching memory but a dud for communicating that information to anyone else.

Finally, the *style* of writer-based prose also has its own logic. Its two main stylistic features grow out of the private nature of interior monologue, that is, of writing which is primarily a record or expression of the writer's flow of thought. The first feature is that in such monologues the organization of sentences and paragraphs reflects the shifting focus of the writer's attention. However, the psychological subject on which the writer is focused may not be reflected in the grammatical subject of the sentence or made explicit in the discussion at all. Second, the writer may depend on code words to carry his or her meaning. That is, the language may be "saturated with sense" and able to evoke—for the writer—a complex but unexpressed context.

Writers of formal written discourse have two goals for style which we can usefully distinguish from one another. One goal might be described as stylistic control, that is, the ability to choose a more embedded or more elegant transformation from variations which are roughly equivalent in meaning. The second goal is to create a completely autonomous text, that is, a text that does not need context, gestures, or audible effects to convey its meaning.

It is easy to see how the limits of short-term memory can affect a writer's stylistic control. For an inexperienced writer, the complex transformation of a periodic sentence—which would require remembering and relating a variety of elements and optional structures such as this sentence contains—can be a difficult juggling act. After all, the ability to form parallel constructions is not innate. Yet with practice many of these skills can become more automatic and require less conscious attention.

The second goal of formal written discourse—the complete autonomy of the text—leads to even more complex problems. According to David Olson the history of written language has been the progressive creation of an instrument which could convey complete and explicit meanings in a text. The history of writing is the transformation of language from utterance to text—from oral meaning created within a shared context of a speaker and listener to a written meaning fully represented in an autonomous text.[9]

In contrast to this goal of autonomy, writer-based prose is writing whose meaning is still to an important degree in the writer's head. The culprit here is often the unstated psychological subject. The work of the "remedial" student is a good place to examine the phenomenon because it often reveals first thoughts more clearly than the reworked prose of a more experienced writer who edits as he or she writes. In the most imaginative, comprehensive and practical book to be written on the basic writer, Mina Shaughnessy has studied the linguistic strategies which lie behind the "errors" of many otherwise able young adults who have failed to master the written code. As we might predict, the ambiguous referent is ubiquitous in basic writing: *he*'s, *she*'s and *it*'s are sprinkled through the prose without visible means of support. *It* frequently works as a code word for the subject the writer had in mind but not on the page. As Professor Shaughnessy says, *it* "frequently becomes a free-floating substitute for thoughts that the writer neglects to articulate and that the reader must usually strain to reach if he can."[10]

> With all the jobs available, he will have to know more of *it* because thire is a great demand for *it*.

For the writer of the above sentence, the pronoun was probably not ambiguous at all; *it* no doubt referred to the psychological subject of the sentence. Psychologically, the subject of an utterance is the old information, the object you are looking at, the idea on which your attention has been focused. The predicate is the new information you are adding. This means that the psychological subject and grammatical subject of a sentence may not be the same at all. In our example, "college knowledge" was the writer's psychological subject—the topic he had been thinking about. The sentence itself is simply a psychological predicate. The pronoun *it* refers quite reasonably to the unstated but obvious subject in the writer's mind.

The subject is even more likely to be missing when a sentence refers to the writer herself or to "one" in her position. In the following examples, again from *Errors and Expectations*, the "unnecessary" subject is a person (like the writer) who has a chance to go to college.

> Even if a person graduated from high school who is going on to college to obtain a specific position in his career [   ] should first know how much in demand his possible future job really is.
> [he]
> If he doesn't because the U.S. Labor Department say's their wouldn't be enough jobs opened, [   ] is a waste to society and a "cop-out" to humanity.
> [he]

Unstated subjects can produce a variety of minor problems from ambiguous referents to amusing dangling modifiers (e.g., "driving around the mountain, a bear came into view"). Although prescriptive stylists are quite hard on such "errors," they are often cleared up by context or common sense. However, the controlling but unstated presence of a psychological subject can lead to some stylistic "errors" that do seriously disrupt communication. Sentence fragments are a good example.

One feature of an explicit, fully autonomous text is that the grammatical subject is usually a precise entity, often a word. By contrast, the psychological subject to which a writer wished to refer may be a complex event or entire network of information. Here written language is often rather intransigent; it is hard to refer to an entire clause or discussion unless one can produce a summary noun. Grammar, for example, normally forces us to select a specific referent for a pronoun or modifier: it wants referents and relations spelled out.[11] This specificity is, of course, its strength as a vehicle for precise reasoning and abstract thought. Errors arise when a writer uses one clause to announce his topic or psychological subject and a second clause to record a psychological predicate, a response to that old information. For example:

> The jobs that are listed in the paper, I feel you need a college degree.
> The job that my mother has, I know I could never be satisfied with it.

The preceding sentences are in error because they have failed to specify the grammatical relationship between their two elements. However, for anyone from the Bronx, each statement would be perfectly effective because it fits a familiar formula. It is an example of topicalization or Y-movement and fits a conventionalized, Yiddish-influenced, intonation pattern much like the one in "Spinach—you can have it!" The sentences depend heavily on certain conventions of oral speech, and insofar as they invoke those patterns for the reader, they communicate effectively.[12]

However, most fragments do not succeed for the reader. And they fail, ironically enough, for the same reason—they too invoke intonation patterns in the reader which turn out to be misleading. The lack of punctuation gives off incorrect cues about how to segment the sentence. Set off on an incorrect intonation pattern, the thwarted reader must stop, reread, and reinterpret the sentence. The following examples are from Maxine Hairston's *A Contemporary Rhetoric* (Boston, Houghton Mifflin, 1974):

> The authorities did not approve of their acts. These acts being considered detrimental to society (society, they . . .).
> Young people need to be on their own. To show their parents that they are reliable (reliable, young people . . .).

(p. 322)

Fragments are easy to avoid; they require only minimal tinkering to correct. Then why is the error so persistent? One possible reason is that for the writer the fragment is a fresh predicate intended to modify the entire preceding psychological subject. The writer wants to carry out a verbal trick easily managed in speech. For the reader, however, this minor grammatical oversight is significant. It sets up and violates both intonation patterns and strong structural expectations, such as those in the last example where we expect a pause and a noun phrase to follow "reliable." The fragment, which actually refers backward, is posing as an introductory clause.

The problem with fragments is that they are perfectly adequate for the writer. In speech they may even be an effective way to express a new idea which is predicated on the entire preceding unit thought. But in a written text, fragments are errors because they do not take the needs of the reader into consideration. Looked at this way, the "goodness" of a stylistic technique or grammatical rule such as parallelism, clear antecedents, or agreement is that it is geared to the habits, expectations, and needs of the reader as well as to the demands of textual autonomy.

Vygotsky noticed how the language of children and inner speech was often "saturated with sense." Similarly, the words a writer chooses can also operate as code words, condensing a wealth of meaning in an apparently innocuous word. The following examples come from an exercise which asks writers to identify and transform some of their own pieces of mental shorthand.

The students were asked to circle any code words or loaded expressions they found in their first drafts of a summer internship application. That is, they tried to identify those expressions that might convey only a general or vague meaning to a reader, but which represented a large body of facts, experiences, or ideas for them. They then treated this code word as one would any intuition—pushing it for its buried connections and turning those into a communicable idea. The results are not unlike those brilliant explications one often hears from students who tell you what their paper really meant. This example also shows how much detailed and perceptive thought can be lying behind a vague and conventional word:

> First draft: "By having these two jobs, I was able to see the business in an entirely different perspective." (Circle indicates a loaded expression marked by the writer.)
> Second draft with explanation of what she actually had in mind in using the circled phrase: "By having these two jobs, I was able to see the true relationship and relative importance of the various departments in the company. I could see their mutual dependence and how an event in one part of the firm can have an important effect on another."

The tendency to think in code words is a fact of life for the writer. Yet the following example shows how much work can go into exploring our own saturated language. Like any intuition, such language is only a source of potential meanings, much as Aristotle's topics are places for finding potential arguments. In this extended example, the writer first explores her expression itself, laying out all the thoughts which were loosely connected under its name. This process of pushing our own language to give up its buried meanings forces us to make these loose connections explicit and, in the process, allows us to examine them critically. For the writer in our example, pushing her own key words leads to an important set of new ideas in the paper.

EXCERPT FROM AN APPLICATION FOR THE NATIONAL INSTITUTE OF HEALTH INTERNSHIP PROGRAM
> First draft: "I want a career that will help other people while at the same time be challenging scientifically. I had the opportunity to do a biochemical assay for a neuropsychopharmocologist at X—Clinic in Chicago. Besides learning the scientific procedures and techniques that are used, I

realized some of the $\boxed{\text{organizational, financial and people problems}}$ which are encountered in research. This internship program would let me pursue further my interest in research, while concurrently exposing me to $\boxed{\text{relevant and diverse}}$ areas of bioengineering."

EXCERPT FROM WRITER'S NOTES WORKING ON THE CIRCLED PHRASES
Brainstorm

How did research of Sleep Center tie into overall program of X—Clinic? Not everyone within dept. knew what the others were doing, could not see overall picture of efforts.

Dr. O.—dept. head—trained for lab yet did 38–40 hrs. paperwork. Couldn't set up test assay in Sleep Center because needed equip. from biochem.

Difficulties in getting equipment
1. Politics between administrators
Photometer at U. of—even though Clinic had bought it.
2. Ordering time, not sufficient inventory, had to hunt through boxes for chemicals.
3. Had to schedule use by personal contact on borrowing equipment—done at time of use and no previous planning.

No definite guidelines had been given to biochem. people as to what was "going on" with assay. Partner who was supposed to learn assay was on vacation. Two people were learning, one was on vac.

No money from state for equipment or research grants.

Departments stealing from each other.

Lobbying, politics, included.

My supervisor from India, felt prejudices on job. Couldn't advance, told me life story and difficulties in obtaining jobs at Univ. Not interested in research at Clinic per se, looking for better opportunities, studying for Vet boards.

REVISION (ADDITIONS IN ITALICS)
As a biomedical researcher, I would fulfill my goal of a career that will help other people while at the same time be challenging scientifically. I had exposure to research while doing a biochemical assay for a neuropsychopharmocologist at X—Clinic in Chicago. Besides learning the scientific procedures and techniques that are used, I realized some of the organizational, financial and people problems which are encountered in research. *These problems included a lack of funds and equipment, disagreements among research staff, and the extensive amounts of time, paperwork and steps required for testing a hypothesis which was only one very small but necessary part of the overall project. But besides knowing some of the frustrations, I also know that many medical advancements, such as the cardiac pacemaker, artificial limbs and cures for diseases, exist and benefit many people because of the efforts of researchers.* Therefore, I would like to pursue my interest in research by participating in the NIH Internship Program. The exposure to many *diverse projects, designed to better understand and improve the body's functioning, would help me to decide which areas of biomedical engineering to pursue.*

We could sum up this analysis of style by noting two points. At times a writer-based prose style is simply an interior monologue in which some necessary information (such as intonation pattern or a psychological subject) is not expressed in the text. The solution to the reader's problem is relatively trivial in that it involves adding information that the writer already possesses. At other times, a style may be writer-based because the writer is thinking in code words at the level of intuited but unarticulated connections. Turning such saturated language into communicable ideas can require the writer to bring the entire composing process into play.

Implications for Writers and Teachers From an educational perspective, writer-based prose is one of the "problems" composition courses are designed to correct. It is a major cause of that notorious "breakdown" of communication between writer and reader. However, if we step back and look at it in the broader context of cognitive operations involved, we see that it represents a major, functional stage in the composing process and a powerful strategy well fitted to a part of the job of writing.

In the best of all possible worlds, good writers strive for reader-based prose from the very beginning: they retrieve and organize information within the framework of a reader/writer contract. Their top goal or initial question is not, "What do I know about physics, and in particular the physics of wind resistance?" but, "What does a model plane builder need to know?" Many times a writer can do this. For a physics teacher this particular writing problem would be a trivial one. However, for a person ten years out of Physics 101, simply retrieving any relevant information would be a full-time processing job. The reader would simply have to wait. For the inexperienced writer, trying to put complex thought into written language may also be task enough. In that case, the reader is an extra constraint that must wait its turn. A reader-based strategy which includes the reader in the entire thinking process is clearly the best way to write, but it is not always possible. When it is very difficult or impossible to write for a reader from the beginning, writing and then transforming writer-based prose is a practical alternative which breaks this complex process down into manageable parts. When transforming is a practiced skill, it enters naturally into the pulse of the composing process as a writer's constant, steady effort to test and adapt his or her thought to a reader's needs. Transforming writer-based prose is, then, not only a necessary procedure for all writers at times, but a useful place to start teaching intellectually significant writing skills.

In this final section I will try to account for the peculiar virtues of writer-based prose and suggest ways that teachers of writing—in any field—can take advantage of them. Seen in the context of memory retrieval, writer-based thinking appears to be a tapline to the rich sources of episodic memory. In the context of the composing process, writer-based prose is a way to deal with the overload that writing often imposes on short-term memory. By teaching writers to use this transformation process we can foster the peculiar strengths of writer-based thought and still alert writers to the next transformation that many may simply fail to attempt.

One way to account for why writer-based prose seems to "come naturally" to most of us from time to time is to recognize its ties to our episodic as opposed to semantic memory. As Tulving describes it, "episodic memory is a more or less faithful record of a person's experiences." A statement drawn from episodic memory "refers to a personal experience that is remembered in its temporal-spatial relation to other such experiences. The remembered episodes are . . . autobiographical events, describable in terms of their perceptible dimensions or attributes."[13]

Semantic memory, by contrast, "is the memory necessary for the use of language. It is a mental thesaurus, organized knowledge a person possesses about words and other verbal symbols, their meaning and referents, about relations among them, and about rules, formulas, and algorithms for the manipulation of these symbols, concepts, and relations." Although we know that table salt is NaCl and that motivation is a mental state, we probably do not remember learning the fact or the first time we thought of that concept. In semantic memory facts and concepts stand as the nexus for other words and symbols, but shorn of their temporal and autobiographical roots. If we explored the notion of "writing" in the semantic memory of someone we might produce a network such as this:

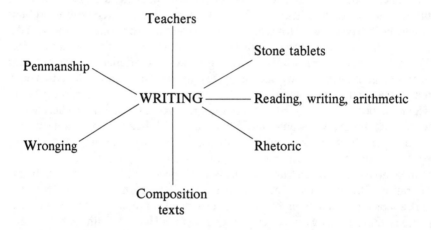

In an effort to retrieve what she or he knew about stone tablets, for example, this same person might turn to episodic memory: "I once heard a lecture on the Rosetta stone, over in Maynard Hall. The woman, as I recall, said that . . . and I remember wondering if . . ."

Writers obviously use both kinds of memory. The problem arises only when they confuse a fertile source of ideas in episodic memory with a final product. In fact, a study by Russo and Wisher argues that we sometimes store our ideas or images (the symbols of thought) with the mental operations we performed to produce these symbols.[14] Furthermore, it is easier to recall the symbols (that fleeting idea, perhaps) when we bring back the original operation. In other words, our own thinking acts can serve as memory cues, and the easiest way to recover some item from memory may be to *reprocess* it, to reconstruct the original thought process in which it appeared. Much writer-based prose appears to be doing just this—reprocessing an earlier thinking experience as a way to recover what one knows.

Writing is one of those activities that places an enormous burden on short-term or working memory. As George Miller put it, "The most glaring result [of numerous experiments] has been to highlight man's inadequacy as a communication channel. As the amount of input information is increased, the amount of information that the man transmits increases at first but then runs into a ceiling. . . . That ceiling is always very low. Indeed, it is an act of charity to call man a channel at all. Compared to telephone or television channels, man is better characterized as a bottleneck."[15]

The short-term memory is the active central processor of the mind, that is, it is the sum of all the information we can hold in conscious attention at one time. We notice its capacity most acutely when we try to learn a new task, such as driving a car or playing bridge. Its limited capacity means that when faced with a complex problem—such as writing a college paper—we can hold and compare only a few alternative relationships in mind at once.

Trying to evaluate, elaborate, and relate all that we know on a given topic can easily overload the capacity of our working memory. Trying to compose even a single sentence can have the same effect, as we try to juggle grammatical and syntactic alternatives plus all the possibilities of tone, nuance, and rhythm even a simple sentence offers. Composing, then, is a cognitive activity that constantly threatens to overload short-term memory. For two reasons writer-based prose is a highly effective strategy for dealing with this problem.

1. Because the characteristic structure of writer-based prose is often a list (of either mental events or the features of the topic), it temporarily suspends the additional problem of forming complex concepts. If that task is suspended indefinitely, the result will fail to be good analytical writing or serious thought, but as a first stage in the process the list structure has real value. It allows the writer freedom to generate a breadth of information and a variety of alternative relationships before locking himself or herself into a premature formulation. Furthermore, by allowing the writer to temporarily separate the two complex but somewhat different tasks of generating information and forming networks, each task may be performed more consciously and effectively.

2. Taking the perspective of another mind is also a demanding cognitive operation. It means holding not only your own knowledge network but someone else's in conscious attention and comparing them. Young children simply can't do it.[16] Adults choose not to do it when their central processing is already overloaded with the effort to generate and structure their own ideas. Writer-based prose simply eliminates this constraint by temporarily dropping the reader out of the writer's deliberations.[17]

My own research suggests that good writers take advantage of these strategies in their composing process. They use scenarios, generate lists, and ignore the reader, but only for a while. Their composing process, unlike that of less effective writers, is marked by constant reexamination of their growing product and an attempt to refine, elaborate, or test its relationships, plus an attempt to anticipate the response of a reader. Everyone uses the strategies of writer-based prose; good writers go a step further to transform the writing these strategies produce.

But what about the writers who fail to make this transformation or (like all of us) fail to do it adequately in places? This is the problem faced by all teachers who assign papers. I think this study has two main and quite happy implications for us as teachers and writers.

The first is that writer-based prose is not a composite of errors or a mistake that should be scrapped. Instead, it is a halfway place for many writers and often represents the results of an extensive search and selection process. As a stage in the composing process, it may be a rich compilation of significant thoughts which cohere *for the writer* into a network she or he has not yet fully articulated. Writer-based prose is the writer's homework, and so long as the writer is also the audience, it may even be a well-thought-out communication.

The second happy implication is that writing reader-based prose is often simply the task of transforming the groundwork laid in the first stage of the process.[18] Good analytical writing is not different in kind from the writer-based thought that seems to come naturally. It is an extension of our communication with ourselves transformed in certain predictable ways to meet the needs of the reader. The most general transformation is simply to try to take into account the reader's purpose in reading. Most people have well-developed strategies for doing this when they talk. For a variety of reasons—from cognitive effort to the illusion of the omniscient teacher/reader—many people simply do not consider the reader when they write.

More specifically, the transformations that produce reader-based writing include these:

Selecting a focus of mutual interest to both reader and writer (e.g., moving from the writer-based focus of "How did I go about my research or reading of the assignment and what did I see?" to a focus on "What significant conclusions can be drawn and why?").

Moving from facts, scenarios, and details to concepts.

Transforming a narrative or textbook structure into a rhetorical structure built on the logical and hierarchical relationships between ideas and organized around the purpose for writing, rather than the writer's process.

Teaching writers to recognize their own writer-based writing and transform it has a number of advantages. It places a strong positive value on writing that represents an effort and achievement for the writer even though it fails to communicate to the reader. This legitimate recognition of the uncommunicated content of writer-based prose can give anyone, but especially inexperienced writers, the confidence and motivation to go on. By defining writing as a multistage process (instead of a holistic act of "expression") we provide a rationale for editing and alert many writers to a problem they could handle once it is set apart from other problems and they deliberately set out to tackle it. By recognizing transformation as a special skill and task, we give writers a greater degree of self-conscious control over the abilities they already have and a more precise introduction to some skills they may yet develop.

EXPLORING THE IDEAS — *Theoretical discussion*

QUESTION 1

Background   Flower argues that writer-based prose "functions as a medium for thinking" (page 24). However, she also maintains that writer-based prose is not necessarily a stage through which a writer must develop (page 31).

Discussion   Refer back to your own analysis of how you typically proceed when you write. Do you typically go through a stage of writer-based prose when you write? When you do go through this stage, is it necessarily written? What benefits do you see in going through a stage of writer-based prose in terms of developing an effective final product?

QUESTION 2

Background   Flower states that "writer-based prose is one of the 'problems' composition courses are designed to correct" (page 31). She seems to suggest that there is no context in which such prose is appropriate or effective.

Application   Can you think of any circumstances in which writer-based prose would be an effective medium of communication? Would you classify literary texts as writer-based prose or reader-based prose?

Applying theoretical concepts

ACTIVITY 1

Background   As Flower points out, one reason why writer-based prose is easier to write is that it uses a narrative framework in which the internal structure of the essay mirrors the order in which the writer perceives the information. Reader-based prose, in contrast, presupposes a rhetorical structure which highlights and relates the information in the text for the reader.

The following essay topics are included in Ann Raimes' *Focus on Composition* (New York, Oxford University Press, 1978, pp. 67, 90–91, 125, 165–166). As you can see, they vary in the degree to which they draw on a narrative framework.

a. Write an explanation of how you wrote any one recent assignment from this book. Give details: where were you, did you make a draft, use a typewriter, did you interrupt the writing process, what equipment did you use?

b. Write a description of what happened in the most exciting class hour in school you have ever experienced. Describe it in detail so that your reader will be able to experience the excitement you felt.

c. Think of a way in which an institution—a school, a hospital, a business, etc.—could and should be changed. Write a letter to the president of the institution, and argue for this change. Give reasons why it is necessary and recommend how the change should be made. What will be the effect of the change?

d. The situation: You are living in an apartment building with badly insulated walls and floors. You hear a great deal of noise at all hours of the day and night from your upstairs neighbor. . . . Write a letter to your landlord making the point that you have to break your lease and move out immediately because of the noise. Explain to him your reasons why, clearly and unemotionally. Tell him about some specific occasions on which you have been disturbed by noise.

Application   Assume that as a composition teacher you were going to use all four topics with your class at some point during the semester. First, specify the order in which you would present them beginning with what you feel is the easiest writing task and ending with the most difficult. Then for each one explain what contributes to its relative ease or difficulty in terms of Flower's writer-based prose/reader-based prose distinction.

ACTIVITY 2

Background   A technique which Flower and Hayes have used to examine the writing process is protocol analysis (L. Flower and J. R. Hayes. 1981. A Cognitive Process Theory of Writing. *College Composition and Communication* 32, 4:367–375). To collect a protocol, Flower and Hayes give writers a topic and ask them to compose out loud near a tape recorder. The authors are "to work on the task as they normally would—thinking, jotting notes, and writing—except that they must think out loud. They are asked to verbalize everything that goes through their minds as they write, including stray notions, false starts, and incomplete or fragmentary thoughts."

The following is a protocol of a nonnative speaker. The student was asked to write an essay in which he gave his definition of a typical American (i.e., citizen of the United States). In the essay he was to elaborate on what characteristics he believed were shared by most Americans. In essence, the protocol reflects the first stage in the development of writer-based prose.

In this transcription, pauses are divided into three categories:

,   = a couple of seconds
. . .   = up to about 30 seconds
(long pause) = more than 30 seconds (several minutes in some cases)

OK . . . OK (long pause) OK, I think that an American have too many . . . too, too different . . . or more than . . . meaning to everybody everybody, will find, find his own definition of an American, cause we discussed that in class once, and eh . . . everybody has a different definition of what an American is . . . for example somebody says like an American is eh who . . . was . . . who is a citizen in the United States . . . and . . . eh . . . that's it, if he's a legal immigration and he got his, a, a, he got his alien card, so this is an American, after he get his citizenship . . . OK, so I'm going to start, eh . . . writing . . . what is an American (long pause) I believe that an American is eh . . . who . . . who isn't the United States and eh . . . he doesn't necessary have to be born here but if he adjust with the way of life in the United States and at the same time he have the legal right

or . . . to be an American, like . . . to be a legal citizen or . . . a legal immigration
. . . immigrant (long pause) so . . . eh . . . for me eh . . . it's, it's two versions, it's
not only being . . . born here . . . is an American and if you was, if you you was
born here in the United States sometimes you might not be an American if you
don't really . . . feel like you belong in . . . this state . . . or in the United States,
for example if there's a . . . somebody who's . . . who's an American but he just
can't adjust with the way of life here and he just don't like it, he won't react with
the . . . with the people, he won't communicate with them, so I don't think, I
don't think, or I don't feel like this is an American . . . because, to be an
American you have to . . . to believe that you are . . . in the right place and the
right . . . with the right people, so you have to be . . . happy in your life and you
have to be . . . in a way you have to adjust with the way of life there . . . there are
too many things that are related to an American, or . . . that makes him different
from, like French or German or something, so . . . I'm trying to find out what are
these things . . . now . . . so, I'm gonna . . . try to think of . . . somethings that
. . . differentiate between an American and . . . non-American . . . to try to find
the real definition of an American . . . so . . . what are Americans different? . . .
I'm not sure if there are . . . related to . . . to the . . . like . . . the politics of the,
that state for example, the United States they believe that it's a free land, and
eh . . . that, yah they are related to this but what I mean is eh . . . does politics
have anything to do with it? like eh . . . eh for example . . . um, I can't think of
something now so I'm trying to find out what it is . . . eh, well . . . I think that an
American . . . especially since the . . . since the . . . American . . . government
. . . or the . . . the United States . . . believe in . . . in certain things that makes
them different from other states, for example that it's a free land, you can do
anything you want . . . you can speak out . . . loudly if you don't really feel
that . . . for example, the president is eh, is right, so you can talk to him, cause in
other states . . . or, from the place where I came from which is eh, I'm a
Palestinian and eh . . . from where I am, since I have a special situation there,
but, there I can't speak out my mind sometimes which . . . that will harm me, for
example if I, if I didn't like, like the government and I talked about it, even if
I . . . they found out that I am thinking this I'd be in trouble . . . so that's, that's a
good point about the American . . . way of life, that's that's . . . that you're free
to say whatever you believe in, and that's . . . that's really good point about
being an American (long pause) I'm trying to now, to . . . to write down
what . . . are the character characteristics that eh . . . differentiate an American
from another . . . nation . . . what's the difference between an American and a
real American . . . cause we discussed that in class once . . . and . . . we had . . .
too many . . . ideas about what they mean by that . . . but I think I'm not, I
shouldn't try to (inaudible) in some, just trying to find now what the
characteristics of an American . . . so I'm not talking about the real American or
an American but just an American now (long pause) and some of the things that
are related to . . . to each American is . . . the way of life they are living
here . . . example like eh . . . umm . . . I was going to say about eh . . . you know

every, every normal . . . day life . . . like eh . . . all that routine, getting up early in the morning if he has, if he . . . must go to work or go to school, and then after that if . . . after he finish school he must go to work if he is really . . . pendent, independent, and eh . . . all these routines . . . it is really rel-related to an American, for example from, from where I came from it's not that . . . hard, maybe because I was dependent on my parents . . . but here I find it . . . it's different . . . since I must go to school . . . and I have to go to work after that and then do my homework, so I feel like . . . I'm dependent no on . . . on . . . acting like an American . . . even though I'm not an American yet legally or eh . . . or eh . . . emotion, emotionally . . . since I don't . . . I don't eh . . . really . . . believe that I . . . I exist, or that I belong in here, at this time, maybe after . . . after while I change my mind . . . but . . . so far I'm not adjusting to the way of life here, even though I'm working and acting like any . . . normal American person . . . so, so far I wrote like, for example, if one believes, believes in and . . . practice freedom of choice, I believe that this is a real American . . . well, that's just one part of it . . . and if he's really, and if he really feels that he belongs . . . here and in the states and eh . . . he act . . . normally, so I believe that he is an American (long pause) I was thinking now of the legal side of an American, which I said something about it before but . . . if, if I'm going to discuss . . . the legal side of an American I have to be . . . either born here in the United States or got an . . . an, immigration or or is a legal immigrant . . . that will be an American, after . . . I stay here five years, as the rule says and . . . and eh . . . so, I don't know if I'm going to . . . write about this, shall I discuss the legal side too, or maybe I should . . . cause . . . it's . . . it's the states government definition of being an American . . . but I'm always trying to concentrate on . . . not the legal side, but . . . on, on what an American are, you know you don't have to be an American citizen to be a real American . . . that's what I believe in (long pause) OK I . . . now I'm trying to find out . . . why . . . what are the reasons that I don't . . . have to be a citizen of the United States to be an American . . . so . . . the only way I can explain it is just by examples . . . according to what I believe . . . for example if there's eh . . . the person who . . . who is an American, he was born here . . . and eh . . . the person who . . . who is an American, he was born here . . . and eh . . . was living all his life in the states but . . . in a way he doesn't feel like he's an American in . . . like he's, he's . . . he doesn't belong here, for example he can't adjust with the way of life, he can't . . . he can't communicate with people, and so . . . he just keep wondering in life, why is he in this place . . . so, he just feel that he's . . . not an American . . . so, what will happen to him is just he . . . he's gonna stay here, but . . . he's gonna keep wondering . . . what am I? what am or why am I doing here, why am I staying here, so . . . so what will happen to him is just he's gonna . . . eh . . . be different than the other Americans . . . and there's too many ways that he can do it . . . by using drugs for example . . . to try to avoid what he is, maybe I went too far off the subject, I don't know (laughs) but it is . . . it has something to do with that, you know why, why all these people are using drugs now you know, especially hard drugs like cocaine and . . . all that stuff, I just can't understand why they're using that, so there should be a reason, so . . . I think the reason is just that they don't eh . . . believe that eh . . . maybe just one part of it . . . that they don't believe that they belong to this place, or they . . . they just can't adjust with it, so they have to find a way to run away from this life . . . I guess . . . because eh . . . I just can't understand why people use drugs . . . well, I'm a waiter, I work at Denny's, and one Sunday morning three guys came into the place, and they were just shaking, I thought they were some kind of . . . sick, or something, you know just something normal like . . . the nervous system or something . . . but after while I found out that they were taking real hard drugs . . . I mean . . . hard that they couldn't even move . . . they, that guy was drinking his coffee and he was shaking, he throw all the coffee on his . . . on his eh . . . pants and all over the place and all . . . and, they couldn't even touch it, and eh . . . so I think why they doing this? you know . . . either they just . . . enjoy this, or they should enjoy I know but . . . I mean what's the reason for doing that? that's what I don't understand, so I think I can just say that they . . . they don't feel that they belong in this . . . place, or in this . . . earth . . . so I don't believe that these guys are Americans, or maybe . . . the, the . . . lots of Americans do this . . . drugs . . . and, all that so . . . so is that the way of life of an American? I don't know, is it? . . . is this . . . is that, somebody might say that this is real American (laughs) and somebody might not, which . . . I don't agree on that . . . and the technology . . . eh, technology is eh . . . especially here, since it's one of the most . . . maybe the most . . . powerful, powerful countries of the world . . . so they have to adjust with technology . . . and technology now . . . is increasing rapidly and eh . . . so I think that is . . . I feel that it's, that they are . . . affected by this thing . . . this technology . . . I just eh . . . got a thought here that there's too many different types of Americans, you know, some of them are really . . . nice . . . and at the same time some of them are really . . . different . . . which is something natural, everybody has the . . . anyplace, in any country there's . . . too many different kinds of . . . people . . . but . . . what . . . when I came here, there was . . . things that . . . that I noticed, that . . . it was . . . quite different for me, or unusual . . . or . . . for example, the behavior of . . . of each person . . . uh, like eh . . . yah, for example, if you just accidentally . . . that's all I just thought of it you know if you accidentally . . . you were running or something or you walking and hit somebody . . . and especially for . . . where I work at, and you hit . . . you know when you're busy and you try to do this and that, and you hit somebody and you said "excuse me" you know, this is just . . . a thought . . . and some of them are very nice, you know and . . . they don't really . . . they accept that, but some of them, they, they . . . uh . . . they don't ac-accept you to have, to make any mistakes and if you do they try to . . . somehow punish you, or just try to . . . let you feel that you are . . . you're different, or you're not from this country, and . . . you shouldn't belong here . . . and some of them on the other hand they just eh . . . normal people, and eh . . . I'm not saying that they, that those other guys are not normal, but I'm saying just they're acting . . . they're not really prejudice (long pause) trying to eh (inaudible whisper) uh, I can't think of it . . . I'm trying to find a word . . . um . . . OK, that's in the sentence, it's, eh . . . I was talking about, about . . . when I found about Americans, some of them are really nice and eh . . . some other are not, and they are not prejudice, and they don't really try to, don't . . . don't try to work to bother something . . . so . . . try to . . . maybe I use "bother" (laughs) I'm going to use it . . . since this is the first time I'm writing something like this, I'm just . . . can't really concentrate on the subject . . . so I'm going here and there now (long pause) those who are prejudiced, they . . . some of them . . . they try to let you feel that . . . that they are prejudiced, for example they just eh . . . don't act like a prejudiced person, but they don't even care, they let you know that . . . "I don't want you to be here" . . . and so . . . that, that's the kind of eh . . . that I don't like . . . and though I, I don't want to be here either you know, but . . . there was some reasons that made me came here . . . and . . . maybe because I couldn't finish school back home . . . since . . . I used to be in a college . . . and eh . . . just the government would close it every two or three months so if I'm going to stay there I'll be at school forever, so . . . I have my reasons why I'm here too . . . and eh . . . I might, I might like it here, or I might go back home after I finish school, so this . . . this is not decided yet . . . in the place I work in . . . we have Americans and we have eh . . . immigrants which, they are legally there but eh . . . you know, they're not Americans . . . yet . . . and what I found out that eh . . . the Americans, not all of them, some of them are . . . irresponsible, you know, they just don't . . . sometimes they just don't show up to work and they . . . don't even call that they gonna . . . they're not eh . . . coming to work . . . on the other hand . . . the . . . the . . . immigrants, or who are not Americans . . . they are more eh . . . eh . . . discipline . . . especially for work, you know . . . I'm talking about work now, so . . . they, if they are sick or something, or . . . they can't show up to work, they call and try to find the reason for that, but . . . I found that the Americans, some of them are . . . irresponsible, or . . . or they just eh . . . don't take it that seriously . . . that's just one point . . . but we have others who have some of them are really responsible, and eh . . . they really care about work and eh . . . all that

Application   The protocol is presented within the narrative framework of writer-based prose. If it were to be transformed into reader-based prose, it would need an organizational framework. In order to make this transformation, list the characteristics which the student seems to be suggesting are central to being an American.

Composition evaluation

ACTIVITY 1

Background   The following is the first draft of this same student's paper.

MY DEFINITION OF AN AMERICAN
    I believe that my definition of an American comes from my observation of a typical American person in his daily life routine. In my opinion, a typical American is a person who feels that he

belongs to the United States no matter of his nationality. At the same time, he must meet the fact that he adjusted to the way of life in that state.

According to my definition there are some characteristics that are essential of being an American. The first characteristic that attracted my attention of an American is being polite. It is natural that people are not the same, but in general most of them are polite. Sometimes they exaggerate of being polite and expect me to do the same thing. For example, I work at Denny's—a restaurant—as a waiter and there is a very polite waitress that drives me crazy with her formality. She expects me to be formal whenever I react with her and sometimes I can feel the heat of prejudication on the air around her.

The second characteristic of an American is being outspoken. One of the things that I like about the United States is having the right to speak freely without fear. This fact attracts many immigrants to come to America reaching for their existance. I believe that if one believes and practices freedom of choice he is truly an American.

The third characteristic in my definition of an American is being flexible. Some of the Americans, especially teenagers and young people, are attracted to the new waves in this country and they are always looking for something new or different. This creates many subcharacteristics which are unfortunately essential to them of being an American like heavy drug abuse and alcoholism.

Application   Reread the essay and do the following.

1. Point out any elements in the essay that were previously explored by the student in his protocol.

2. Write out several questions or comments you could put on the essay to help the student revise his essay to make it a better model of reader-based prose. You might begin, as Flower suggests, by circling code words or loaded expressions in the text or in the protocol which convey only vague meaning but seem to represent a large body of facts and experiences for the student (page 29).

NOTES

1. Lev Vygotsky, *Thought and Language*, ed. and trans. Eugenia Hanfmann and Gertrude Vakar. Cambridge, Mass., MIT Press, 1962, p. 15.

2. Jean Piaget, *The Language and Thought of the Child*, trans. Marjorie Gabin. New York, Harcourt, Brace, 1932), p. 49.

3. Herbert Ginsberg and Sylvia Opper, *Piaget's Theory of Intellectual Development*. Englewood Cliffs, N.J., Prentice-Hall, 1969, p. 89.

4. John Flavell, *The Developmental Psychology of Jean Piaget*. New York, D. Van Nostrand, 1963, p. 275. For these studies see the last chapter of Piaget's *Language and Thought of the Child* and *Judgment and Reasoning in the Child*, trans. M. Warden. New York, Harcourt, Brace, 1926.

5. *Thought and Language*, p. 75. See also the paper by Gary Woditsch which places this question in the context of curriculum design, Developing Generic Skills: A Model for a Competency-Based General Education, available from CUE Center, Bowling Green State University.

6. The seminal paper on frames is M. Minsky's A Framework for Representing Knowledge. In P. Winston (ed.). *The Psychology of Computer Vision*. New York, McGraw-hill, 1973. For a more recent discussion of how they work see B. Kuipers, A Frame for Frames. In D. Bowbow and A. Collins (eds). *Representation and Understanding: Studies in Cognitive Science*, New York, Academic Press, 1975, pp. 151–184.

7. L. Flower and J. Hayes, Plans That Guide the Composing Process. In *Writing: The Nature, Development and Teaching of Written Communication*, C. Frederikson, M. Whiteman, and J. Dominic (eds.). Hillsdale, N.J., Lawrence Erlbaum, 1980.

8. C. Linde and W. Labov, Spatial Networks as a Site for the Study of Language and Thought. *Language*, 51 (1975), 924–939.

9. David R. Olson, From Utterance to Text: The Bias of Language in Speech Writing, *Harvard Educational Review*, 47 (1977), 257–281.

10. Mina Shaughnessy, *Errors and Expectations*, New York, Oxford University Press, 1977, p. 69.

11. "Pronouns like *this, that, which,* and *it* should not vaguely refer to an entire sentence or clause," and "Make a pronoun refer clearly to one antecedent, not uncertainly to two." Floyd Watkins et al., *Practical English Handbook*. Boston, Houghton Mifflin, 1974, p. 30.

12. I am greatly indebted here to Thomas Huckin for his insightful comments on style and to his work in linguistics on how intonation patterns affect writers and readers.

13. Edel Tulving, Episodic and Semantic Memory. In Edel Tulving and Wayne Donaldson (eds.). *Organization of Memory*. New York, Academic Press, 1972, p. 387.

14. J. Russo and R. Wisher, Reprocessing as a Recognition Cue. *Memory and Cognition*. 4 (1976), 683–689.

15. George Miller, *The Psychology of Communication*. New York, Basic Books, 1967, p. 48.

16. Marlene Scardamalia, "How Children Cope with the Cognitive Demands of Writing," in *Writing: The Nature, Development and Teaching of Written Communication*, C. Frederikson, M. Whiteman, and J. Dominic, eds.

17. Linda Flower and John R. Hayes, "The Dynamics of Composing: Making Plans and Juggling Constraints," in *Cognitive Processes in Writing: An Interdisciplinary Approach*, Lee Gregg and Irwin Steinberg, eds. (Hillsdale, N.J.: Lawrence Erlbaum, 1979).

18. For a study of heuristics and teaching techniques for this transformation process see L. Flower and J. Hayes, Problem-Solving Strategies and the Writing Process. *College English*, 39 (1977), 449–461.

3

Cultural Thought Patterns in Intercultural Education

Robert B. Kaplan

The teaching of reading and composition to foreign students does differ from the teaching of reading and composition to American students, and cultural differences in the nature of rhetoric supply the key to the difference in teaching approach.

Rhetoric is a mode of thinking or a mode of "finding all available means" for the achievement of a designated end. Accordingly, rhetoric concerns itself basically with what goes on in the mind rather than with what comes out of the mouth. . . . Rhetoric is concerned with factors of analysis, data gathering, interpretation, and synthesis. . . . What we notice in the environment and how we notice it are both predetermined to a significant degree by how we are prepared to notice this particular type of object. . . . Cultural anthropologists point out that given acts and objects appear vastly different in different cultures, depending on the values attached to them. Psychologists investigating perception are increasingly insistent that what is perceived depends upon the observer's perceptual frame of reference.[1]

Language teachers, particularly teachers of English as a second language, are latecomers in the area of international education. For years, and until quite recently, most languages were taught in what might be called a mechanistic way, stressing the prescriptive function of such teaching. In recent years the swing has been in the other direction, and the prescriptive has practically disappeared from language teaching. Descriptive approaches have seemed to provide the answer. At the present moment, there seems to be some question about the purely descriptive technique, and a new compromise between description and prescription seems to be emerging. Such a compromise appears necessary to the adequate achievement of results in second-language teaching. Unfortunately, although both the prescriptivists and the descriptivists have recognized the existence of cultural variation as a factor in second-language teaching, the recognition has so far been limited to the level of the sentence—that is, to the level of grammar, vocabulary, and sentence structure. On the other hand, it has long been known among sociologists and anthropologists that logic per se is a cultural phenomenon as well.

Even if we take into account the lexical and grammatical similarities that exist between languages proceeding from a common hypothetical ancestor, the fact remains that the verbal universe is divided into multiple sectors. Sapir, Whorf, and many others, comparing the Indian

43

languages with the Occidental languages, have underlined this diversity very forcefully. It seems, indeed, as if the arbitrary character of language, having been shown to be of comparatively little significance at the level of the elements of a language, reasserts itself quite definitely at the level of the language taken as a whole. And if one admits that a language represents a kind of destiny, so far as human thought is concerned, this diversity of languages leads to a radical relativism. As Peirce said, if Aristotle had been Mexican, his logic would have been different; and perhaps, by the same token, the whole of our philosophy and our science would have been different.

The fact is that this diversity affects not only the languages, but also the cultures, that is to say the whole system of institutions that are tied to the language . . . [and] language in its turn is the effect and the expression of a certain world view that is manifested in the culture. If there is causality, it is a reciprocal causality . . .

The types of structures characteristic of a given culture would then, in each case, be particular modes of universal laws. They would define the Volksgeist. . . .[2]

LOGIC AND RHETORIC

Logic (in the popular, rather than the logician's sense of the word) which is the basis of rhetoric, is evolved out of a culture; it is not universal. Rhetoric, then, is not universal either but varies from culture to culture and even from time to time within a given culture. It is affected by canons of taste within a given culture at a given time.

Every language offers to its speakers a ready-made *interpretation* of the world, truly a Weltanschauung, a metaphysical word-picture which, after having originated in the thinking of our ancestors, tends to impose itself ever anew on posterity. Take for instance a simple sentence such as 'I see him . . .' This means that English and, I might say, Indo-European, presents the impressions made on our senses predominantly as human *activities*, brought about by our *will*. But the Eskimos in Greenland say not 'I see him' but 'he appears to me. . . .' Thus the Indo-European speaker conceives as workings of his activities what the fatalistic Eskimo sees as events that happen to him.[3]

The English language and its related thought patterns have evolved out of the Anglo-European cultural pattern. The expected sequence of thought in English is essentially a Platonic-Aristotelian sequence, descended from the philosophers of ancient Greece and shaped subsequently by Roman, Medieval European, and later Western thinkers. It is not a better or a worse system than any other, but it is different.

As human beings, we must inevitably see the universe from a centre lying within ourselves and speak about it in terms of a human language by the exigencies of human intercourse. Any attempt rigorously to eliminate our human perspective from our picture of the world must lead to absurdity.[4]

A fallacy of some repute and some duration is the one which assumes that because a student can write an adequate essay in his native language, he can necessarily write an adequate essay in a second language. That this assumption is fallacious has become more and more apparent as English-as-a-second-language courses have proliferated at American colleges and universities in recent years. Foreign students who have mastered syntactic structures have still demonstrated inability to compose adequate themes, term papers, theses, and dissertations. Instructors have written, on foreign-student papers, such comments as: "The material is all here, but it seems somehow out of focus," or "Lacks organization," or "Lacks cohesion." And these comments are essentially accurate. The foreign-student paper is out of focus because the foreign student is employing a rhetoric and a sequence of thought which violate the expectations of the native reader.

> A personality is carved out by the whole subtle interaction of these systems of ideas which are characteristic of the culture as a whole, as well as of those systems of ideas which get established for the individual through more special types of participation.[5]

The fact that sequence of thought and grammar are related in a given language has already been demonstrated adequately by Paul Lorenzen. His brief paper proposes that certain linguistic structures are best comprehended as embodiments of logical structures.[6] Beyond that, every rhetorician from Cicero to Brooks and Warren has indicated the relationship between thought sequence and rhetoric.

> A paragraph, mechanically considered, is a division of the composition, set off by an indentation of its first sentence or by some other conventional device, such as extra space between paragraphs. . . . Paragraph divisions signal to the reader that the material so set off constitutes a unit of thought.
>
> For the reader this marking off of the whole composition into segments is a convenience, though not a strict necessity. . . . Since communication of one's thought is at best a difficult business, it is the part of common sense (not to mention good manners) to mark for the reader the divisions of one's thought and thus make the thought structure visible upon the page. . . .
>
> Paragraphing, obviously, can be of help to the reader only if the indicated paragraphs are genuine units of thought. . . . For a paragraph undertakes to discuss one topic or one aspect of a topic.[7]

PARAGRAPH DEVELOPMENT IN ENGLISH

The thought pattern which speakers and readers of English appear to expect as an integral part of their communication is a sequence that is dominantly linear in its development. An English expository paragraph usually begins with a topic statement, and then, by a series of subdivisions of that topic statement, each supported by example and illustrations, proceeds to develop that central idea and relate that idea to all the other ideas in the whole essay, and to employ that idea in its proper relationship with the other ideas, to prove something, or perhaps to argue something.

> A piece of writing may be considered unified when it contains *nothing* superfluous and it omits nothing essential to the achievement of its purpose. . . . A work is considered coherent when the sequence of its parts . . . is controlled by some principle which is meaningful to the reader. Unity is the quality attributed to writing which has all its necessary and sufficient parts. Coherence is the quality attributed to the presentation of material in a sequence which is intelligible to its reader.[8]

Contrarily, the English paragraph may use just the reverse procedure; that is, it may state a whole series of examples and then relate those examples into a single statement at the end of the paragraph. These two types of development represent the common *inductive* and *deductive* reasoning which the English reader expects to be an integral part of any formal communication.

For example, the following paragraph written by Macaulay demonstrates normal paragraph development:

Whitehall, when [Charles the Second] dwelt there, was the focus of political intrigue and of fashionable gaiety. Half the jobbing and half the flirting of the metropolis went on under his roof. Whoever could make himself agreeable to the prince or could secure the good offices of his mistress might hope to rise in the world without rendering any service to the government, without even being known by sight to any minister of state. This courtier got a frigate and that a company, a third the pardon of a rich offender, a fourth a lease of crown-land on easy terms. If the king notified his pleasure that a briefless lawyer should be made a judge or that a libertine baronet should be made a peer, the gravest counsellors, after a little murmuring, submitted. Interest, therefore, drew a constant press of suitors to the gates of the palace, and those gates always stood wide. The king kept open house every day and all day long for the good society of London, the extreme Whigs only excepted. Hardly any gentleman had any difficulty in making his way to the royal presence. The levee was exactly what the word imports. Some men of quality came every morning to stand around their master, to chat with him while his wig was combed and his cravat tied, and to accompany him in his early walk through the Park. All persons who had been properly introduced might, without any special invitation, go to see him dine, sup, dance, and play at hazard and might have the pleasure of hearing him tell stories, which indeed, he told remarkably well, about his flight from Worcester and about the misery which he had endured when he was a state prisoner in the hands of the canting meddling preachers of Scotland.[9]

The paragraph begins with a general statement of its content, and then carefully develops that statement by a long series of rather specific illustrations. While it is discursive, the paragraph is never digressive. There is nothing in this paragraph that does not belong here, nothing that does not contribute significantly to the central idea. The flow of ideas occurs in a straight line from the opening sentence to the last sentence.

CONTRAST WITH OTHER SYSTEMS

Without doing too much damage to other ways of thinking, perhaps it might be possible to contrast the English paragraph development with paragraph development in other linguistic systems.

For the purposes of the following brief analysis, some seven hundred foreign student compositions were carefully analyzed. Approximately one hundred of these were discarded from the study on the basis that they represent linguistic groups too small within the present sample to be significant.[10] But approximately six hundred examples, representing three basic language groups, were examined.[11]

In the Arabic language, for example (and this generalization would be more or less true for all Semitic languages), paragraph development is based on a complex series of parallel constructions, both positive and negative. This kind of parallelism may most clearly be demonstrated in English by reference to the King James version of the Old Testament. Several types of parallelism typical of Semitic languages are apparent there because that book, of course, is a translation from an ancient Semitic language, a translation accomplished at a time when English was in a state of development suitable to the imitation of those forms.

1. Synonymous parallelism; The balancing of the thought and phrasing of the first part of a statement or idea by the second part. In such cases, the two parts are often connected by a coordinating conjunction.

   Example: His descendants will be mighty in the land
       and
       the generation of the upright will be blessed.

2. Synthetic parallelism: The completion of the idea or thought of the first part in the second part. A conjunctive adverb is often stated or implied.

   Example: Because he inclined his ear to me
       therefore
       I will call on him as long as I live.

3. Antithetic parallelism: The idea stated in the first part is emphasized by the expression of a contrasting idea in the second part. The contrast is expressed not only in thought but often in phrasing as well.

   Example: For the Lord knoweth the way of the righteous:
       But the way of the wicked shall perish.

4. Climactic parallelism: The idea of the passage is not completed until the very end of the passage. This form is similar to the modern periodic sentence in which the subject is postponed to the very end of the sentence.

   Example: Give unto the Lord, O ye sons of the mighty,
       Give unto the Lord glory and strength.[12]

The type of parallel construction here illustrated in single sentences also forms the core of paragraphs in some Arabic writing. Obviously, such a development in a modern English paragraph would strike the modern English reader as archaic or awkward, and more importantly it would stand in the way of clear communication. It is important to note that in English, maturity of style is often gauged by degree of subordination rather than by coordination.

  The following paper was written as a class exercise by an Arabic-speaking student in an English-as-a-second-language class at an American university:

The contemporary Bedouins, who live in the deserts of Saudi Arabia, are the successors of the old bedouin tribes, the tribes that was fascinated with Mohammad's massage, and on their shoulders Islam built it's empire. I had lived among those contemporary Bedouins for a short period of time, and I have learned lots of things about them. I found out that they have retained most of their ancestor's characteristics, inspite of the hundreds of years that separate them.

They are famous of many praiseworthy characteristics, but they are considered to be the symbol of generosity; bravery; and self-esteem. Like most of the wandering peoples, a stranger is an undesirable person among them. But, once they trust him as a friend, he will be most welcome. However, their trust is a hard thing to gain. And the heroism of many famous figures, who ventured in the Arabian deserts like T. E. Lawrence, is based on their ability to acquire this dear trust!

Romance is an important part in their life. And "love" is an important subject in their verses and their tales.

Nevertheless, they are criticized of many things. The worst of all is that they are extremists in all the ways of their lives. It is there extremism that changes sometimes their generosity into squandering, their bravery into brutality, and their self-esteem into haughtiness. But in any case, I have been, and will continue to be greatly interested in this old, fascinating group of people.

Disregarding for the moment the grammatical errors in this student composition, it becomes apparent that the characteristics of parallelism do occur. The next-to-last element in the first sentence, for example, is appositive to the preceding one, while the last element is an example of synonymous parallelism. The two clauses of the second sentence illustrate synonymous parallelism. In the second "paragraph" the first sentence contains both an example of antithetic parallelism and a list of parallel nouns. The next two sentences form an antithetic pair, and so on. It is perhaps not necessary to point out further examples in the selection. It is important, however, to observe that in the first sentence, for example, the grammatical complexity is caused by the attempt to achieve an intricate parallelism. While this extensive parallel construction is linguistically possible in Arabic, the English language lacks the necessary flexibility. Eight conjunctions and four sentence connectors are employed in a matter of only fourteen "sentences." In addition, there are five "lists" of units connected by commas and conjunctions.

Another paper, also written by an Arabic-speaking student under comparable circumstances, further demonstrates the same tendencies:

At that time of the year I was not studying enough to pass my courses in school. *And* all the time I was asking my cousin to let me ride the bicycle, *but* he wouldn't let me. *But* after two weeks, noticing that I was so much interested in the bicycle, he promised me that if I pass my courses in school for that year he would give it to me as a present. *So* I began to study hard. *And* I studying eight hours a day instead of two.

My cousin seeing me studying that much he was sure that I was going to succeed in school. *So* he decided to give me some lessons in riding the bicycle. After four or five weeks of teaching me and ten or twelve times hurting myself as I used to go out of balance, I finally knew how to ride it. And the finals in school came *and* I was very good prepared for them *so* I passed them. My cousin kept his promise *and* give me the bicycle as a present. *And* till now I keep the bicycle in a safe place, *and* everytime I see it, It reminds me how it helped to pass my courses for that year.

In the first paragraph of this example, four of the five sentences, or 80 percent of the sentences, begin with a coordinating element. In the second paragraph, three of the six sentences, or 50 percent of the total, also begin with a coordinating element. In the whole passage, seven of the eleven sentences, or roughly 65 percent, conform to this pattern. In addition, the first paragraph contains one internal coordinator, and the second contains five internal coordinators; thus, the brief passage (210 words) contains a total of thirteen coordinators. It is important to notice that almost all of the ideas in the passage are coordinately linked, that there is very little subordination, and that the parallel units exemplify the types of parallelism already noted.

Some Oriental[13] writing, on the other hand, is marked by what may be called an approach by indirection. In this kind of writing, the development of the paragraph may be said to be "turning and turning in a widening gyre." The circles or gyres turn around the subject and show it from a variety of tangential views, but the subject is never looked at directly. Things are developed in terms of what they are not, rather than in terms of what they are. Again, such a development in a modern English paragraph would strike the English reader as awkward and unnecessarily indirect.

The following composition was written, as a class exercise, by a native speaker of Korean, under the same circumstances which produced the two previous examples. Obviously, this student is weaker in general English proficiency than the students who produced the two prior examples.

DEFINITION OF COLLEGE EDUCATION
College is an institution of an higher learning that gives degrees. All of us needed culture and education in life, if no education to us, we should to go living hell.
One of the greatest causes that while other animals have remained as they first man along has made such rapid progress is has learned about civilization.
The improvement of the highest civilization is in order to education up-to-date.
So college education is very important thing which we don't need mention about it.

Again, disregarding the typically Oriental grammar and the misconception of the function of "parts of speech," the first sentence defines college, not college education. This may conceivably be a problem based upon the student's misunderstanding of the assignment. But the second sentence appears to shoot off in a totally different direction. It makes a general statement about culture and education, perhaps as *results* of a college education. The third sentence, presented as a separate "paragraph," moves still farther away from the definition by expanding the topic to "man" in a generic sense, as opposed to "nonman." This unit is tied to the next, also presented as a separate paragraph, by the connecting idea of "civilization" as an aspect of education. The concluding paragraph-sentence presents, in the guise of a summary logically derived from previously posited ideas, a conclusion which is in fact partially a topic sentence and partially a statement that the whole basic concept of the assignment is so obvious that it does not need discussion. The paper arrives where it should have started, with the added statement that it really had no place to go to begin with.

The poorer proficiency of this student, however, introduces two other considerations. It is possible that this student, as an individual rather than as a representative native speaker of Korean, lacks the ability to abstract sufficiently for extended definition. In the case under discussion, however, the student was majoring in mathematics and did have the ability to abstract in mathematical terms. While the demands of mathematics are somewhat different from the demands of language in a conventional sense, it is possible to assume that a student who can handle abstraction in one area can also probably handle it at least to some extent in the other. It is also possible that the ability to abstract is absent from the Korean culture. This appears quite unlikely in view of the abundance of Korean art available and in view of the fact that other native speakers of Korean have not demonstrated that shortcoming.

The examples cited so far have been student themes. The following example is from a professional translation. Essentially, the same variations can be observed in it. In this case, the translation is from French.

> The first point to which I would like to call your attention is that nothing exists outside the boundary of what is strictly human. A landscape may be beautiful, graceful, sublime, insignificant, or ugly; it will never be ludicrous. We may laugh at an animal, but only because we have detected in it some human expression or attitude. We may laugh at a hat, but we are not laughing at the piece of felt or straw. We are laughing at the shape that men have given to it, the human whim whose mold it has assumed. *I wonder why a fact so important has not attracted the attention of philosophers to a greater degree. Some have defined man as an animal that knows how to laugh. They could equally well have defined him as an animal which provokes laughter; for if any other animal or some lifeless object, achieves the same effect, it is always because of some similarity to man.*[14]

In this paragraph, the italicized portion constitutes a digression. It is an interesting digression, but it really does not seem to contribute significant structural material to the basic thought of the paragraph. While the author of the paragraph is a philosopher, and a philosopher is often forgiven digressions, the more important fact is that the example is a typical one for writers of French as well as for writers of philosophy. Much greater freedom to digress or to introduce extraneous material is available in French or in Spanish than in English.

Similar characteristics can be demonstrated in the writing of native French-speaking students in English. In the interests of keeping this report within some bounds, such illustrations will be inserted without comment. The first example was written under circumstances similar to those described for the preceeding student samples. The writer is a native speaker of French.

AMERICAN TRAFFIC LAW AS COMPARED WITH
TRAFFIC LAW IN SWITZERLAND

> At first glance the traffic law in the United States appeared to me simpler than in Switzerland.
> The American towns in general have the disposition of a cross, and for a driver who knows how to situate himself between the four cardinal points, there is no problem to find his way. Each street has numbers going crescendo from the center of the town to the outside.
> There are many accidents in Switzerland, as everywhere else, and the average of mortality comparatively to the proportion of the countries is not better than in United States. We have the problem of straight streets, not enough surveillance by policemen on the national roads, and alcohol. The country of delicious wines has made too many damages.

The following illustration, drawn from the work of a native speaker of Latin American Spanish, was produced under conditions parallel to those already cited:

THE AMERICAN CHILDREN

In America, the American children are brought differently from the rest of the children in other countries. In their childhood, from the first day they are born, the parents give their children the love and attention they need. They teach their children the meaning of Religion among the family and to have respect and obedience for their parents.

I am Spanish, and I was brought up differently than the children in America. My parents are stricter and they taught me discipline and not to interrupt when someone was talking.

The next and last example is again not a piece of student writing, but a translation. The original was written in Russian, and the translation attempts to capture the structure of the original as much as possible, but without sacrificing meaning completely.

On the 14th of October, Khrushchev left the stage of history. Was it a plot the result of which was that Khrushchev was out of business remains not clear. It is very probable that even if it were anything resembling a plot it would not be for the complete removal of Khrushchev from political guidance, but rather a pressure exerted to obtain some changes in his policies: for continuations of his policies of peaceful co-existence in international relations or making it as far as possible a situation to avoid formal rupture with the Chinese communist party and at any rate not to go unobstructed to such a rupture—and in the area of internal politics, especially in the section of economics, to continue efforts of a certain softening of "dogmatism," but without the hurried and not sufficiently reasoned experimentation, which became the characteristic traits of Khrushchev's politics in recent years.[15]

Some of the difficulty in this paragraph is linguistic rather than rhetorical. The structure of the Russian sentence is entirely different from the structure of the English sentence. But some of the linguistic difficulty is closely related to the rhetorical difficulty. The above paragraph is composed of three sentences. The first two are very short, while the last is extremely long, constituting about three quarters of the paragraph. It is made up of a series of presumably parallel constructions and a number of subordinate structures. At least half of these are irrelevant to the central idea of the paragraph in the sense that they are parenthetical amplifications of structurally related subordinate elements.

There are, of course, other examples that might be discussed as well, but these paragraphs may suffice to show that each language and each culture has a paragraph order unique to itself, and that part of the learning of a particular language is the mastering of its logical system.

One should join to any logic of the language a phenomenology of the spoken word. Moreover, this phenomenology will, in its turn, rediscover the idea of a logos immanent in the language; but it will seek the justification for this in a more general philosophy of the relations between man and the world. . . . From one culture to another it is possible to establish communication. The Rorschach test has been successfully applied to the natives of the island of Alor.[16]

This discussion is not intended to offer any criticism of other existing paragraph developments; rather it is intended only to demonstrate that paragraph developments other than those normally regarded as desirable in English do exist. In the teaching of paragraph structure to foreign students, whether in terms of reading or in terms of composition, the teacher must be himself aware of these differences, and he must make these differences overtly apparent to his students. In short, contrastive rhetoric must be taught in the same sense that contrastive grammar is presently taught. Now not much has been done in the area of contrastive rhetoric. It is first necessary to arrive at accurate descriptions of existing paragraph orders other than those common to English. Furthermore, it is necessary to understand that these categories are in no sense meant to be mutually exclusive. Patterns may be derived for *typical* English paragraphs, but paragraphs like those described above as being atypical in English do exist in English. By way of obvious example, Ezra Pound writes paragraphs which are circular in their structure, and William Faulkner writes paragraphs which are wildly digressive. The paragraph being discussed here is not the "literary" paragraph, however, but the expository paragraph. The necessities of art impose structures on any language, while the requirements of communication can often be best solved by relatively close adhesion to established patterns.

Superficially, the movement of the various paragraphs discussed above may be graphically represented in the following manner:

English　　　*Semitic*　　　*Oriental*　　　*Romance*　　　*Russian*

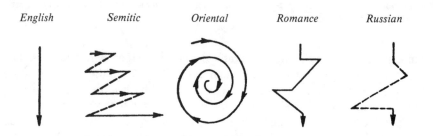

Much more detailed and more accurate descriptions are required before any meaningful contrastive system can be elaborated. Nonetheless, an important problem exists immediately. In the teaching of English as a second language, what does one do with the student who is reasonably proficient in the use of syntactic structure but who needs to learn to write themes, theses, essay examinations, and dissertations? The "advanced" student has long constituted a problem for teachers of English as a second language. This approach, the contrastive analysis of rhetoric, is offered as one possible answer to the existing need. Such an approach has the advantage that it may help the foreign student to form standards of judgment consistent with the demands made upon him by the educational system of which he has become a part. At the same time, by accounting for the cultural aspects of logic which underlie the rhetorical structure, this approach may bring the student not only to an understanding of contrastive grammar and a new vocabulary, which are parts of any reading task, but also to a grasp of idea and structure in units larger than the sentence. A sentence, after all, rarely exists outside a context. Applied linguistics teaches the student to deal with the sentence, but it is necessary to bring the student beyond that to a comprehension of the whole context. He can only understand the whole context if he recognizes the logic on which the context is based. The foreign student who has mastered the syntax of English may still write a bad paragraph or a bad paper unless he also masters the logic of English. *"In serious expository prose, the paragraph tends to be a logical, rather than a typographical unit."*[17] The understanding of paragraph patterns can allow the student to relate syntactic elements within a paragraph and perhaps even to relate paragraphs within a total context.

Finally, it is necessary to recognize the fact that a paragraph is an artificial thought unit employed in the written language to suggest a cohesion which commonly may not exist in oral language. "Paragraphing, like punctuation, is a feature only of the written language."[18] As an artificial unit of thought, it lends itself to patterning quite readily. In fact, since it is imposed from without, and since it is a frame for the structuring of thought into patterns, it is by its very nature patterned. The rhetorical structures of English paragraphs may be found in any good composition text.[19] The patterns of paragraphs in other languages are not so well established, or perhaps only not so well known to speakers of English. These patterns need to be discovered or uncovered and compared with the patterns of English in order to arrive at a practical means for the teaching of such structures to nonnative users of the language.

In the interim, while research is directed at the rhetorics of other languages, certain practical pedagogical devices have been developed to expedite the teaching of rhetorical structures to nonnative speakers of English. An elementary device consists simply of supplying to the students a scrambled paragraph. A normal paragraph, such as the one cited from Macaulay above, may be arbitrarily scrambled, the sentences numbered, and the students asked to rearrange the sentences in what appears to them to be a normal order. Frequently, the results of such an assignment will demonstrate the diversity of views or cultures represented in the classroom. The exercise can be used effectively to point out the very disparity. The students must then be presented with the original version of the paragraph, and the instructor must be able to explain and justify the order of the original.

[Instructions: Arrange the sentences below into some normal order.]

SCRAMBLED ORDER

1. A jackass brays; a turkey cock gobbles; a dog yelps; a church bell clangs.

2. The narrow streets and lanes leading into the market are crammed with Indians, their dark skins glistening like copper or bronze in the bright sun, their varicolored cloaks looking like a mass of palette colors smeared together.

3. There is the smell of animal dung mingled with the order of carnations and heliotrope from the flower stalls.

4. In the open plaza outside the market the crowd mills about.
5. Mothers sit on the curb nursing their babies.
6. A kind of blending of Indian talk in various dialects creates a strange droning noise.
7. On the narrow sidewalks, merchandise is spread so haphazardly that in order to pass, pedestrians have to press against the wall or leap the displays.
8. Wrinkled old women squat over charcoal braziers cooking corn cakes, or black beans, or pink coconut candy.

[This is the order in which the author arranged his sentences. Can you detect his reason?]

NORMAL ORDER

The narrow streets and lanes leading into the market are crammed with Indians, their dark skins glistening like copper or bronze in the bright sun, their varicolored cloaks looking like a mass of palette colors smeared together. In the open plaza outside the market the crowd mills about. A kind of blending of Indian talk in various dialects creates a strange droning noise. A jackass brays; a turkey cock gobbles; a dog yelps; a church bell clangs. On the narrow sidewalks, merchandise is spread so haphazardly that in order to pass, pedestrians have to press against the wall or leap the displays. Wrinkled old women squat over charcoal braziers cooking corn cakes, or black beans, or pink coconut candy. Mothers sit on the curb nursing their babies. There is the smell of animal dung mingled with the odor of carnations and heliotrope from the flower stalls.[20]
[This paragraph is descriptive, presented in the present tense, and arranged perceptually in the order of sight, hearing, and smell.]

A second device consists of giving the students carefully written topic sentences, arranged in some convenient way such as that suggested below, and then asking the students to fill out the subdivisions of the topic sentence with examples and illustrations chosen to support the point. Depending upon the relative difficulty of the topic, the examples may be supplied by the instructor in scrambled order.

AMERICAN TELEVISION

American commercial television appears to consist of three principal classes of material: programs of serious interest, such as news broadcasts and special features; programs intended primarily as entertainment, such as variety shows, situation comedies, and adventure tales; and the advertisements which link all of these.

I. Programs of serious interest:
   A. News Broadcasts:
      1. _____
      2. _____
   B. Special Features:
      1. _____
      2. _____
II. Programs intended primarily as entertainment:
   A. Variety Shows:
      1. _____
      2. _____
   B. Situational Comedies:
      1. _____
      2. _____

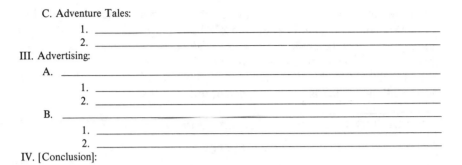

C. Adventure Tales:
    1. _____
    2. _____
III. Advertising:
  A. _____
    1. _____
    2. _____
  B. _____
    1. _____
    2. _____
IV. [Conclusion]:

[Instructions: The student is to supply contrasting examples for each of the spaces provided under items I and II. In item III the student must also supply the main subdivisions, and in item IV the point of the whole essay must also be supplied by the student. Obviously, item IV will vary considerably depending upon the kinds of illustrations selected to fill the blanks.]

The illustration constitutes a very simple exercise. Greater sophistication may be employed as the student becomes more familiar with the techniques. Obviously, too, the outline must be introduced and taught simultaneously. A simple technique for teaching the outline may be found illustrated in a number of texts for both American and foreign students.[21]

It is important to impress upon the student that "A paragraph is *clear* when each sentence contributes to the central thought . . . [and that] clarity also demands coherence, that is, an orderly flow of sentences marked by repetition of key ideas."[22]

While it is necessary for the nonnative speaker learning English to master the rhetoric of the English paragraph, it must be remembered that the foreign student, ideally, will be returning to his home country, and that his stay in the United States is a brief one. Under these circumstances, English is a means to an end for him; it is not an end in itself. Edward Sapir has written:

An oft-noted peculiarity of the development of culture is the fact that it reaches its greatest heights in comparatively small, autonomous groups. In fact, it is doubtful if a genuine culture ever properly belongs to more than such a restricted group, a group between the members of which there can be said to be something like direct intensive spiritual contact. This direct contact is enriched by the common cultural heritage on which the minds of all are fed. . . . A narrowly localized culture may, and often does, spread its influence far beyond its properly restricted sphere. Sometimes it sets the pace for a whole nationality, for a far flung empire. It can do so, however, only at the expense of diluting the spirit as it moves away from its home, of degenerating into an imitative attitudinizing.[23]

He is absolutely correct in pointing out the dangers of spreading a culture too thin and too far from home. However, in the special case of the foreign student learning English, under the conditions stipulated above, the imitation which would be an error in most cases is the sought aim. The classes which undertake the training of the "advanced" student can aim for no more. The creativity and imagination which make the difference between competent writing and excellent writing are things which, at least in these circumstances, cannot be taught. The foreign student is an adult in most cases. If these things are teachable, they will already have been taught to him. The English class must not aim too high. Its function is to provide the student with a form within which he may operate, a form acceptable in this time and in this place. It is hoped that the method described above may facilitate the achievement of that goal.

EXPLORING THE IDEAS—*Composition evaluation*

ACTIVITY 1

Background   The essays included here were written by students from three of the language groups characterized by Kaplan: Romance, Oriental, Semitic. They were all written in response to the following topic:

> Most people have one possession that is especially important to them. For example, someone may value a musical instrument because of the many hours she spends playing music on it. Another person may value a piece of jewelry because it belonged to a relative. Finally, another person may value a photograph, a teapot or a wall hanging because it reminds him of home.
>
> Think about a possession you have that is very important to you. Write a paper in which you: first describe it, and then explain why it is so important to you.
>
> In the first part, be so specific that the reader will have a picture of it in his or her mind. In the second part, provide sufficient examples so that the reader understands exactly why the object is valuable to you.

In his article, Kaplan did not indicate the topic that his students wrote on. It may be that a highly structured writing topic, such as the one listed above, would encourage students to adhere to the linear development of English rhetoric. Thus, any deviation from a typical English pattern would be even more significant.

Application

SEMITIC

Kaplan (page 47) distinguishes the following types of parallelism that he believes are typical of Semitic languages.

> 1. Synonymous parallelism: The balancing of the thought and phrasing of the first part of a statement or idea by the second part. In such cases, the two parts are often connected by a coordinate conjunction.
> Example: His descendants will be mighty in the land *and* the generation of the upright will be blessed.
> 2. Synthetic parallelism: The completion of the idea or thought of the first part in the second part. A conjunctive adverb is often stated or implied.
> Example: Because he inclined his ear to me *therefore* I will call on him as long as I live.
> 3. Antithetic parallelism: The idea stated in the first part is emphasized by the expression of a contrasting idea in the second part. The contrast is expressed not only in thought but often in phrasing as well.
> Example: For the Lord knoweth the way of the righteous: But the way of the wicked shall perish.

4. Climactic paralellism: The idea of the passage is not completed until the very end of the passage. This form is similar to the modern periodic sentence in which the subject is postponed to the very end of the sentence.
Example: Give unto the Lord, O ye sons of the mighty, Give unto the Lord glory and strength.

List any sentences in the essays of the Arabic students which demonstrate parallelism. In addition, since Kaplan is arguing that parallelism is evident not only on a sentence level but also on a discourse level, point out examples of parallelism on a discourse level.
Which of the essays do you feel most closely adheres to the English rhetorical pattern? Which of the essays did you find most interesting to read? Why?

STUDENT A

Even though I am not the materialistic type of person and even though I don't like to use the word possession because I feel kind of a selfish person. But I have something special, it is a ring my mother gave me around four years ago before I left my country to the U.S. for my education.

The ring is 18 K gold with my initial engraved in it, it is a very small and simple ring and looks like a wedding ring.

I consider the ring important to me not because I like gold or any fancy jewlery, but because it was given to me by somebody whom I love and respect. And because every time I look at it I remember my mother, family, my country and people.

It took me a while before I adopted to the American culture, so I felt lonely and the ring was my only companion.

Everytime I look at the ring I also remember the advice my mother gave with it. She told me, "Son, you are going to a country with different language and culture. You are going to face problems but be strong and struggle to get your education and come back to us."

So as you can conclude it is not the materialistic value of the ring that is important to me, it is the memory with the ring.

STUDENT B

Music is very important for humans. It takes you to a different atmosphere and relax your mind. Every culture has its own set or kinds of music both fast and slow. Most instruments are used for both types of music, that is fast and slow. There is an instrument in the Arabic culture called "Lute." Lute is made of thin wood in a shape of almost half a sphere with a piece of wood in a shape of a ruler at one side of it. It has five doubled strings to make the sound louder and you can control the sound of each string just like the gitar. The cavity in the half sphere gives it better sound. Because Lute is made of wood, it can be a piece of art with drawings on it. To play the lute you have to have a great skill because you have to judge the place at which you press to shorten the string.

Lute is very important to me because when I play it, I really loose myself in all kinds of imaginations. If I am tired or depressed all I have to do is to play the Lute and after that I relax mentally. My father is the one who taught me how to play it. When you play the Lute you hug it so to speak. Lute is the main instrument in my culture and it is mainly used for eastern music. There is a thing called "Lute Solo" which is type of music you play on the Lute but it does not have rythm and you play it by yourself and not companied by other instruments. Lute is used mainly for the solo.

STUDENT C

Since I am an artist, one of the possession I value a lot is my paintings. The fact is, of all my work, I'm strickly attached to one drawing of a man holding his little sons hand and standing by his wife's grave, in a windy day, just about sunset time, where the sky was colored with red, and the darkness had covered the land.

Actually, there's not much to describe in the physical appearance of the painting, to me it's more than just a sunset in a windy day, it's love standing against nature's will and a renewall of all the promesses by the father to his wife. I happen to be Lebanese where almost every family have lost a member in the last eight years of war, therefore I see all my people feelings comming to reality. As to me personaly it reminds me of the sentimental state I was in, I was sad and sadness to me is like the beauty of a sunset, and I was optimistic and that's like the man's will to keep going.

STUDENT D

Three years ago when I came to America, I brought a small persian rug which was very valuable to me. It was made up by people who lived in villages in Iran. It has a rectanglar shape, containing a mixture of bright colors. The colors are very unique and peaceful. A good combination of different colors such as blue, white, green, red and some other colors showing the rug's picture nicely. The picture on the rug was made by some beautiful birds, flying in the sky. The material which was used for making the rug is soft and delicate. So the rug is light and too easy to carry it.

The reason I love this particlur rug described above is first that was a gift from my grandmother when I was 15 years ago. Since then I always took care of it. It was kept in my room all the time. I used to look at it every morning when I woke up. It was a very beautiful rug I have ever seen. When I look at it carefully I can't stop admiring all the effort and art which were applied by people who made it. Second I have another memory of my rug, I used to pray on that rug every day. That's why it is very valuable to me. Third when my grandmother died I always felt I was not alone because I have somthing from her to remind of her. I know it was very important to my grandmother so I try to keep and take care of it well. And I don't want to exchange it with anything else in this world.

ORIENTAL

The following essays were all written by native Japanese speakers. In his article, Kaplan defines Oriental as specifically Chinese and Korean, but not Japanese. After studying the essays of the Japanese students, point out specific things which either support or refute a model of Oriental indirection in their writing. If you can provide an alternate characterization of a prevalent pattern in their essays, be sure to do so.

Which of the essays do you feel most closely adheres to an English rhetorical pattern? Which of the essays did you find most interesting to read? Why?

STUDENT A

The most important possession to me has been always cats. They are sometimes friends, and on the other times, they are mysterious creature from the other world. Cat is very nice animal to talk with when I'm alone (of course it is only one way talking) and affectionate with budding his body to me. On the other hand, his figure is smooth and sexy. His eyes shines in the dark. He is a animal of nights, who walks around without making any sounds. Because of these traits, some people have strong fear of cats. Mysterious stories have been associated to cats for long time in a lot of countries. I believe in strange things—super natural power like E.S.P. Cats reminds me those a sort of fantacies which make human beings separate from materialism.

In western countries and westernized countries, society gets very complicated and people tend to be mechanic and forget about spiritual values. The relationships are dry because people stay in their own small world to avoid troubles and disturbance from others.

When I look at a cat watching the movement of the outer world just by the window in my house, I feel like I have a beautiful visitor from the unknown world with super natural power. He has a nonverbal language talking or telling me something always. Cats are great friends and tellers.

STUDENT B

Money may be the most important one that I need. Well, people usually make wry faces when they know a person who talks about money; however, I feel that almost everyone wants to get money as much as they can. Without money, we cannot make our lives comfortably. You can imagine if you do not have money enough, who is going to give you a room, food, clothes, and some other things that you need to live. Sometimes money may cure a person of a disease. Rich man can easily visit his doctor when he feels he get a sick. On the other hand, poor man may stay at home and be patient even when he is under a serious condition. I can say money can buy everything. Of course money makes people ugly when it is the reason that people fight. Nevertheless, it is the one many people work for and so do I.

STUDENT C

I have a very nice camera which is indispensable to my life. My camera is called Nikon F2, which itself reminds me something that I had experienced before.

I had a camera from my elder sister three years ago when she married. I was asked to take pictures of my sister's wedding pictures. When my sister saw the pictures that I took for her, she was so surprised to see the pictures and thanked to me so much, and she gave her camera to me. That is, now, my camera Nikon F2. So, whenever I use my camera, I remember my sister and her wedding vividly. I don't need to see pictures. I just look at the camera for a while and I recall my sister. My camera is the memory of my sister who left my house three years ago. So, I won't sell my camera to anybody, even if somebody give me thousands and hundreds dollars. I remember not only my sister but also my father, my mother and my friend. Putting my camera on the desk now, I recall everything what I had experienced for three years.

After I got a camera from my sister I began to take many kinds of pictures when I felt to be inspired to take pictures. I had been taken pictures just for fun or just casually. But I found out that I was taking pictures what I wished to be, not casual.

STUDENT D

I have one tennis racket that is important to me for a long time. I would like to describe my tennis racket and explain why it's important to me.

My tennis racket that I bought when I was in high school is a steel racket. The shape is everybody can imagine because I guess everybody knows how a tennis racket looks like. One particular thing of my racket is it's made from steel which differs from the wood racket. The color of the racket is silver and the end of the glip has red color on which a white letter "W," which is a beginning letter of bland name, "Wilson." The red color seems that this racket belongs to female player.

The racket is very important to me because it has been teaching me something special. Since I got the racket, I have been playing a lot of games with other players. Sometimes I won several games and sometimes I lost; however, everytime the racket seemed to tell me something special. I don't know what it is exactly, but I think it might be a kind of patience. It didn't matter if I won the game or not. The important thing was that I had patience while I was playing. When I was winning, I had patience to win the game. When I was defeated by the player, I had also patience to the player and myself, I think.

Of course, I brought the racket when I came to the United States. Sometimes I play tennis with my friend. Whenever I see my tennis racket, it reminds me of that I should have patience to every body with whom I'm related and everything which happens to me.

ROMANCE

The following essays were written by native Spanish speakers. Kaplan contends that more freedom to digress is allowed in French and Spanish than in English. List specific examples from the essays which either support or refute this contention.

Which of the essays do you feel most closely adheres to an English rhetorical pattern? Which of the essays did you find the most interesting to read? Why?

STUDENT A

I am an electrical engineer and normally works with a lot of instrument but for me, the most important is the voltmeter. This instrument has several parts: the reading scale, two terminals that you use to measure the voltage, and there is a knob for changing the measurer's scale and the type of current you have (continuous or alternative). Besides, there are two holes in front of the voltmeter, one is the positive terminal and the other is the negative one (only use for continuous current) that hold the two terminals.

This instrument is very important for me because, every time I have to be in contact with electrial equipment, I have to be sure that the equipment is not connected although you see the mainswitch is off and it is unpluged (Could be a condenser), and the way to check any equipment safety is with the voltmeter. One of my friend, an electrical engineer too, had an accident because he didn't check the equipment before he started to work on it. It was not very bad, but enought to show me not to trust to anything that I'm not sure has voltage or not, and even if I am sure, better is to check twice than have an "electrical shock."

STUDENT B

I love our old family picture album. It is full of old pictures; babies, young couples in love, old couples and more babies, that were born before the first world war. Of all those pictures there are some that for some reasons I like them the most. Those are my grandparents pictures. I never had the chance to meet them when they were alive. Throught those photographs I learned how they were and how they looked. My grandmother how arrogant she was, perfect hair, fancy clothes. She loved parties, friends. How ironic to learn that she died in rags, insane. Her husband (my grandfather) a dignified, very well educated man, always looked mean, or unhappy maybe. He died too young. Just he looking at those pictures I could write a book if I new how to, but then I think what is the big thing about it, what is so special about them. In a century from now only pictures would be left from us on blurry memories perhaps, because we all be gone. And maybe another young person (like me) will be looking at the same type of pictures and thinking similar things.

STUDENT C

As a rule I don't keep anything that brings me memories from the past. I don't know why, but I almost always get rid of my things and replace them for new ones. Friends tell me that my places (very often) has a different look and that's because I'm constantly changing my furniture. However there is one thing that I have kept over the years and it is a picture of a big portion of my family and relatives. This is not a big picture, it is rather small. It was taken on Mothers' Days a few years ago. There are so many people in this picture that is hard to recognize their faces. Starting from left to right you could see my four uncles, followed my mother (smiling as usual), my two sisters, who look like they have been fighting, my grandmother is right in the center of the picture, I noticed her face and it is like she is saying "When are you going to finish taking this picture," three of my aunts are in the right side of my grandmother. Now this is the first row, because in the second one I could see (they are in front sitting down) my four brothers who look like angels. (They must be up to something), my father who looks bord, my four cousins are also here. And I could see their big teeth. Everybody is in my mother's living room which looks beatiful with all those flowers given by her children. I could see the walls which had been painted recently of white they look so clean, I can not see any chairs in the living room, but in the left side (down) of the picture I could see part of the table with a big cake that looks like a wedding cake. It is too bad that the picture is a little bit too dark because you can't apreciate very well the guy in the front row sitting down on the very right (guess who?*) Why do I like this picture? because it was taken on a day that all of us were very happy, especially me. Everytime I look at this picture brings me good feelings about my people back home. This is the only picture that I have of all of them together. This is the picture of my beatiful family.

*myself

Teaching strategies

ACTIVITY 1

Background   According to Kaplan, one distinctive characteristic of English paragraph development is that it is not digressive; everything in a paragraph contributes to the central idea. There are undoubtedly many exceptions to this pattern in published expository prose. However, if this is a prevalent pattern that we want our students to be familiar with, it is important to teach the idea of relevancy of support.

Application   Design two exercises to help students develop the concept of relevancy of support. One possibility is to have students identify irrelevant sentences within a paragraph. Another possibility is to list a topic sentence with supporting details, some of which are relevant and some of which are not. Students could then be asked to identify the irrelevant sentences.

NOTES

1. Robert T. Oliver, Foreword. Maurice Nathanson and Henry W. Johnstone, Jr. (eds.). In *Philosophy, Rhetoric and Argumentation.* University Park, Pa., 1965, pp. x–xi.

2. Mikel Dufrenne, *Language and Philosophy.* trans. Henry B. Veatch. Bloomington, 1963, pp. 35–37.

3. Leo Spitzer, Language—The Basis of Science, Philosophy and Poetry. In George Boas et al. (eds.). *Studies in Intellectual History.* Baltimore, 1953, pp. 83–84.

4. Michael Polanyi, *Personal Knowledge: Towards a Post-Critical Philosophy.* Chicago, 1958, p. 9.

5. Edward Sapir, Anthropology and Psychiatry. *Culture, Language and Personality.* Los Angeles, 1964, p. 157.

6. *Logik und Grammatik.* Mannheim, Germany, 1965.

7. Cleanth Brooks and Robert Penn Warren, *Modern Rhetoric,* 2d ed. New York, 1958, pp. 267–268.

8. Richard E. Hughes and P. Albert Duhamel, *Rhetoric: Principles and Usage.* Englewood Cliffs, N.J., 1962, pp. 19–20.

9. From *The History of England from the Accession of James the Second.* London, 1849–1861.

10. The following examples were discarded: Afghan–3, African–4, Danish–1, Finn–1, German–3, Hindi–8, Persian–46, Russian–1, Greek–1, Tagalog–10, Turk–16, Urdu–5; Total–99.

11. The papers examined may be linguistically broken down as follows: Group I–Arabic–126, Hebrew–3; Group II–Chinese (Mandarin)–110, Cambodian–40, Indochinese–7, Japanese–135, Korean–57, Laotian–3, Malasian–1, Thai–27, Vietnamese–1; Group III–(Spanish-Portuguese) Brazilian–19, Central American–10, South American–42, Cuban–4, Spanish–8 (French) French–2, African–2 (Italian) Swiss–1. Group I total–129; Group II total–381; Group III total–88; Total–598. These papers were accumulated and examined over a 2-year period, from the beginning of the fall 1963 semester through the fall 1965 academic semester.

12. I am indebted to Dr. Ben Siegel for this analysis.

13. *Oriental* here is intended to mean specifically Chinese and Korean but not Japanese.

14. From *Laughter, An Essay on the Meaning of the Comic.* trans. Marcel Bolomet, Paris, 1900.

15. From S. Schwartz, After Khrushchev. trans. E. B. Kaplan, *The Socialist Courier.* April 1965, p. 3.

16. Dufrenne, *Language and Philosophy,* pp. 39–40.

17. Hans P. Guth, *A Short New Rhetoric.* Belmont, Calif., 1964, p. 205.

18. Edward P. J. Corbett, *Classical Rhetoric for the Modern Student.* New York, 1965, p. 416.

19. Important work in the rhetoric of the paragraph is being done by Francis Christensen, among others. See especially A Generative Rhetoric of the Paragraph. *College Composition and Communication.* October 1965, pp. 144–156.

20. Hudson Strode, The Market at Toluca. *Now in Mexico.* New York, 1947.

21. At the risk of being accused of immodesty, I would recommend in particular the section entitled Outlining in Robert B. Kaplan, *Reading and Rhetoric.* New York, 1963, pp. 69–80.

22. Francis Connolly, *A Rhetoric Casebook.* New York, 1953, p. 304.

23. Edward Sapir, Culture, Genuine and Spurious. *Culture, Language and Personality.* Los Angeles, 1964, pp. 113–114.

4

Reading Research and the Composition Teacher: The Importance of Plans[1]

Bonnie J. F. Meyer

A plan consists of a goal and steps to achieve that goal. Plans are obviously a central component of the processes of communicating and understanding. A writer must evolve some general plan of what to say; and a reader must somehow be able to follow the plan along. However, there has so far been only a small amount of work which relates the psychology of planning to the act of writing.[2] It might be helpful to consider some research on *reading* as a potential means of exploring the role of planning.

Reading research has demonstrated the important role played by the *mental representation* formed in the mind of human beings who read texts. This representation cannot be the text itself; that is, it cannot be a linear series of individual words as presented on the page. Although this mental representation is important for many tasks, such as writing, reporting, summarizing, and commenting, readers will seldom be able to provide a word-for-word account of the original text. Therefore, a better understanding of what this mental representation is and how it forms in *long-term memory* should help writers plan texts which enable their readers to create representations that better match the writer's purpose in the communication.

For a writer, the *plan* is like a set of directions about how to present one's materials. I shall be concerned here with three important *functions* that writing plans have. In their *topical function*, they help a writer conceive and organize main ideas on a topic. In their *highlighting function*, they help the writer show the reader how some ideas are of greater importance than others. In their *informing function*, they help the writer see how to present new knowledge while keeping readers aware of the old.

THE TOPICAL FUNCTION OF PLANS

Evidence shows that a communication is vastly more efficient (it saves effort) and effective (it gets results) if it follows a topical plan instead of being a miscellaneous sequence of sentences or paragraphs.[3] That is, people remember more and read faster information which is logically organized with a topical plan than they do when the same information is presented in a disorganized, random fashion. One study compared readers' ability to comprehend paragraphs in normal sequences with their comprehension of the paragraphs arranged in a scrambled order.[4] Students read a narrative passage of 1,400 words and then wrote summaries. The scrambled versions were much more time-consuming to read. Interestingly, the summaries produced by the two groups were much the same. No doubt the readers were using the extra time to unscramble the content. Under severe time limitations, they were no longer able to do so and produced inferior summaries.

Such findings suggest that the presence of a visible plan for presenting content plays a crucial role in assuring the interpretability of a passage. Differences in *text types* are in part a result of differences in writing plans. The same content can be recast according to various plans and plan functions, and the impact on communication will vary. Thus, the plan of a discourse can be considered apart from content, and deserves separate consideration from researchers, as from those who are planning a composition.

My own work has been largely in reading and comprehension, with particular emphasis on the notion of the *hierarchy*. A text is not just a series of sentences or paragraphs precisely because it displays a hierarchy of content, so that some facts (statements, etc.) are superordinate or subordinate to others.[5] It seems plain that the process of creating such a hierarchy must be governed by some plan. But it is not at all plain how writers and readers *form* and carry out their plans, nor is it plain that in dealing with the same text writers and readers are following the same plan. As will be remarked below, readers who use a plan different from the author's may be at a disadvantage.

Drawing upon linguistics and rhetoric, I have gathered empirical evidence that five basic writing plans have specific kinds of impact on reading comprehension.[6] These five types are designated as follows: *antecedent/consequent, comparison, description, response,* and *time-order.* The typology is not intended to be exhaustive or definitive, but there is good support for the belief that significant distinctions are present here.

The *antecedent/consequent* plan is devoted to presenting *causal relationships* (like the "if/then" of antecedent/consequent statements in logic). The *comparison* plan presents *two opposing viewpoints,* and can be subdivided accordingly: the *alternative* view gives equal weight to the two sides, whereas the *adversative* view clearly favors one side over the other. The *description* plan develops a topic by describing its component parts, for instance, by presenting attributes, specifications, or settings. For example, on the topic of whales, descriptive texts could be generated by describing the physical characteristics of whales as a group, by describing one particular type of whale, by describing the environment of whales, etc. The *response* plan contains some kind of statement followed by a response, such as remark and reply; question and answer; problem and solution; and so on. Finally the *time-order* plan relates events or ideas according to chronology.

These five basic plan types are familiar in various contexts. Political speeches are often of the comparison type, and, in particular, its adversative subtype. Newspaper articles are often of the description type, telling us who, where, how, and when. Scientific treatises often adhere to the response type, first raising a question or problem and then seeking to give an answer or solution. The typical article in a psychological journal follows a quite specific version of the response plan, having well-marked sections for "problem," "method," "results," and "discussion." History texts frequently follow the time-order plan.

Of course, many texts will reflect more than one of these basic five plans. Folktales contain description and time-order within a general response plan where the protagonist confronts and resolves a problem.[7] Whenever the protagonist is placed in a difficult or dangerous situation, the audience is supposed to be imagining possible solutions; however, the use of magical events enables a storyteller to outsmart the audience sometimes. Finally, folktales may carry a comparison plan, such as demonstrating the contrast between good vs. evil, selfishness vs. altruism, industry vs. slothfulness, and much more.

My research group has used expository texts to probe how these five plans affect reading comprehension. In one study, 102 ninth graders each read two texts; one text was written with a comparison plan, while the other had a response plan. The students wrote down whatever they remembered, first right after reading, and then one week later. The *recall protocols* (the documents thus obtained) were examined to see if the readers were organizing their reports along the *same type of plan* as was used by us, the authors of the texts. We then correlated the results of this analysis with the *amount* that the readers could recall.

The findings were impressive. Only 46 percent of the students organized protocols written right after reading along the same plan as was used by the authors; one week later only 30 percent of the 102 students organized their protocols according to the authors' plan. Those who did remembered far more content, retaining the main ideas especially well, even a week after reading, but recovering more details also. These students performed much better on a true/false test on the content of the passage; and they were also the students who had shown good reading comprehension skills on standardized tests. Conversely, students who did not use the authors' plan tended to make disorganized lists of ideas, so that they couldn't recover either main ideas or details very well. These were also the students who had lower scores on standardized reading tests.[8]

There are two sides to this kind of evidence. First, it indicates a need to gear reading instruction around identification of plans, so that readers can effectively learn and remember the materials they study. Second, it indicates a parallel need in writing instruction, so that writers can offer readers this support in some recognizable way. Schooling involves a confrontation with many new topics about which students are not yet knowledgeable. In that situation, organizational plans are far more crucial to teaching than they would be otherwise, because unfamiliar content must be thoroughly organized in order to be learned.

To drive this point home, we gave a group of ninth-graders a week of training in identifying and using the four plan types of antecedent/consequent, comparison, description, and response. This group read and was tested for recall of texts on three occasions: before training, a day after training, and three weeks after training. A control group did the same tasks but received no instruction about the plans. The trained group could remember nearly twice as much content from the texts after their instruction (both one day after and three weeks after) than they could before; and on the tests after instruction, the trained group performed nearly twice as well as the control group. Moreover, those students in both groups who identified and used the author's plan remembered more information from the texts than those who did not find the plan.[9]

Similar studies have begun now with older readers. In a sample of junior college students, slightly more than 50 percent recognized and used the author's response plan in pieces on the topics of energy demands and schizophrenia; they retained more than did those who failed to recognize that plan.[10] In tests of Cornell undergraduates with these passages, a higher percentage recognized and used the author's plan; in studies of college graduates of varying ages (young, middle-aged, and older adults), the percentage was still higher (80 to 100 percent). When students do not use the author's plan for organizing what they remember from a text, they usually use a list plan and simply list ideas remembered from the text without trying to organize the information according to any of the five previously discussed topical plans. For all samples of students, the amount of information recalled by students who recognized and used the author's plan was greater than the amount recalled by students who failed to recognize a plan and recalled text by listing in sentence form information from the text. Interestingly enough, a sample of college graduates was able to use effectively a different topical plan from that of the writer, whereas ninth-graders were found unable to do so:[11] a group of graduate students organized their recall protocols (for a piece about loss of water from the body) with comparison or antecedent/consequent plans, whereas the author had used a muddled response plan which proposed an offensive solution to a problem of concern to the students. The amount of information remembered did not differ among the students who used the comparison, the antecedent/consequent, or the author's response plan.

These and similar studies may provide support for composition teachers who assign papers that describe, compare, raise problems, and so forth.[12] However, such topical plans should be effectively taught to students; teaching would include identification of the plans apart from content as well as practice with using the different plans on a variety of topics. Such plans can be empirically shown to provide benefits for both writers and readers. When they are used, content is better integrated and organized during writing, and readers retain more with less time and effort.

However, we still need to inquire further whether one plan type is more or less effective than another for different communication goals. For example, we have taken a given block of content, on topics such as "dehydration" or "the characteristics of whales," and cast it into four different versions, each of which was dominated by either an antecedent/consequent, comparison, description, or response plan. Some of our ongoing studies suggest that the descriptive plan is the least effective when people read or listen to text for the purpose of remembering it. For example, when two passages presenting the same topic and detailed content, but following different plans, were read aloud, listeners to the comparison version did better on recall (immediately and a week later) and answering questions than listeners to the description version. Similar findings emerged from tests with ninth-graders and with adults of various ages. Also, a study showed that the antecedent/consequent plan yielded superior recall of the identical information, as compared with the description plan. Some interesting data concerning the suitability of different topical plans for different purposes come from a recent study in which a text was presented to one group of expert adult readers with a comparison plan and to another such group with a time-order plan. The text with the comparison plan, entitled Disagreement Over Early American Railroad Development, emphasized the efforts of early American businessmen which resulted in improvements in railroads, contrasted with the views and actions of those who opposed development of railroads. The text with the time-order plan, entitled Early Development of Railroads in America, contained basically the same information but highlighted a historical sequence of specific developments in railroads and deemphasized the causal actions of the businessmen. When the comparison plan was highlighted (by words like "in contrast") and the time-order plan deemphasized (by removal of dates, e.g., changing "1829" to "early last century" and "1832" to "soon after that"), expert readers used the comparison plan to remember the text; when the comparison plan was deemphasized and the time-order plan was emphasized, readers' use of the comparison plan decreased and use of the time-order plan increased. There were no differences in total amount of information recalled when we varied the features of text that influenced which plan was identified as the overall topical plan. However, there was a big difference in the kinds of information remembered; if readers identified and used the comparison plan, the readers remembered causal and comparative relationships and related the content in this manner, but recalled few specific facts, e.g., names, historical events. In contrast, expert readers who recognized and used the time-order plan remembered the specific facts very well but recalled less of the information that was closely related to the comparative and causal logic in the text. Thus, depending on the goals of the writer and reader for the topic, different topical plans would be recommended.[13]

Deliberate attention to plans in composition training is, indeed, well justified, in view of our research. (Of course, there is a difference between *consciously* using a plan, as writing students will do if so instructed, and *unconsciously* using one, as expert writers presumably will do on their own.) As was already proposed above, the choice of plan is particularly crucial if the topic is not a familiar one. Perhaps the tendency of basic writers to fall back on trite, commonplace topics is a defense mechanism resulting from insufficient ability to use different writing plans and thus to develop original topics.

THE HIGHLIGHTING FUNCTION OF PLANS

Two modes of highlighting will be discussed here: *subordination* and *signaling*. *Subordination* creates dependencies among subtopics, as has been discussed in Christensen's rhetoric. For example, a writer can create a main idea and support it with reasons for a reader to believe it. Or a writer may describe an object in steadily greater detail; the greater detail is subordinate to the general statement about the object. *Signaling* is done with explicit markers, such as "on the one hand/on the other," "three things must be stressed here," and other expressions indicating how content is organized.

Psychologists have already explored the role of hierarchical subordination in enabling people to recall what they have read.[14] My own work centers around methods for constructing a model for describing reading and comprehending that recognizes the presence of a hierarchy among items mentioned in the text. Figure 1 shows a tree diagram for a passage about the problems caused by oil supertankers (such as that they spill oil and destroy wildlife) and about the possible solutions for these problems (training officers, redesigning ships, installing control stations on land, discontinuing use). This tree is postulated as a representation of the hierarchy, so that main ideas are above subtopics and details.

The relationships among the items in the tree are stipulated according to the terms of recent work on semantic relations like "cause-of" (like the antecedent/consequent plan previously discussed), "attribute-of" (in a description of an object or idea), "time-of" (the time when the event or idea occurred), and so on.[15] Some of these relations indicate movement down a level in a hierarchy, e.g., "attribute-of," "specification-of" (labeled *"description* [specifics, attributes]" in Figure 1), and so on. I have gathered some support for my inferences about these hierarchies by having independent judges make informal outlines of the content elements of text.

Research with various text materials, learners, and tasks generally indicates that content at the top of the hierarchy is better recalled and retained over time than content at the lower levels. One explanation of this effect is that readers make heavier use of this top-level content, calling it to mind frequently and tying it in with large amounts of material coming from the text.[16] Hence, this content is more frequently rehearsed in the mind and is easier to get at.

Recognizing that there is a hierarchy in the content of most texts, some teachers emphasize the outlining of essays. Less skilled writers profit from an outline precisely because it returns them periodically to high levels of their content hierarchy. However, directions for outlining are often vague regarding how the various entries further down in the hierarchy are (or should be) related to the top level. For example, some of our tests found that confusion arises among readers about whether events are related causally or temporally; by using express signaling and by simplifying relationships, we were able to eliminate the confusion. Perhaps student writers might enrich their outlining by trying to label the relations among the various entries in the outline.

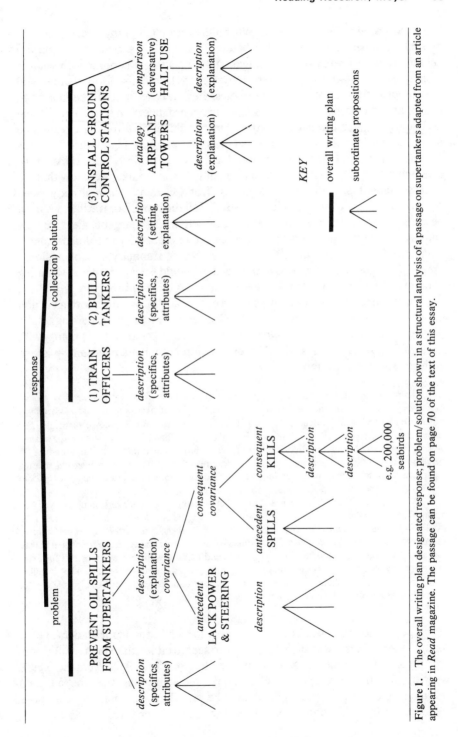

Figure 1.   The overall writing plan designated response; problem/solution shown in a structural analysis of a passage on supertankers adapted from an article appearing in *Read* magazine. The passage can be found on page 70 of the text of this essay.

The normal order followed in giving information in writing appears to be to present the superordinate materials before the subordinate. Such a procedure is helpful because it provides easy means to connect new content with what is already known. Unskilled writers may depart from this normal order and thereby obscure their content hierarchies. In that case, it could be helpful to rearrange their statements or paragraphs in accordance with some hierarchical outline made after the act of writing. Superordinate materials could then be moved to earlier stages of the presentation and properly highlighted.

Signaling can clarify both hierarchical and semantic relationships. If we encounter "thus," "therefore," "consequently," and the like, we know that the next statement should follow logically from whatever has already been presented. If we see "nevertheless," "still," "all the same," or the like, we must be prepared for a statement that reverses direction. On a larger scale, signaling can indicate how whole blocks of content are related, e.g., as "illustrations," "evidence," "further details," or the like. Or a "summary," "conclusion," "preview," or whatever may be announced. It should be expected that signaling operates as a significant aid to clear writing and effectual reading.

To probe this expectation, we carried out a study of signaling with a version of the passage about supertankers.[17] One group of ninth-graders read the passage as shown below—it follows a response (problem-solution) plan—with the signaling words (italics added here). A control group read the same passage with the signaling deleted.

A *problem of vital concern is* the prevention of oil spills from supertankers. A typical supertanker carries a half-million tons of oil and is the size of five football fields. A wrecked supertanker spills oil in the ocean; this oil kills animals, birds, and microscopic plant life. *For example,* when a tanker crashed off the coast of England, more than 200,000 dead seabirds washed ashore. Oil spills *also* kill microscopic plant life which provide food for sea life and produce 70 percent of the world's oxygen supply. Most wrecks result from the lack of power and steering equipment to handle emergency situations, *such as* storms. Supertankers have only one boiler to provide power and one propeller to drive the ship.

The solution to the problem is not to immediately halt the use of tankers on the ocean since about 80 percent of the world's oil supply is carried by supertankers. *Instead, the solution lies in the training of officers of supertankers, better building of tankers, and installing ground control stations to guide tankers near shore. First,* officers of supertankers must get top training in how to run and maneuver their ships. *Second,* tankers should be built with several propellers for extra control and backup boilers for emergency power. *Third,* ground control stations should be installed at places where supertankers come close to shore. These stations would act like airplane control towers, guiding tankers along busy shipping land and through dangerous channels.

The deletions had no effect on the ability to recall content for readers at both ends of the proficiency scale, i.e., those who scored either quite high or quite low on standardized reading tests (notably the Stanford Achievement Test). Apparently, the very good readers could recognize and use the author's problem-solution plan, whether or not the signaling was present. The poor readers, on the other hand, couldn't use the plan either way.

However, the signaling expressions did make a difference for the middle group of *average* readers, as well as for readers whose comprehension scores on the Stanford Achievement Test fell into a category below their vocabulary scores. With the signaling, these readers recalled more and produced better-planned protocols. A similar effect was found for students in junior college, but not for those in regular college.[18]

It would be wrong to conclude from such findings that signaling doesn't matter. True, if you write with one distinct topical plan for an audience of skilled, well-informed readers, you can dispense with signaling, because they will have no trouble identifying and applying the proper highlighting plan. Indeed, much scientific writing is badly organized and yet understood by the target audience. But to reach the much larger audiences of average readers, a writer ought to include signaling at strategic points, to reveal the major hierarchy of super-ordination and subordination. When so used, the elements of highlighting support each other.[19]

THE INFORMING FUNCTION OF PLANS

Communication would be pointless if a writer did not convey to the audience something they didn't know or believe before. However, often not all the content is radically new in the sense that the audience knows nothing whatsoever about it beforehand. Frequently, the writer will select a topic which the audience knows something about and will offer new details, specifications, perspectives, illustrations, and so on. Thus, the audience often has some frame of reference for making sense of any particular new fact or statement.

In their *informing* function, discourse plans guide presentation of new content while known or predictable content is kept in the reader's mind. The greater the ratio of new to known content, the higher the degree of informativeness.

This consideration had been studied for some years as an influence on the organization of English sentences.[20] Recently, Susan Haviland and Herbert Clark have undertaken to gather information on this feature of planning from laboratory experiments.[21] They constructed contrasting pairs such as this:

Horace got some beer out of the car. The beer was warm.
Horace got some picnic supplies out of the car. The beer was warm.

Readers would read each sentence and press a button when they felt they had understood it. The experimenters reasoned that it should take extra time to process the second sequence, because readers would need to take the additional step of inferring a relationship (in this case, that the "beer" was a part of the "picnic supplies"). And, in fact, readers spent an average of 180 milleseconds additional time on sequences of the second type, as compared with those of the first.

Such a result can be explained by appealing to the organization of *memory stories*. To write or read a text, people must access knowledge from *long-term memory* and make it *active*, i.e., place it in *working memory*. To understand the second sequence in the pair shown above, readers must infer the extra fact (that picnic supplies would include beer) and get it into working memory.

In longer texts, concepts may fade from working memory before the writer refers to them again. In such cases, the concepts must be *reinstated* in order to integrate new content about them. Such an operation consumes more time and effort than if the concept is still in working memory, e.g., if the concept has been activated in the immediately preceding sentence. The operation is facilitated if the concept happens to be high in a content hierarchy of the kind discussed previously in this essay, presumably because such concepts are frequently reinstated as reading progresses.[22]

Walter Kintsch and Douglas Vipond have worked out a model of reading based on these considerations.[23] The capacity of working memory is assumed to be six to ten *propositions* (each proposition being a "predicate" with one or more "arguments," e.g., "Socrates is Greek," where the predicate is "Greek" and "Socrates" the argument). When new content arrives, the reader tries to find out how it overlaps with these already active propositions inside working memory. If no overlap is found, readers may *reinstate* earlier propositions or may make *inferences* that bridge propositions. Such activities, especially if needed frequently and extensively, drain away readers' mental resources and render comprehension unduly difficult: the result is thus a decrease in *readability*.

Here again, psychological findings corroborate what composition teachers know to be a major problem among unskilled writers, namely, gaps or abrupt transitions in the presentation of content. Teachers intuitively sense the problem because of their own memory exertions; less experienced readers would be taxed even more severely. To combat such problems, writers need to reactivate the relevant concepts from time to time. That is, in order to inform readers successfully—or present new information to them—writers frequently need to provide links to information already presented in the text; they must remind readers about what they have read previously so that readers can efficiently interrelate new and old information. Indeed, Barbara Hayes-Roth suggests that the same expression should be repeated periodically in complex discourse to ensure that the concept in question is activated the same way each time.[24] But such repetition should be limited to key concepts, lest the text become tiresome.

CONCLUSION

I have briefly reviewed some findings in reading research that are relevant for instruction in composition. These findings lend support to the teaching of organizational techniques for planning a text in such a way that it can be read and recalled by wide audiences without undue effort. Planning can fulfill the strategic functions of organizing data and ideas, highlighting relationships, and informing readers about topics. Different plan types, such as antecedent/ consequent, comparison, description, response, and time-order, can be introduced so that they can be used by both writer and reader, so that resources like attention and memory are deployed to best advantage.

Explicit instruction in the identifying and using of plans can be included in the curriculum for both reading and writing. For example, composition classes could be devoted to analyzing prose passages in terms of the types of plan and the functions of the plans that the writer has selected. Students might gain insights by applying such an analysis to their own writings (or that of fellow students) in order to determine if the plan and its functions (goals or purposes) are clear and consistent in a particular case. Where they are not, students should have guides to follow for revision: presenting concepts high in the hierarchy before lower ones; inserting explicit signalings; reactivating major concepts periodically; using the same expressions for this reactivating; and so on.

The relevance of research on reading for that on writing (and vice versa) should be obvious, since the two processes are complementary. However, attempts to correlate the two research domains have become prominent only recently. It is to be hoped that this trend will become stronger and more productive in the coming years.

EXPLORING THE IDEAS — *Theoretical Discussion*

QUESTION 1

Background   Based on her research, Meyer argues for the need to gear reading instruction around the identification of plans and to offer a similar type of instruction in composition classes so that students learn to organize their ideas according to a plan.

Discussion   Do you think that students who are skillful readers and can identify the plans in a reading text will necessarily be able to organize their own writing according to a plan? On the other hand, do you believe that writers who are capable of producing effective reader-based prose will necessarily be efficient readers? If so, why? If not, why not?

QUESTION 2

Background   Meyer argues for the importance of giving deliberate attention to plans in composition training. However, she points out that "there is a difference between *consciously* using a plan, as writing students will do if so instructed, and *unconsciously* using one, as expert writers presumably will do on their own" (page 67).

Discussion   Do you feel it is a good idea to instruct students to write a paper which adheres to a particular rhetorical plan such as comparison or antecedent/consequent? If so, why? If not, why not? What do you see as the advantages of giving deliberate attention to plans in a composition class? What do you see as the disadvantages?

QUESTION 3

Background   Meyer maintains that "the relevance of research on reading for that on writing (and vice versa) should be obvious, since the two processes are complementary" (page 73).

Discussion   In what ways do you think the process of reading and writing are complementary? Do you feel that speaking and writing are complementary processes? If so, in what particular ways are they similar processes?

Applying Theoretical Concepts

ACTIVITY 1

Background   As Meyer points out, folktales often contain more than one type of plan, as is evident in the following folktale.

THUNDER AND LIGHTNING

A long time ago, both thunder and lightning lived on this earth, among all the people. Thunder was an old mother sheep and Lightning was her son, a handsome ram, but neither animal was very popular.

When anybody offended the ram, Lightning, he would fly into a furious rage and begin burning down huts and corn bins, and even knock down large trees. Sometimes he damaged crops on the farms with his fire and occasionally he killed people who got in his way.

As soon as his mother, Thunder, knew he was behaving in this evil way, she would raise her voice and shout as loudly as she could, and that was very loud indeed.

Naturally the neighbours were very upset, first at the damage caused by Lightning and then by the unbearable noise that always followed his outbursts. The villagers complained to the king on many occasions, until at last he sent the two of them to live at the very edge of the village, and said that they must not come and mix with people any more.

However, this did no good, since Lightning could still see people as they walked about the village streets and so found it only too easy to continue picking quarrels with them. At last the king sent for them again.

"I have given you many chances to live a better life," he said, "but I can see that it is useless. From now on, you must go right away from our village and live in the wild bush. We do not want to see your faces here again."

Thunder and Lightning had to obey the king and left the village, angrily cursing its inhabitants.

Alas, there was still plenty of trouble in store for the villagers, since Lightning was so angry at being banished that he now set fire to the whole bush, and during the dry season this was extremely unfortunate. The flames spread to the little farms which the people had planted, and sometimes to their houses as well, so that they were in despair again. They often heard the mother ram's mighty voice calling her son to order, but it made very little difference to his evil actions.

The king called all his councillors together and asked them to advise him, and at last they hit on a plan. One white-headed elder said:

"Why don't we banish Thunder and Lightning right away from the earth? Wherever they live there will be trouble, but if we sent them up into the sky, we should be rid of them."

So Thunder and Lightning were sent away into the sky, where the people hoped they would not be able to do any more damage.

Things did not work out quite as well as they had hoped, however, for Lightning still loses his temper from time to time and cannot resist sending fire down to the earth when he is angry. Then you can hear his mother rebuking him in her loud rumbling voice.

Occasionally even his mother cannot bear to stay with him and goes away for a little while. You will know when this happens, for Lightning still flashes his fire on the earth, but his mother is so far away that she does not see, and her voice is silent.

[From *African Myths and Legends* retold by Kathleen Arnott, Copyright 1962 by Kathleen Arnott. Reprinted by permission of Oxford University Press. pp. 32–34.]

Application   Many texts contain both a macro- and micro-level plan. For example, on a macro level a text could be a problem solution essay, yet within the text there could be a comparison of the various solutions. Begin by characterizing the overall plan of "Thunder and Lightning." Then point out examples of any other of the five plans delineated by Meyer which are illustrated in the text: antecedent/consequent, comparison, description, response, or time-order.

ACTIVITY 2

Background   Meyer contends that certain types of discourse rely more heavily on one type of plan than another. She points out, for example, that political speeches are often of the adversative plan, newspaper articles of the description plan, scientific treatises of the response plan, and history texts of the time-order plan.

Application   Select two passages of at least three paragraphs from texts that illustrate different discourse types (e.g., a newspaper article as opposed to a history text). Identify all the plans contained in the text. Then discuss whether or not you believe the plans in the text are typical of this type of discourse.

ACTIVITY 3

Background   Meyer points out that the same information can be presented in a variety of plans. Furthermore, the type of plan seems to affect the amount and type of information which is retained by the reader.

Application   Write two short passages which contain similar information but utilize different plans. Then specify what techniques you used to make a distinction in the type of plan used. (Cohesive devices are one way to make this distinction clear.) Also discuss the problems you encountered in rewriting the same information in two different rhetorical structures.

Teaching Strategies

ACTIVITY 1

Background   Meyer maintains that topical plans should be taught to students. Such instruction would include identification of the plans apart from content. If Kaplan is correct that different cultures tend to favor different rhetorical patterns, it seems important to include some formal training in the identification of typical English rhetorical patterns in ESL classes.

Application   Select a reading passage that would be appropriate for an intermediate- or advanced-level ESL class which illustrates at least three of the plans delineated by Meyer. Then design an exercise to accompany the text which would help students identify the plans that are included. Be certain to precede the exercise with some type of explanation or illustration of the five basic plans.

ACTIVITY 2

Background   Meyer points out that outlining may help students perceive the hierarchy of content in a text but that unfortunately the directions for such outlining are often vague. She suggests having students label the relationship among the entries in the outline.

Application   Design an exercise which requires students to outline a reading passage using a tree diagram. Begin the exercise by providing a model outline which includes, as Meyer suggests, a way of indicating the relationship among the entries. In order to expose students to a variety of plans, select passages for both the introductory material and the student exercise which include several of the plan types.

ACTIVITY 3

Background   Meyer provides a tree diagram for an article about the problems caused by oil supertankers (page 69). As she points out, one advantage of using a tree diagram is that this technique clearly illustrates the hierarchy of ideas. Tree diagrams can also be used to help students generate ideas and organize these ideas before they begin to write. For example, you could put the diagram shown on page 77 on the board as a strategy for helping students explore a specific topic. In this case, you could ask the students to tell you about some personal problem that they have such as not being able to find a job or an apartment. Then students could suggest possible causes for their problem. Finally, they could discuss a possible solution for each of the causes of the problem.

Application   Draw a tree diagram which could be used as a prewriting strategy for brainstorming and organizing ideas. Then list several topics which could be explored using your tree diagram.

NOTES

1. This research was supported in part by faculty grants from the Arizona State University. An earlier version was presented at the Conference on College Composition and Communication, Minneapolis, April 1979. I am grateful to Robert de Beaugrande and Richard L. Larson for carefully working through a previous draft.

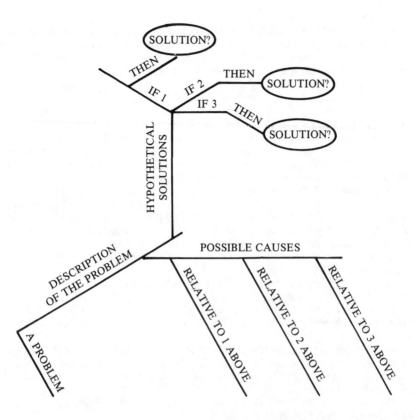

2. For example, Linda Flower and John Richard Hayes, The Dynamics of Composing: Making Plans and Juggling Constraints. In Lee Gregg and Erwin Steinberg (eds.) *Cognitive Processes in Writing.* Hillsdale, N.J., Erlbaum, 1980, pp. 31–50; Robert de Beaugrande, *The Science of Composition: A Program for Research in Theory and Method.* Norwood, N.J., Ablex, 1982; Ann Matsuhashi, Pausing and Planning: The Tempo of Written Discourse Production. *Research in the Teaching of English* 15 (May 1981), 113–134.

3. See Lawrence Frase, Paragraph Organization of Written Materials: The Influence of Conceptual Clustering upon Level of Organization. *Journal of Educational Psychology* 60 (October 1969), 394–401; and reference in following note.

4. Walter Kintsch, Theodore Mandel, and Ely Kozminsky, Summarizing Scrambled Stories. *Memory and Cognition* 5 (September 1977), 547–552.

5. For exactly this reason, the expansion of sentence linguistics to text linguistics has not been very productive; see survey in Robert de Beaugrande and Wolfgang Dressler, *Introduction to Text Linguistics.* London, Longman, 1981. Compare also works cited below in notes 6, 14, 16, and 23.

6. Bonnie J. F. Meyer, *The Organization of Prose and Its Effects on Memory.* Amsterdam, North Holland, 1975. My linguistic source-work was Joseph Grimes, *The Thread of Discourse.* The Hague, Mouton, 1975, which was available to me in manuscript during my dissertation work at Cornell.

7. See, for instance, David Rumelhart, Understanding and Summarizing Brief Stories. In David Laberge and Jay Samuels (eds.). *Basic Processes in Reading.* Hillsdale, N.J., Erlbaum, 1977, pp. 265–303; Robert de Beaugrande and Benjamin Colby, Narrative Models of Action and Interaction. *Cognitive Science* 3 (January–March 1979), 43–46.

8. Specifics can be found in Bonnie J. F. Meyer, David M. Brandt, and George J. Bluth, Use of Top-Level Structure in Text: Key for Reading Comprehension of Ninth Grade Students. *Reading Research Quarterly* 16 (winter 1980), 72–103. Compare Brendan J. Bartlett, *Use of Top-Level Structure as an Organizational Strategy in Prose Recall*, and David M. Brandt, *Prior Knowledge of the Author's Schema and Prose Comprehension*, both dissertations at the Department of Educational Psychology, Arizona State University, 1978.

9. On the points discussed in this and the previous paragraph, see Bartlett's and Brandt's dissertations (note 8) and B. J. F. Meyer, Following the Author's Top-Level Structure. In Robert J. Tierney et al. (eds.). *Understanding Readers' Understanding*. Hillsdale, N.J., Erlbaum, 1981.

10. Bonnie J. F. Meyer, G. Elizabeth Rice, Vance Woods, and Brendan J. Bartlett, *Facilitative Effects of Passages with Same Structure and Different Content on Prose Recall*. Unpublished Arizona State University manuscript, 1978.

11. Compare the findings on ninth-graders in Brandt's dissertation (note 8) with those on college graduates in Bonnie J. F. Meyer and Roy Freedle, Effects of Discourse Type on Recall. *American Educational Research Journal*, in press, and high verbal older adults with college degrees in B. J. F. Meyer, Text Dimensions and Cognitive Processing. In H. Mandl et al. (eds.). *Learning and Comprehending Texts*. Hillsdale, N.J., Erlbaum, 1982.

12. See, for instance, Frank D'Angelo, *Process and Thought in Composition*. Cambridge, Mass., Winthrop, 1977.

13. See Brandt (note 8); Meyer and Freedle (note 11); Meyer (note 11); and Bonnie J. F. Meyer, G. Elizabeth Rice, Catharine C. Knight, and Janice L. Jessen, *Effects of Comparative and Descriptive Top-Level Structures on the Reading Performance of Young, Middle, and Old Adults* (Prose Learning Series 7), Department of Educational Psychology, Arizona State University, 1979.

14. See Meyer (note 6); Jean Mandler and Nancy Johnson, Remembrance of Things Parsed. *Cognitive Psychology* 9 (January 1977), 111–151; Perry Thorndyke, Cognitive Structures in Comprehension and Memory of Narrative Discourse. *Cognitive Psychology* 9 (January 1977), 77–110; Kintsch and van Dijk (note 16); Kintsch and Vipond (note 23).

15. Compare classifications in Grimes (note 6); and Robert de Beaugrande, *Text, Discourse, and Process*. Norwood, N.J., Ablex, 1980.

16. Walter Kintsch and Teun van Dijk, Toward a Model of Discourse Comprehension and Production. *Psychological Review* 85 (September 1978), 363–394.

17. Meyer et al. (note 8). On the notion of signaling, see the volumes of Grimes and Meyer (note 6).

18. Compare Nancy Marshall, The Structure of Semantic Memory for Text, Dissertation, Cornell University, 1976; and Meyer (note 6).

19. See Ely Kozminsky, Altering Comprehension: The Effect of Biasing Titles on Text Comprehension. *Memory and Cognition* 5 (July 1977), 482–490; and Meyer (note 6).

20. The usual designation was "functional sentence perspective": cf. Frantisek Danes (ed.). *Papers on Functional Sentence Perspective*, Prague: Academia, 1974, and references there.

21. Susan Haviland and Herbert Clark, What's New? *Journal of Verbal Learning and Verbal Behavior* 13 (October 1974), 512–521.

22. On these various accounts, see Kintsch and van Dijk (note 16); Alan Lesgold and Charles Perfetti, Interactive Processes in Reading Comprehension. *Discourse Processes* 1 (October–December 1978), 323–336; Carol H. Walker and Bonnie J. F. Meyer, Integrating Information from Text: An Evaluation of Current Theories. *Review of Educational Research* 50 (fall 1980), 421–437; and Perry Thorndyke, Integration of Knowledge from Text. *Journal of Verbal Learning and Verbal Behavior* 18 (February 1979), 91–108.

23. Walter Kintsch and Douglas Vipond, Reading Comprehension and Readability in Educational Practice. In Lars Nilsson (ed). *Perspectives on Memory Research*. Hillsdale, N.J., Erlbaum, 1979, pp. 329–365.

24. Barbara Hayes-Roth, *Structurally Integrated versus Structurally Segregated Memory Representations: Implications for the Design of Instructional Materials*. Santa Monica, Calif., Rand Corporation Paper P-5841, 1977.

2 TEACHING STRATEGIES

The idea of *teaching* composition suggests that composition is a skill which consists of subprocesses that can be sequenced, presented, and tested. Yet the articles included in the preceding section illustrate that writing is an active process, a way of learning. Because of this fact, there are limits to what we as composition teachers can do. In some ways our role is similar to that of an art instructor. Like an art teacher, we can encourage our students to carefully observe certain details of their environment; in this way, they will have something to write about. And as Raimes points out in her article, providing students with writing topics is one of the most important tasks of a writing teacher.

Furthermore, like art teachers, we can present our students with examples of good models. Indeed one rationale for the use of reading models in composition classes is the belief that people learn through imitation. Thus, it is thought that if students read examples of well-developed "reader-based prose," they will learn what is involved in the creation of such prose. This assumption provides the basis of Watson-Reekie's article on the use of models in ESL classes.

Finally, art teachers devote a great deal of time to teaching their students various techniques which contribute to the success of a final product. In terms of writing, linking devices are one element that is essential for a well-developed essay. However, as Zamel points out, attention to such devices has unfortunately generally been neglected in ESL composition classes.

Thus, the articles in this section set forth specific things that we as composition teachers can do in the classroom. In the follow-up activities you will be asked to design exercises that deal with such things as writing topics, reading models, and linking devices. The teaching exercises that you design require that your students have a certain level of proficiency in English. There are many types of highly controlled exercises which require students to do such things as make simple substitutions or transformations in a text or to answer a series of highly structured questions so as to generate a short paragraph. While such kinds of exercises may have value in teaching students something about the grammatical structure of English, their value in helping students learn to effectively express and organize their own thoughts is questionable. Composing in either a first or second language presupposes that an individual has sufficient competency in the language to give form to his or her ideas. Because of this, instruction in composition, as opposed to grammar, requires that students have a basic foundation in English so that attention can be given to both content and form.

The activities which follow present a variety of teaching strategies to help you achieve a balance between content and form in your teaching. Which of these strategies you select to actually use in your teaching will greatly depend upon the particular writing needs of your students. If you are fortunate enough to have students who share similar professional goals, you will be able to design materials to meet your students' particular occupational needs such as those suggested in the article by Weissberg and Buker. In any case, the needs of your students should always be foremost in your mind as you decide what strategies you will use in helping your students learn to compose.

5

Anguish as a Second Language?
Remedies for Composition Teachers

Ann Raimes

When I first started composing this paper, I felt some anguish myself. I knew I was dealing with the general topic of the problems of ESL composition, but I couldn't decide what to narrow it down to. I felt overwhelmed and went off to Macy's to buy my kids some underwear while my family played havoc with my title: luggage as a second baggage, penguin as a second bandage, and sausage as a second sandwich.

Then I decided to begin, at least, in the way that I advise my own ESL students to begin: to observe and describe. So I watched my students and examined their written work. In both I saw the signs of anguish. Student writers chew their pencils, they shuffle their feet, they sigh, groan and stretch, they ask, "How much do we have to write?" They thumb through their little dictionaries. They write a sentence, read back over it, cross out a word and substitute another—often a wrong one—and then attack the next sentence. They produce dry, flat, mechanical prose, full of unsupported generalizations, repeated concepts, and errors. When asked what they find difficult about composition they invariably reply, "I don't know the right words," "I don't know how to organize," "I worry about grammar," or "I can't think of anything to write." Their anguish becomes our anguish as we read more and more pieces of writing not only filled with grammatical errors but empty of life and content.

Native speakers suffer in the same way, those whom Mina Shaughnessy (1977) calls "basic writing students." She first talked of their "written anguish" (1976, p. 235). I am using and extending her term to explore what makes composing even more agonizing in a second language and what we can do to relieve the pain a little.

Teaching and learning ESL composition spreads over two huge fields: composing and second-language acquisition, separate fields of research and pedagogy. These fields do not meet often in professional conferences or publications—this one is an exception—but they *must* merge in the classroom for teachers and students.

Composition theory and research are almost exclusively devoted to examining the products and processes of native-speaker writers, skilled and unskilled. When unskilled native speakers write, they do, however, have to learn what amounts to a new language for them: the language of standard edited

English or academic English. Many of these student writers are, as Janet Emig points out in her study of composing processes, "enervated by worries over peripherals" such as spelling, punctuation, and length(1971, p. 99). ESL student writers have all the worries of the native speaker and many more besides, for all of them have to acquire or consciously learn the phonology, grammar, syntactic structure, vocabulary, rhetorical structure, and idiom of a new language in addition to learning the mechanics of prose. With so much to be done, it is hardly surprising that many of our ESL composition courses have stressed the acquisition of the rule-governed forms of the second language. We accept and strive for compositions that show mastery over grammar, syntax, and mechanics. And this job is so vast that there is often little time left over for attention to the ideas and the meaning of a piece of writing. Yet we all know how we welcome the composition that says something to the reader, even if it has some incorrect verb forms. For then communication of ideas becomes primary and the rest is truly peripheral.

So why do we emphasize the acquisition of grammar and syntax first in our sequence of learning and our hierarchy of priorities? Peter Elbow explains why when he says, "It's no accident that so much attention is paid to grammar in the teaching of writing. Grammar is the one part of writing that can be straightforwardly taught" (1973, p. 138). Feeling slightly uneasy about this emphasis, we disguise it by the language we use: we say we assign guided or controlled *compositions*. These, however, have more to do with control than with composition. Students are copying, substituting, transforming, and manipulating prose written by someone else. They are not composing. But we like to think they are.

We keep our task straightforward when we deal with paragraphs and essays, too. We give paragraphs to be amplified, unscrambled, or written according to specific guidelines. But ESL students who are not skilled readers and writers in their first language need more than patterns, even if these are presented as a study of contrastive rhetoric. It's not a different paragraph form that is the problem so much as lack of experience with the concept of any written paragraph and with the mental processes needed to express ideas for a reader rather than a listener. The students who do read and write well in their first language also need to work on the new creative activity of forming ideas in English for English-speaking readers.

Yet most of us ESL composition teachers have emphasized structure (a good old ESL word), first syntactic and then rhetorical structure, implying as we did so: "Here's the way to do it. Now go ahead and do it." So after careful teaching of, for example, coordinating conjunctions, sentence connectors, and chronological order in a paragraph, we get back this:

Louie rushed and got ready for work, but, when he went out the door, he saw the snowstorm was very heavy. Therefore, he decided not to go to work. Then, he sat down to enjoy his newspaper. However, he realized his boss might get angry because he did not go to the office. Finally, he made another decision, that he must go to work. So, he went out the door and walked to the bus stop.

Many of us, at one time or another, have praised a student for such a piece of writing. No grammatical mistakes. I have seen such flat paragraphs as this applauded as excellent and I, too, have assessed similar papers with a check mark and the comment "very good." Most of us have. We teach a discrete item of grammar in class and test it in a writing exercise. If the students get it right, we feel we have taught something, and we offer praise to the students who have learned. We respond to the piece of writing as item checkers, not as real readers.

Why does this happen? I think it's because we have stressed the ESL part of ESL composition at the expense of the composition part, and we have done so because we have thought that students need mastery over the sentence before proceeding to the paragraph, and mastery over the paragraph before proceeding to the essay. So we have provided controls and limits which make the task easier for us. The question is, do they make it easier for the students too? We have, I fear, trapped our students within the sentence. They worry about accuracy; they stop after each sentence and go back and check it for inflections, word order, spelling, and punctuation, breathe a sigh of relief and go on to attack the looming giant of the next sentence. Research such as Nancy Sommers's on native speaker student writers shows how their revision consists primarily of rewording. They are concerned with vocabulary and not with concepts. We don't have the same body of research on the composing process for ESL students, but I suspect that the prison of the word and the sentence has even stronger bars. And when we have tried to move beyond the sentence, our emphasis on patterns—patterns of the paragraph and of the essay—has reinforced the restraints. Students begin with a given topic sentence and thus lock themselves into a semantic and rhetorical prison. This first sentence restricts them before they have begun to develop their ideas. But they wonder why, when they have the pattern of the mold, they fill the mold, and they proofread, why isn't this an A paper? After all, they have done what was asked for!

What we need to ask for as well is the composing side of ESL composition. Grammatical accuracy and rhetorical formulas have little force if the piece of writing is not expressing the writer's ideas clearly and forcefully, with an involved imagination. Students who are asked to write an essay on "Holidays in My Country" with no sense of purpose or audience try to guess what the teacher wants, try to find the words and the correct grammar, but have no intellectual or emotional investment in what they are writing about. They are saying something that nobody cares about in order to practice something else. Communication must surely be as important in the composition classroom as it is now becoming in the spoken English classroom.

Composing means expressing ideas, conveying meaning. Composing means thinking. Let us look at a master writer and teacher's definition of composing. For Tolstoy, the mechanism of composing consists in "the ability to combine what follows with what precedes, all the while keeping in mind what is already written down . . . in thinking and writing at the same time without having one of these acts interfere with the other." Although one past U.S. President might have found it difficult to walk and chew gum at the same time, thinking and writing should be (in spite of much ESL pedagogy) inseparable when our students compose. That thinking/writing process is also a way of discovering what we know, a way of "form-finding" (Berthoff 1978, p. 254). The very act of writing itself has a creative function. Writing helps us find out what we want to say.

How many of us pay attention to that function in our ESL classes? Don't we often assign a piece of writing, collect it, correct or indicate errors and return it, perhaps with a request for correction? We stress editing skills rather than the creative act of communicating meaning. We exhort our students to apply learned conscious rules as they edit: to turn sentences into *yes/no* questions, to check sentence boundaries, to combine sentences, to check inflections. Many of our students need that. They cry out for rules, for something concrete to monitor their writing performance with. So we give them grammatical Band-Aids and doses of paragraph models. We must then realize that we are teaching editing and imitating. We're not teaching composing.

There is, of course, no one remedy, no panacea for all teachers in all classrooms. But all of us can examine what we have been doing in our classes, we can ask "What's going wrong?" "Why?" and "What can we do that is better?" It is certainly time to move away from what some ESL books for teachers say about ESL composition. We read in one the rationale that "writing is one way of providing variety in classroom procedures" (Paulston and Bruder 1976, p. 203). We are told that free writing is useful for students to "give vent to their feelings" (Paulston and Bruder 1976, p. 230). However, we are reminded in another that "not all students have the gift of imagination" (Rivers and Temperley 1978, p. 317). Yet another recommends checklists to note errors in (of course) spelling, punctuation, structure, and vocabulary, with the magnanimous concession: "You may prefer, if ideas are important, to give two points for ideas," and then the addendum: "If you think four ideas are necessary, give half a point for each" (Finocchiaro 1974, p. 88).

If ideas are important and necessary! Let's now assume they are, and let's switch focus from elimination of error to thinking and communicating ideas. I'm going to suggest some approaches we might try in place of the old one of controls before freedom, sentences before paragraphs, and pattern practice and accuracy above all. I'm not offering a miracle cure by any means, but I am proposing a change in treatment. We can't cure arthritis by giving treatment for a stomach ulcer. We won't improve composing in any language if we teach only rules of grammar and models of form. I have discussed elsewhere some strategies for helping students with their difficulties in grammar, syntax, and rhetoric as they compose (Raimes 1978a). I have also published teaching materials that include many grammatical exercises to back up each writing assignment (Raimes 1978b). Grammar *is* important for ESL students, but it has been well covered in the literature. Let us turn now to the neglected areas of the process of composing in a second language and the writer's generating of ideas throughout that process. I'll be discussing how we can pay attention to those areas when we do three of our composition teacher's jobs: give assignments, mark papers, and provide readings.

GIVING ASSIGNMENTS

A carefully chosen assignment generates its own many varied classroom activities and paper-marking procedures; so it is worth putting the work in at this early point. Giving an assignment involves more than selecting a topic for students to write on. It means giving suggestions as to how to go about writing it. At this point we can build in the chance for students to pay attention to the writing and revision process: we can give them time to work on a paper, time alone and with each other, time to deal first with content, then with organization, and only finally, at the proofreading stage, with grammar (though that will, of course, crop up in discussion of content if it is preventing clarity of expression). Researchers on composing for native speakers are pointing out that the process is not the linear one of prewriting, writing, and revising. These three activities are, rather, inseparable and intertwined, all going on all the time throughout the process. When we devise assignments, we need to avoid forcing students into three separate activities. I tell my students *not* to begin with an outline, and *not* to begin with the introduction. Instead, they make a list of ideas, they write about words in that list, they observe, describe, define, and classify objects, actions, and concepts in that list. They write a paragraph and then shorten it by two sentences. They write a paragraph, then throw it away and write another. While this writing is going on it is prewriting, writing, and revision all rolled into one.

Students will only see the importance of revision if the teacher expects it, too. I show students drafts, give them time and opportunity for revision, in class discussion and in conferences, so that they don't see writing as a one-shot deal, put down on paper and marked right or wrong. Five minutes spent helping a student with revision even during the class when everyone else is writing can do more good than another whole essay assignment. Praise and honest criticism of ideas can make students want to revise and, ultimately, want to proofread. And that is when proofreading is done effectively.

While we give time for the process of revision, we can also give advice on what students use to engage in the process. I ask my students to use legal notepaper with wide margins for their lists, notes, and all drafts. They, their fellow students, or I can then write questions and comments in the margin. I suggest different color pens for changes on drafts, scissors and tape for rearranging.

From the process and the tools to the topics themselves: what do we ask ESL students to write about? An ongoing ungraded and uncorrected journal in which they record their observations about objects, people, and events, or write stories and poems, can help generate ideas for further writing and increase fluency. For academic purposes, however, I move away from the expressive mode to the referential, persuasive, and heuristic functions of writing. A shared classroom experience gives everyone something to respond to; they make their own observations and their own connections. We look at a photograph of an accident and write an accident report. We write instructions and letters. We look at a Peanuts cartoon in which Lucy exhorts Linus to add a waterfall, a sunset, a forest, and a deer to his drawing of a log cabin and lake because, as she says in her loudly charming way, "That's art!" Students describe the cartoon, writing their own responses and questions in the wide left margin. Then we look at a Cézanne still life, a Cubist Picasso guitar, and an Andy Warhol soup can. Students observe, describe, ask questions, and react, writing all the time. Only after they have many pages down on paper do they begin to devise their own topic and to work on an essay, but by now they have vocabulary, structures, and ideas to put in it.

What I try to do with assignments like this is what any good assignment must do: provide "a bridge from the familiar to the unfamiliar," as Ann Berthoff so aptly puts it (1978, p. 250). Early ESL lessons at elementary and intermediate levels are rooted firmly in the familiar and the concrete: "This is a book," "I'm reading a magazine," "The van is longer than the sportscar," and teachers carry bags of pictures and realia around with them to provide this familiarity. But at more advanced levels and particularly in composition classes students need to deal with causes, categories, and relationships. We must give them the opportunity to use this new language of theirs to form concepts, not just to ask for the salt. Many of us, from the worthiest of motives, have assigned topics we think will be easy enough so that our students will be able to concentrate on their ESL grammar and sentence structure. Such topics, even in freshman composition (e.g., describe a custom of your country), offer invitations to writing that *should* receive the response that Edith Wharton's Anson Warley used to decline dinner invitations: "I decline the boredom." We assign these because we feel that grammar and syntax are enough of a challenge: with a familiar topic the student can wrestle with them unimpeded. But when we realize that what we are really saying is that ideas are impediments to what we call "good" writing, it's time to reexamine what we are doing.

Some teachers try hard to establish a purpose and a specific reader for every piece of writing. I've done it, too: Write to the people in the apartment above you complaining about the noise and asking them to stop—first politely and then, three weeks later, angrily; now write to the landlord terminating your lease. Write to a magic genie in his "Have three famous people to dinner" competition and convince him that your reasons for wanting your three are the most compelling. Students like these assignments and usually do them well. But they are aware of the artificiality. They know in their heart of hearts, as we do too, that their readers are only the teacher and perhaps their classmates, too. If a system of credit and grades is involved, then you can be sure they know all that. The teacher is the reader, and the purpose is to improve the students' written English. There's nothing wrong with that. But somehow we don't use it. We circumvent it and pretend it isn't there. Students are usually eager to improve their writing. They distinguish clearly between good and bad writing or even between good and less good. They are like the students in Robert Pirsig's *Zen and the Art of Motorcycle Maintenance* who balk at defining quality in writing but are amazed to discover they can recognize it. Pirsig, a teacher of rhetoric, writes about a student who was stuck on an assignment to write about her home town. He didn't prescribe a fictional purpose or reader. He told her to begin by looking at the upper left block of the Opera House on Main Street. Unblocked, she now wrote 5,000 words just on the front of the Opera House (Pirsig 1975, p. 185).

So our assignments should provide our students with the opportunity to "look and see freshly" for themselves (Pirsig 1975, p. 186), to write to form their ideas, to work as long as necessary to express those ideas as clearly as possible to a real and responsive reader. Choosing topics should be the teacher's most responsible activity. Yet I've observed teachers who, in the last minute at the end of a class, say, "Oh, yes, the assignment for next time . . . ,' flip through the book, pause, and continue, "Try essay number 2 on page 85. Hand it in on Monday." I've done that myself, too.

Choosing topics with care will not only nurture the development of composing abilities but will also pay attention to our ESL concerns of grammar and syntax. James Moffett sees "cognitive stimulation" as the "best developer of syntax." He noticed third graders using *If . . .* or *When . . .* structures in their journals, both unusual structures for eight-year-old writers. But they were reporting on their observations of candle flames and needed the structure to express concepts like: "If I cover the candle with a jar, then it goes out." In ESL composition classes the teacher can predict what syntactic structures the topic is likely to generate and review these before the composing begins and stress them again in the proofreading. A recent assignment of mine asked students to comment on an excerpt from John Cheever's *Bullet Park* in which a father, annoyed by his son's addiction to TV, has a long argument with him and throws the TV set out of the back door. He then pours himself his fifth drink of the day. A week before we began discussion of this, I reviewed structures like: *should have . . . ; shouldn't have . . . ; could have . . . ; rather . . . ; if. . . .* And students used them when they wrote about the moral dilemma.

The assignments chosen can make or mar a composition class. They can turn it solely into a grammar class, or an imitation class, or a "following directions" class. Or they can unite form and content, ideas and organization, syntax and meaning, writing and revising, and, above all, writing and thinking. But here, too, as elsewhere in life, we are not free from the consequences of our actions. We assign, students write. And our chickens come home to roost. We have to mark the papers we assign.

MARKING PAPERS

There is no one prescription. There are as many as there are teaching styles. The way you would mark an essay would inevitably be different from the way I would mark it. We adapt our marking to fit what we teach and what we emphasize. Our topics and our marking reflect our philosophy as well as our pedagogy.

Those who see teaching composition as mainly teaching grammar look for errors, which they either correct or indicate. Some mark all the errors, while some mark only those that have been discussed in class. Some use checklists to indicate errors or to reinforce correct usage. A few use peer correction, with students working in pairs.

But correcting is not all there is to do. If we want our students to keep on writing, to take pleasure in expressing ideas, then we should always respond to the ideas expressed and not only to the number of errors in a paper. Some ESL teachers I know no longer correct or even indicate errors in grammar and syntax at least on the first two drafts. I try not to, but force of habit sometimes wins. I prefer to note what problems each individual student is having, to explain in conference or in a small group the grammatical or syntactic point, and then to assign some exercises that move from recognition to production. Then, a little later, I assign another topic for which the student is likely to generate the structure in question. Understanding and producing accurate grammatical forms is a parallel activity to composing. It should not be allowed to inhibit and interfere. Paul Diederich, author of the classic work *Measuring Growth in English*, believes that "noticing and praising whatever a student does well improves writing more than any kind or amount of correction of what he does badly" (1974, p. 20). There is no reason for us to assume that ESL students should not be included. Good beginnings, felicitous phrases, pertinent word choice, smooth transitions, sound logic, humor, realistic and lively detail should all be praised so that students feel that what they have to say is of prime importance and get a sense of what they can do well.

When my students get their first draft back from me, they gasp in horror because there is writing all over it. They assume from past experience that these are all corrections. Then they look more closely and see that there is praise—"I like this point"—a response—"The same thing once happened to me"—or a question—"Can you tell me more about this?" Here is one student's paragraph:

Ever since I was a small child the magic of tricks always were mysterious to me. One person who I believed was a master of it is Harry Houdini. He was the greatest, and his magic will live on as the greatest. If I was to meet him at my magic dinner, all my mysteries would be answer. Maybe he will even teach me a trick to amaze my friends. I feel I'm the person who should find out the secrets that were buried with him.

These are the comments I made:

What did he *do* that was so great? What mysteries do you want to have answered? What were the secrets that were buried with him? I'd like to know.

The student then revised, and really improved on her first version, even correcting the faulty subject-verb agreement without being prompted. She included details and rearranged sentences. That is revising—and it's a lot more than just correcting errors. Here is the revised paragraph:

Ever since I was a child the magic of tricks always was mysterious to me. One person who I believed was a master is Harry Houdini. All his escapes from chains and from jails shocked millions. His death in the water tank truly was a mystery. Some people think he did not know how to escape; others believe he suffered a bad cramp. I will find out at my dinner. I would like him to even teach me a trick to amaze my friends.

The student then admitted that she had just been to the library to check her facts and had found that Houdini had died of peritonitis. So she revised again.

It is not only the teacher who can respond with questions. Fellow students can too, if a student's writing is presented as a "reading" to the class. Students in a writing class seldom view their own writing as "reading" for someone else (that's a lot of what is wrong with it). Once they see it is, they look at it differently. So when we engage in our third major activity, providing readings, the Xerox or ditto machine is invaluable for presenting student writing for close and critical reading.

PROVIDING READINGS

I think I can almost hear some of you muttering, "But why provide readings at all in a writing class?" I am not urging readings as models for imitation (Look at this topic sentence and support and now write one just like it) or simply as springboards for discussion and ultimately for writing topics, or as a base for true/false questions and exercises on prepositions and synonyms, though readings can of course be used for these purposes too. I am urging examination of what a writer says, of why and how she or he says it. Such close reading entails determining the writer's intent, extricating and paraphrasing the meaning, asking questions like: "How is this related to what comes next and to what has gone before?" and examining the words and structure used to produce the meaning. In this way students see exactly what is involved in writing well, and learn more about what is expected of them when they write for a reader.

Readings can be adapted for an ESL class in a number of ways. They can be presented first as a kind of cloze test, with words omitted. When function words are omitted, this is purely an exercise in idiom and correct usage. But when content words are omitted, students try to come up with as many alternatives for the slot as possible, discussing the tone and connotations of each word choice. Then we can give them a choice of three or four words, one of which is the original author's choice. This prediction of the author's choice of words can be extended to predicting much larger chunks of form and content. Students see that they really know a lot about tone and textual and thematic development when they are asked, "What do you think comes next?" We can do this on a large scale, giving students the first lines of ten different novels and asking: Which one would you want to read? Why? What can you say about the novel?

When students read an opening sentence like:

The great fish moved silently through the night water propelled by short sweeps of its crescent tail.
(Peter Benchley, *Jaws*)

they make accurate, sensitive and sensible predictions, for writers often begin as they mean to go on; we sense the voice, the movement and direction of the piece. It is important for student writers to realize this. Movement and direction are rarely mentioned in ESL composition textbooks, and not too often in ESL composition classes, either.

How ideas are linked logically in shorter passages of prose can be examined by prediction also. If you were given the following section of text, what would you predict for the subsequent two or three sentences?

Music in Other People's Clock Radios
    There are times when I find myself spending the night in the home of another. Frequently the other is in a more reasonable line of work than I and must arise at a specific hour. Ofttimes the other, unbeknownst to me, manipulates an appliance in such a way that I am awakened by Stevie Wonder. On such occasions I announce that if I wished to be awakened by Stevie Wonder I would sleep with Stevie Wonder.
                                    Fran Lebowitz, *Metropolitan Life* (Dutton 1978)

This is what actually does come next:

I do not, however, wish to be awakened by Stevie Wonder and that is why God invented alarm clocks. Sometimes the other realizes that I am right, sometimes the other does not. And that is why God invented many others.

With appropriate passages, ESL students can predict and explain their predictions just as you would have done.

A related exercise in prediction is one applied to close reading of a short one- or two-page essay. Students are given the first lines of paragraphs and predict how each one will be developed and what the body of each paragraph might contain. Michael Donley suggests a technique that combines prediction and close analysis. He dictates a paragraph to a class one line at a time, with discussion after each line of what the subsequent sentence might be. When the complete paragraph has been dictated in this way it is analyzed for its grammatical and lexical links (1976).

It is important for ESL students to look at prose as a woven fabric rather than as strands of meaning. If they have been through ESL classes, they have written their obligatory pattern sentences, practicing the sentence grammar that is necessary for effective communication. But when they compose, they have to control their sentence grammar, at the same time dealing with links between sentences, with cohesion. Now if any grammar is to be taught in a composition class, it should surely be the grammar of cohesion. Halliday and Hasan in their book *Cohesion in English* show how the internal logic of the ideas is revealed in the surface structure of the ordering of the sentences, in the stated or implied relationships between sentences, and in the grammatical and lexical system: in pronouns, articles, demonstratives, omissions, substitutions, conjunctions, and vocabulary ties. Halliday and Hasan categorize the types of cohesive devices, showing that cohesion is "part of the system of a language . . . expressed partly in the grammar and partly through the vocabulary" (1976, p. 5).

ESL teachers usually love systems, and for composition this one is especially relevant, for it deals with connected discourse and textual movement. Teachers who feel it imperative to continue teaching grammar in an ESL composition course will find that this grammar at least gets students looking at sentence links and thus logic; it provides a framework for analyzing a piece of writing so that we see what Tolstoy is after in composing: "the ability to combine what follows with what precedes." It gets students looking beyond the sentence.

Let me here just illustrate briefly what this grammar of cohesion entails, with lines from *The New York Times:*

An upstate utility company spent several months and who knows how much money dunning a man who had moved from Greenwood Lake to Brooklyn. It finally succeeded in locating him and the man paid. He had owed the company one cent.

The New York Times, December 15, 1978

In these four lines alone there are a great many different cohesive links:

reference: pronouns—*it, him, he*
    articles—*the* man, *the* company (previously *a* man, *a* company)
conjuncts: *finally*
verb tense indicating time sequence: *had moved, had owed*
lexical links: repetition of *man* and *company*
    association of *paid-owed, money-cent*

Students can go through such a passage, circling the links and connecting them to referents. In this case, this involves looking at pronouns, articles, conjuncts, tenses, and vocabulary. That's a lot of grammar for any composition class.

Let me emphasize that study of this grammar of cohesion is not an end in itself; it is a tool for close examination of a text, of how writers get their words to work for them. And indeed this applies to all I have been saying here about giving topics, marking papers, and choosing readings: that in an ESL composition course we have got to make sure that we emphasize composing and not just ESL. And when we do, much of the necessary work on grammar, sentence structure, and rhetoric begins to take care of itself. Lucy proclaims that once you have trees, a lake, a log cabin, a waterfall, a deer, and a sunset, that's art; textbooks similarly proclaim that once you have an introduction, a body, a conclusion, and correct grammar and punctuation, that's a composition. We know our students need more than that placebo. Virginia Woolf prescribed £500 a year and a room of one's own to relieve a writer's anguish. That kind of relief we can't provide. But we can change our prescription. Our ESL students in composition classes are engaged in the complex linguistic exercise of making meaning without which no language can truly be said to be learned. One remedy for the anguish of composing is to concentrate on that making of meaning, to concentrate on the act of composing instead of peripherals. When we deal with ESL composition, when we give assignments, mark papers, and provide readings, we are dealing not just with ESL on the one hand and with composition on the other. We are dealing with TSL: Thinking in a Second Language. If we can get our students to do just that, we have surely taught them something.

EXPLORING THE IDEAS — *Teaching Strategies*

ACTIVITY 1

Background   Raimes argues persuasively for devoting a great deal of time in a composition class to activities that provide students with writing topics. As she says, "grammatical accuracy and rhetorical formulas have little force if the piece of writing is not expressing the writer's ideas clearly and forcefully with an involved imagination" (page 83). She points out that a shared classroom experience provides something for everyone to respond to in writing.

Application   Select a visual or series of visuals such as a photograph, a painting, an advertisement, a slide, or a cartoon that could be used as a basis for a shared classroom experience. Describe in detail how you would use the visual in class to give the students something to write about. In addition, specify the writing topic that would be generated from the visual. Be sure to indicate the level of class that the activity is intended for. Since visuals do not depend on linguistic competency, they are a highly effective medium to use with lower-level classes.

ACTIVITY 2

Background   Raimes contends that "at more advanced levels and particularly in composition classes, students need to deal with causes, categories, and relationships" (page 86).

Application   Select a visual such as a diagram or chart that could be used as a basis for exploring "causes, categories, and relationships." Describe in detail how you would use the visual in class. Then specify the writing topic that would be generated from this discussion.

ACTIVITY 3

Background   One valuable resource book for another type of prewriting activity is Simon, Howe, and Kirschenbaum's *Values Clarification* (New York, Hart Publishing, 1972). The following are some techniques described by the authors to help students clarify their values.

Rank Order Questions (page 59)
1. Where would you rather be on a Saturday afternoon?
_____ at the beach
_____ in the woods
_____ in a discount store

Either-or Forced Choice (page 94)
    Are you
_____ 1. More of a saver or a spender?
_____ 2. More of a breakfast or a dinner?
_____ 3. More like summer or winter?

Strongly Agree/Strongly Disagree (page 253)
    Instructions: Circle the response which most closely indicates the way you feel about each
    item.
SA – Strongly Agree   AS – Agree Somewhat
DS – Disagree Somewhat   SD – Strongly Disagree

1. Students are losing respect for their teachers.   SA   AS   DS   SD
2. Man is basically good.   SA   AS   DS   SD
3. Giving grades encourages meaningful learning in school. SA AS   DS   SD

Application   Design a value-clarification exercise which would help
students explore a specific topic such as male/female roles, attitudes toward
growing old, or a current controversial issue. Describe in detail how you would
use the exercise in class to give the students something to write about. Then
specify the writing topic that would be generated from the value-clarification
exercise.

ACTIVITY 4

Background   Raimes maintains that "in ESL composition classes the
teacher can predict what syntactic structures the topic is likely to generate and
review these before the composing begins and stress them again in the
proofreading" (page 89).

Application   Specify the syntactic structure or structures that you believe
would be generated by the writing topics you devised in the assignments listed
above (numbers 1, 2, and 3). Then design an exercise that could be used with
one of these assignments to help students practice a relevant syntactic structure
before they start to compose. Be certain to keep the content of the exercise
related to the topic of the writing assignment.

ACTIVITY 5

Background   According to Raimes, "choosing topics should be the
teacher's most responsible activity" (page 87). In addition, class time should be
spent providing students with ideas about these topics and reviewing relevant
syntactic structures. As a teacher, however, frequently you will not be devising
these activities yourself, but rather relying on the format of a text.

Application   Listed below are several writing topics taken from the text, *Writing as a Thinking Process* (Lawrence, Mary. 1972. Ann Arbor, University of Michigan Press, page 195). Assume that you are using this text. Select one of the topics to use with your class. Then design two exercises to accompany the text, one which would help students generate ideas on the topic and another which would help them review a relevant grammatical structure.

Personal Opinion

1. If you could spend one day with one famous person, whom would you choose? Write a composition in which you explain your choice.

2. If you could have changed one event in history, what would you have changed? Write a composition in which you tell what you would have changed and why.

3. Write a composition in which you explain whether you prefer to live in a large city or a small town.

Composition Evaluation

ACTIVITY 1

Background   As Raimes points out, in responding to students' compositions, "correcting is not all there is to do. If we want our students to keep on writing, to take pleasure in expressing ideas, then we should always respond to the ideas expressed and not only to the number of errors in a paper" (page 88). Basically she supports Paul Diederich's conclusion that praising what a student does well improves writing more than any amount of correction.

Application   Assume that the following essays describing a memorable experience were written by students in your ESL composition class. Write comments and questions for the students, but be certain to deal primarily with the positive elements of the essays.

SAILING ON THE BAY

It happened in my country, in one of the most beatiful beaches that I had ever seen, El Espino. I was only 7 years old and my oldest brother was 10. My mother had prevented us from sailing in a motor boat because it was too dangerous. Even though my mother had told us not to do so we decide to sail for a while. Minutes later we were with a group of friends sailing in the Espino Bay enjoying the view, the waves and the sun. After almost 2 hours of sailing, the outboard motor broke because it was too small for 11 children. It was still early, about 4 o'clock. The sun was burning us, so we were all red. The oldest person of the group was 16 years old. He took the oars and worked hard. Unfortunately the direction of the waves was stronger than us and we didn't make any progress. The wind pulled us away from the shore.

Although almost everybody knew how to swim; we were afraid of the sea and its animal life. I was too young to understand what was really going on, but I figure it out because I remember my oldest brother close to tears.

We struggled for 2 hours trying to advance to the shore. It was getting darker and darker. Suddenly and I still don't know how and why, a rescue boat of the Green Cross save us. This is one of that experiences that one can not forget. I remember it as if it were yesterday.

MY EXPERIENCE

Getting older, I have various experiences. Although they contain good experiences and bad experiences, both of them teach me the knack of living.

Four years ago, I lived alone in an apartment in Tokyo. The apartment was on the narrow sideway from the main street. My room was on the first floor. The apartment had a wall deviding the street and the apartment. There was a narrow space where only one person could walk between the wall and my room facing window. One summer night, when I was going to bed, I heard something rustle. At first, I thought leaves or insects made a rustling sound. But I heard louder sound again. I felt something strange. Then I remembered that I kept my window open because it was sultly night. I darted to the window and I caught my breath when I saw a man with a bat standing between the wall and my room. But at once, I noticed that the man was living near my apartment and I met sometimes on the street. However, I had never talked with him and, of course, I didn't know his name.

I asked covering my fear, "What are you doing here?"

"Hush!" he said, "Phew! As you made a sound, he ran away. I was chasing a wolf."

"Eh! A wolf? Where? What's happened?"

"A young girl was attacked three blocks away from here. He was a young thin guy."

I said to him that he should report to the police and he answered that he would and walk away. I was relieved and I closed the window surely. Getting ready to go to bed, I heard a siren. A few minutes later, I heard someone call me from the window. It was that man. He said, "I'm sorry I surprised you but don't worry because the wolf was arrested. You heard the siren of the police, didn't you?" And he went away. I thought it was very strange thing by recalling that event.

Suddenly I was seized with fear. Wait a minute. A siren of the police? Was that sound the silen of the police? No! It was the siren of the fire engine. Oh, what shall I do? Well, I should ask the police. Then I went to the police box which was located near my apartment. I explained a policeman that event and asked whether someone was arrested for attacking a young girl. As I expected, the answer was "No." When I came home with the policeman, that man was calling me toward the window of my room. The policeman asked him some questions. He answered immediately and he added that he worked at the Metoropolitan Government Office and he knew the policeman's superior officer. Unfortunately, since the policeman was very young, he believed what the man said. The event was over and I entered into my room with dissatisfaction.

By this event I knew to live on the first floor was dangerous and a policemen were weak by authority I regret I didn't report it to a newspaper. Before long I moved to the room on the second floor of another apartment.

ACTIVITY 2

Background   Raimes points out that one way to deal with the grammatical problems that a student is having is to explain them in conference, assign some exercises, and then assign another topic that is likely to generate the same syntactic structures which are causing the problem.

Application   Select one of the compositions printed above and specify one or more grammatical problems that reoccur throughout the essay. Then either select a grammar exercise from a text or design your own exercise to deal with these problems. Finally, devise another writing topic which would likely generate the particular grammatical points in question.

REFERENCES

Berthoff, A. 1978. Tolstoy, Vygotsky, and the Making of Meaning. *College Composition and Communication*, 29, 249–255.

Diederich, P. 1974. *Measuring Growth in English.* Champaign, Ill.: National Council of Teachers of English.

Donley, M. 1976. The Paragraph in Advanced Composition: A Heuristic Approach. *English Language Teaching Journal*, 30, 224–235.

Elbow, P. 1973. *Writing Without Teachers.* New York: Oxford University Press.

Emig, J. 1971. *The Composing Process of Twelfth Graders.* NCTE Research Report No. 13. Urbana, Ill.: National Council of Teachers of English.

Finocchiaro, M. 1974. *English as a Second Language: From Theory to Practice.* New York: Regents.

Halliday, M. A. K., and Hasan, R. 1976. *Cohesion in English.* London: Longman.

Moffett, J. 1968. *Teaching the Universe of Discourse.* Boston, Mass.: Houghton Mifflin.

Paulston, C., and Bruder, M. 1976. *Teaching English as a Second Language: Techniques and Procedures.* Cambridge, Mass.: Winthrop.

Pirsig, R. 1975. *Zen and the Art of Motorcycle Maintenance.* New York: Bantam Books.

Raimes, A. 1978a. Problems and Teaching Strategies in ESL Composition. In Language in Education Series. Washington, D.C.: Center for Applied Linguistics.

Raimes, A. 1978b. *Focus on Composition.* New York: Oxford University Press.

Rivers, W., and Temperley, M. 1978. *A Practical Guide to the Teaching of English.* New York: Oxford University Press.

Shaughnessy, M. 1976. Diving in: An Introduction to Basic Writing. *College Composition and Communication*, 27, 234–239.

Shaughnessy, M. 1977. *Errors and Expectations: A Guide for the Teacher of Basic Writing.* New York: Oxford University Press.

Sommers, N. 1978. Revision Strategies of Student Writers and Experienced Writers. Paper presented at the annual meeting of the Modern Language Association.

6

The Use and Abuse of Models in the ESL Writing Class

Cynthia B. Watson-Reekie

The use of model passages, usually extracts or paragraphs, is widespread in ESL writing texts at all levels and is largely unquestioned by ESL teachers. The simplistic notion that people learn to speak a language mainly by imitating others has been abandoned; yet it is still assumed that the study and imitation of a model, a sample of writing that is by definition successful, is a valid means of helping students to learn to write in their first or second language. The model-based tradition of composition goes back a long way. For centuries boys learned to write Latin by imitating the flowing style of Cicero or the terse, witty epigrams of Seneca. In turn, English writers of the sixteenth and seventeenth centuries tried to reproduce in their vernacular the style of admired classical Latin writers. By the late eighteenth century the models of prose style used in school in both Britain and the United States included the works of those very writers and their more confident successors. People felt that they now knew who the best writers were in English too and that there was no surer guide to good writing than careful study and imitation of their products. Thus evolved a tradition which, with a certain increase in sophistication and refinement of the notion of imitation, continues yet in many composition texts intended for American college students and is particularly strong in second and foreign language teaching.

Why this continuing reliance upon models? What case can be made out for them? Most ESL teachers would probably agree on at least the following points: (1) Models provide exposure to the lexical items, structural patterns, and conventions of the target language at all levels of discourse; in particular, they take us beyond sentence level. (2) They demonstrate many modes of rhetorical organization and stylistic variety, related to variables such as communicative purpose and anticipated audience. (3) They are, especially when authentic rather than composed to order, windows onto culture in its widest sense, revealing customs, values, assumptions, and attitudes toward the world and man as perceived by speakers of the target language.

Models, then, provide powerful input. But what about intake (Corder 1967; Krashen 1978)? How much of this input can students actually take in, utilize, and incorporate in their own work? Models are chosen as examples of good writing, but how far can study and analysis of these products strengthen students' understanding of how good writing is actually made, let alone help them to produce some for themselves? Yet these are, or should be, the aims of a writing lesson. And teachers who use models in that context presumably believe that models can contribute significantly to students' own participation in the writing process by providing both resource and support, both stimulus and guidance, both experience (linguistic, rhetorical, cultural) and reassurance.

But this is where doubts creep in. Model-based composition teaching is product-based composition teaching. Gerald Dykstra has pointed out (Paulston and Dykstra 1973: vii) that the model "is the product of other people's writing, not the student's own product, and it is the product—not the process—of writing that is observed." Here he focuses sharply on writing teachers' dilemma: How can they ensure transfer to the students' own writing of the features of the model that are considered desirable? And, since product and process are two very different things, how can study and analysis of the former contribute to understanding of and participation in the latter?

Textbook writers have tackled these problems in very different ways. They reveal sharply contrasting underlying notions of what writing is for the ESL student. For some authors, student writing is apparently envisaged primarily as transference into the written medium of lexical items and patterns already presented and practiced orally. Thus writing becomes merely a reinforcement of grammar teaching, with error-free sentence production as its prime target. This approach treats the model largely as a source of patterns to be reproduced or manipulated in various ways. One disadvantage of this is that the student product that results is likely to be very artificial: a collection of sentences rather than a text, something that no experienced writer would ever produce.

Other textbook writers take a broader view. They wish to encourage genuine composition and choose models for their potential appeal in theme or topic. They also use analytical discussion, exercises, and writing tasks to increase student awareness of how the product has been put together, of exactly what contribution particular features (lexical, syntactic, organizational) make to its appeal or communicative effectiveness. Students are shown how they can themselves adopt or adapt these features to produce compositions which are in some sense their own and yet acceptable specimens of the target language in use.

Whichever of these approaches is taken, the sequence of materials and classroom activities is usually as follows: In every chapter or unit, first the model, then discussion/exercises on particular features, and finally, suggested topics on which students can work to produce a parallel text.

The tradition of using models raises many important issues for the ESL teacher and materials writer. An evaluation of their use, including the principles on which they are chosen or constructed, the various ways in which ESL writing materials exploit them, and the basic question of how far alien product can stimulate original process, is the concern of this paper.

CHOICE OF MODEL

Models fall into two main types, authentic and specially written, each of which has both virtues and disadvantages. Particularly at the elementary level, where authentic models are often thought too difficult to serve as intake, there is a very strong case for the use of specially written models. The materials writer can thus control totally the language to which students are exposed in the classroom and can shape individual units to show how particular communicative functions are realized through particular structures and rhetorical strategies. Such tight integration must surely be helpful to the beginning student, in that it provides maximum support and reassurance.

There are, however, two objections to this kind of specially written model, objections that apply even at the elementary level. First, the model can become depressingly artificial. The following (adapted from a recent elementary composition text) provides evidence:

Jane gets up at 7:30 every morning. She gets dressed before she eats breakfast. She usually has orange juice, toast and coffee for breakfast. She usually watches television while she eats breakfast. After breakfast she reads the newspaper for a few minutes. Then she goes to work. She goes to work by car.
    She arrives at work at 9 o'clock . . .

Here we have a typical piece of tightly controlled writing. The paragraph contains seven single-clause sentences. Four consecutive sentences contain the word *breakfast*, while the last two (and the first of the next paragraph) contain the word *work*. For this writer, clarity is so important that it leads to the serious overuse of lexical repetition as a cohesive device. Since the writer assumes that students have already been taught personal pronouns (*she* occurs in every sentence except the first and is used initially in five), greater use could surely be made of pro-forms, such as *it* and *that*, to link sentences and produce a more convincing English paragraph. While agreeing that the model must remain accessible, i.e., not of a forbidding level of difficulty even for elementary students, one might wonder whether artificial models of this sort are not to some extent responsible for the short, repetitive sentences one often encounters in student work long after the elementary level is passed. If elementary level students were not encouraged to imitate this kind of text, perhaps we would not need to put so much emphasis on teaching connectives and achieving variety in sentence length later on.

A second and related risk is that such an unduly sheltered environment may offer false reassurance. Some exposure to authentic English is desirable, and perfectly feasible, from the start. Brochures, official forms, menus, notices, timetables—all these can be used to stimulate student writing which is not necessarily directly imitative. Even at the elementary level, the aim should be to introduce students to the living language in as wide a variety of styles, formats, and genres as possible. To be successful, student work must be based on an internalized knowledge of accepted conventions—lexical, grammatical, organizational, and graphic.

At every level, too, an attempt should be made to introduce students to literature in the target language. This does not mean Shakespeare and Wordsworth in the first month but rather a careful choice of poems and extracts from contemporary plays (including TV and film scripts), short stories, and novels which are thematically relevant and provocative, culturally rich and linguistically challenging, yet appropriate to the students' level of competence. Provided the principle of accessibility is always kept in mind, literature is invaluable in producing an affective response in the student. Writing thus stimulated, whether it takes the form of a personal reaction to a theme or a point of view exercise, proceeds from at least partial empathy with the characters and events narrated. In other words, if students' own feelings are involved, as well as their efforts to comprehend and respond to the world of the literary piece, then alien product really has informed original process and the result is likely to be genuine composition.

Whether it will also be a piece of fairly acceptable English in grammatical, rhetorical, and mechanical terms, however, depends not only on an appropriate initial choice of model but also on how carefully integrated the whole writing lesson has been. In-class discussion of human issues, especially in small groups, is particularly important here. Students have to be given the chance to explore the motivation of characters and the nature of the moral/social conflicts in the piece, as well as the linguistic and rhetorical means through which these are realized. The result will be what James Britton (1978:14) has called *involved* rather than *perfunctory* writing. He defines the latter as "minimal attempts to satisfy demands the writers did not themselves endorse," whereas the former represents "performances in which writers made demands of themselves." Britton was concerned with the L1 situation, but in ESL teaching too the aim should always be to encourage—indeed force our students through the very format of the writing lesson—to make such demands of themselves. Responding to literature is experiencing vicariously at one remove from real life. And that response can be translated into genuine composition.

MODEL-BASED TASKS AND EXERCISES

These vary enormously, from tightly controlled to completely free, from those that require little actual writing and no composition (such as cloze-type and other blank-filling exercises) to the stark injunction to "Write an essay on X." All, except possibly the last, have their place in the writing lesson. They can be categorized in at least two ways: by focus, which may relate to structural points in the model, to its rhetorical organization, or to its communicative function; or by emphasis, which may be placed on comprehension and analysis of the model, or on the student's own production. Cloze-type exercises, for example, are certainly very useful for directing attention to features on various levels of discourse, but they should be considered as prewriting tasks, reinforcing more general discussion of the model and how it achieves its effect.

Exercises that emphasize production, however, are by no means all equally useful. Most controlled exercises involve more or less copying the model with a greater or lesser amount of structural manipulation. One might reasonably doubt whether such exercises give students new insight into how the model was constructed because what they are being asked to do is change it in various arbitrary ways, e.g., changing declaratives to interrogatives, singular subjects to plurals, and so on. And do they help students much at all with the business of their own writing? It is often suggested that such manipulations build confidence and fluency in the use of sentence-patterns and encourage attention to intersentential relations, as in the use of pronouns to agree with and refer back to NPs in preceding sentences. It may be so, but the risk of boredom is great and, as Rivers and Temperley (1978:297–307) have amply shown, there are better, more imaginative ways of achieving the same ends.

There are, moreover, two further and even more weighty objections to such manipulative exercises. The focus on structural manipulation often means that the communicative purpose of the model is ignored or perverted and also that students are asked to produce entirely unnatural discourse that no native speaker would ever produce. They may, for example, be required to convert a paragraph of descriptive prose made up of a series of short, single-clause declarative sentences (A sandy beach is an interesting place in summer. There is a happy atmosphere. Also, there is a lot of noise . . .) into a parallel series of yes/no questions (Is a sandy beach an interesting place in summer? Is there a happy atmosphere? Is there a lot of noise?, or of negative statements (A sandy beach isn't an interesting place in winter. There isn't a happy atmosphere. There isn't a lot of noise . . .). They are thus producing nontexts, for what native speaker would ask such a series of questions (without a single response) or describe a sandy beach in winter in purely negative terms?

Completion exercises based on the notion of guidance rather than control are more helpful. Students may be asked to answer a series of questions or to complete individual sentences which together amount to a retelling or summary of the model. Sometimes the first few sentences of summary or paraphrase are given and students supply the rest of the parallel text. In any case, real comprehension of at least parts of the model is required, including the capacity to pick out its communicatively salient features. Students must also, of course, be able to relate the given stimulus questions or incomplete sentences to the relevant portions of the model (a task which often invokes transformational competence). Finally, they are forced into a certain limited amount of actual composition as they make their completions. They can always refer back to the model for help in finding out how it's done but, if the exercise is well designed, they will not be able to make the completion simply by copying. A further significant step toward composition is taken when, following the principle of analogy, a new but closely related topic is suggested and at least some of the relevant lexis supplied. Students have more to do for themselves now; they can follow the model in overall organization and syntactic patterning but must relate these to the new theme. They are thus simultaneously challenged yet reassured as they become aware of the possibilities for generalizing the syntactic and rhetorical features of the model.

In all these tasks, however, the primary focus of the materials writer is on comprehension and reproduction of, above all, the structural patterns of the model. Structural patterns always realize deeper levels of discourse planning. Greater awareness of this fact has led to the production of ESL writing materials that adopt a rhetorically based approach. This assumes that effective writing (especially of expository prose) is based on conscious thought about logical and other relationships. This approach requires that students become skilled at differentiating, for example, opinions from facts, implications from inferences, generalizations from supporting material, and then that they produce these to order.

But the validity of this assumption is open to question. Taylor, for example in his useful survey of the implications of writing and second-language acquisition research for ESL teaching, expresses strong doubts about the value of the rhetorical approach when he suggests that

we have no more right to assume that analyzing written models with an eye toward teaching the explicit structure of discourse will necessarily improve writing ability any more than to assume that grammar drills will necessarily improve speaking ability (1981:8).

Nonetheless the rhetorical approach has some merits. It at least focuses attention on the way successful writers handle units of discourse larger than the sentence. At all times, writers must be aware not only of the details of a particular sentence but also of the place of that sentence in their overall argument. A student who cannot do this is never going to write well. There seem, moreover, to be as yet largely unstudied interlingual and cultural differences of a rhetorical nature (Kaplan 1966) which make this approach especially valuable in second and foreign language teaching.

Rhetoric, however, serves a communicative purpose, and many recently produced ESL writing texts focus primarily on this. Most, though not all, use models and ask students to write with the same purpose but within different, though analogous situations; that is, they hold purpose constant but vary topic, participants, or setting. Changes of role and participant relationships often require so many stylistic adjustments that the students may now be said to be writing a truly new composition. Basically they are still being asked to reproduce, but the task is much richer, more meaningful, since now they have to think about why they are using certain structures and what their effect is likely to be on the envisaged audience. Contrasting pairs of models can be used, e.g., an informal personal letter of apology (I'm very sorry that . . .) and a formal impersonal one (We greatly regret that . . .). Thus students are made aware of the existence of stylistic options that have social meanings. When they, in their turn, write, they can make their own choices knowledgeably and appropriately—true evidence of communicative competence in the target language.

USING PRODUCT WITHIN PROCESS

The last decade has seen growing dissatisfaction with traditional model-based writing lessons, especially in the L1 teaching situation, for reasons strongly presented and summarized by Paul Eschholz (1980). The models used tend to be too long, too remote from students' own writing problems, too likely to promote reading comprehension and rhetorical analysis rather than writing. The traditional sequence of activities in model-based writing lessons (read, analyze, write) is also criticized, for it involves an "underlying assumption that advance diagnosis of writing problems promotes learning." Detailed analytical work tends to encourage students to "see form as a mold into which content is somehow poured" and results in "mindless copies of a particular organizational plan or style." In general, the imitation of models is seen as "stultifying and inhibiting writers rather than empowering them or liberating them" (1980:24).

Eschholz relates how, prodded by the process-oriented writing research that stemmed from the work of Donald Murray (1968), he and his colleagues at the University of Vermont developed new courses in which models are used as problem-specific resources, i.e., within the students' writing process, rather than outside it or initiating it. "Students must be permitted to discover their own writing problems" (1980:35), but once they have made that discovery models may be very helpful, demonstrating solutions that others have found and that students can utilize for themselves.

In ESL teaching too, learner-centered approaches that stress communicative achievement rather than correctness have had their effect. Some teachers have abandoned models altogether, preferring an experiential approach in which themes for writing originate in students' own concerns and are developed interactionally (cf. Taylor 1981), the teacher supplying linguistic resources as and when necessary. For others, the model has become merely one kind of cue for writing; visual and graphic devices are used either instead of or alongside it. Students may even have to discover the model for themselves, as when sentences are presented in muddled sequence, on separate slips of paper, and the class has to work out the original sequence with the help of pictures, diagrams, or graphs. Thus students are actively and simultaneously involved in comprehension, analysis, and re-creation. (See White (1980:51–52) for a lesson plan that integrates model analysis and student production very tightly indeed.)

The model has thus in a sense been demoted by being brought within the process. But surely this is entirely desirable. If students can treat the model as a resource rather than an ideal, if they can explore it with each other as well as with the teacher, if they can comfortably compare their own products at various stages of composition with that of the professional, then the alien product is truly involving them in original process.

Models should be introduced and utilized in the writing lesson, then, in such a way as to allow for collaborative activity, both oral and written, for both prewriting discussion and postwriting critique, for both analysis of the model and evaluation of students' own productions. The suggested sequence of activities within each unit in Raimes (1978) exemplifies such an integrated approach to the business of writing. Models are there but not in their traditional place at the beginning of the unit. Students focus first on communicative purpose (e.g., describing what happened) and the linguistic and rhetorical features needed to realize this. Exposure to the model is deliberately delayed. Only when they have already embarked on the process of their own composition—producing a rough draft by group effort or pair work—are they invited to read the model, for the sake of comparison rather than imitation.

Thus Raimes achieves that close and fruitful integration of reading and writing which helps writers to understand "that writing is the making of reading" (Eschholz 1980:28) and develops that "special eye for craft" (Murray 1968:173) that makes them read like writers. Students working from this kind of text are asked to be readers and writers, critics and listeners, actively involved in all four roles, whether engaged with their own work or that of a peer or a professional. They do not have to imagine the needs of a reader throughout, for they are each other's readers and can make the reader's needs plain. Since they write first, they are not overawed or cast down by exposure to a smooth professional production. And when they do read the model, it is presented to them as one way to realize a particular communicative purpose, certainly not the only or necessarily the best way.

Models can, then, still contribute a very great deal to the teaching of composition, especially in the second or foreign language situation. Indeed, they are an indispensable resource. They should not be completely abandoned in favor of visual and graphic cues, however much these may brighten up the pages of textbooks. But the traditional use of them in the writing lesson as ideals for discussion, dissection, and imitation (in that order) has indeed been discredited in the last decade. Process-oriented writing research suggests instead that models can be most useful when fully integrated into the sequence of activities within the writing lesson.

Teachers should first help student writers define their own communicative purposes in the written medium, then select appropriate writing tasks and introduce relevant models for stimulus, guidance, and support. Exploration and analysis of models should involve students actively working together, in the expectation that shared discoveries and reactions will stimulate individual involvement and that this will result in genuine composition. When models are used within the writing process, students can easily perceive their purpose and utility. In a sense, the student writers thus control the total process, including recourse to the model, because their own writing has quite clearly become the central concern of the lesson. And that, of course, is exactly what it always ought to be.

EXPLORING THE IDEAS — *Theoretical Discussion*

QUESTION 1

Background   As Watson-Reekie points out, models have traditionally been used in the classroom on the assumption that people learn to speak and write mainly by imitation.

Discussion   What evidence are you aware of from research in first or second language acquisition which would either support or refute the theory of imitation as central to language acquisition?

QUESTION 2

Background   Watson-Reekie points out that most controlled exercises which are based on models involve more or less copying the model with some degree of structural manipulation. She continues that "one might reasonably doubt whether such exercises give students new insight into how the model was constructed because what they are being asked to do is change it in various arbitrary ways, e.g., changing declaratives to interrogatives, singular subjects to plurals, and so on. And do they help students much at all with the business of their own writing?" (pages 100–101).

Discussion   Do you think such exercises help students with "the business of their own writing"? If so, what are some benefits of using such exercises? What do you see as the danger of using highly controlled exercises?

Teaching Strategies

ACTIVITY 1

Background   Watson-Reekie argues that there are three major advantages to the use of models: first, they provide exposure to the vocabulary and structure of the language; second, they illustrate rhetorical organization and stylistic variety; and third, they provide insight into the culture.

Application   Select a reading passage which you believe would be appropriate to use as a model for a writing class. Indicate what type of class you feel it would suit and why. Then analyze the passage in terms of what it illustrates for each of the areas delineated by Watson-Reekie: structural patterns and lexical items, rhetorical organization and stylistic variety, and cultural insights.

ACTIVITY 2

Background   Watson-Reekie discusses two major approaches to the use of models in ESL textbooks. The first approach is to treat the model primarily as a source of patterns to be manipulated by the students; the second is to explore the theme and topic for discussion and writing tasks.

Application   Analyze two writing texts which use reading models. Select several representative exercises as a basis for determining which of the approaches discussed by Watson-Reekie is primarily used in each of the texts. If the exercises fit into neither category, characterize the type of activities that are included.

ACTIVITY 3

Background   Watson-Reekie maintains that one advantage of using models is that "they take us beyond sentence level" (page 97). As connected discourse, models are valuable resources for illustrating cohesive devices such as pronouns, articles, conjunctions, and vocabulary ties.

Application   Select a short reading passage and design an exercise that helps students identify the cohesive devices within the text. One possibility for the exercise is to use a cloze technique in which certain cohesive devices have been omitted. Another possibility is to have students identify the referent for the pronouns or demonstratives in the text. In any case, be certain to select a text which illustrates a variety of cohesive devices.

ACTIVITY 4

Background   As Watson-Reekie points out, models are useful in illustrating stylistic variation. One technique she suggests is to use contrasting pairs of models such as an informal personal letter of apology as opposed to a formal impersonal one.

Application   Write a contrasting pair of models which illustrates two different levels of formality. Then describe how you would use the models in class to help students become aware of stylistic options.

ACTIVITY 5

Background   Watson-Reekie discusses two major approaches to the use of models in ESL textbooks. The first approach is to treat the model primarily as a source of patterns to be manipulated by the students; the second is to explore the theme and topic for discussion and writing tasks.

Another way to use a model, one proposed by Patricia Taylor, is creative imitation (Creative Imitation—The Earliest Art. In P. Taylor, F. Peitzman, and J. R. McCuen (eds.). *In the Trenches.* Los Angeles, University of California Press, 1982). Taylor suggests that students be given a model and asked to change the content but to maintain the particular forms of the original in terms of its sentence structure, tone, and figures of speech. One of her examples is an expository essay topic, "School Means Different Things to Different People," in which the students are to use the following model (page 61).

Mountaineering, to be sure, means different things to different practitioners. For an adventurous few, it means ambitious expeditions and first ascents: Alaska, the Andes, the Himalayas. For another comparatively small group, it means an interest in complex climbing problems and the development and refining of techniques. For the rest of us, most of us, it means simply to visit mountains when and where we can and to climb them according to our opportunities and abilities, whether it be the Alps or the Adirondacks, the Catskills or the Rockies.

Application   First, use the paragraph above as a model for your own creative imitation. You may replace the topic sentence with "School means different things to different people" or with any other topic of your choosing. Next, write a passage which could be used as a model for creative imitation with a group of intermediate-level ESL students, and if possible, use the passage with such a group. Then, discuss what you see as the strengths and weaknesses of this technique.

Applying Theoretical Concepts

ACTIVITY 1

Background   Watson-Reekie delineates two types of models: authentic and specially written. H. G. Widdowson (in *Teaching Language as Communication*. Oxford University Press, 1978:77–93) further refines this distinction by describing three major types of models. The first is an *extract* or a piece of genuine discourse. The second is a *simplified version* or a passage which is derived from an extract by a process of lexical and syntactic substitution. The third is a *simple account* which is the recasting of information abstracted from some source to suit a particular kind of reader. Widdowson advocates presenting the same topic in a series of simplified texts that gradually increase in linguistic complexity.

Watson-Reekie's main objection to specially written models is that they may be artificial and provide students with a sheltered environment. The first objection, artificiality, can be countered by writing texts which do contain a variety of sentence patterns and cohesive devices. The second objection, false security, can be met by Widdowson's suggestion of using a series of progressively more difficult texts.

Application   The following are three different accounts of silicon chips. Rank the three of them according to level of difficulty. Then specify what criteria you used in determining their relative difficulty.

Finally, write three of your own accounts of the same information but in increasing levels of difficulty. In writing the texts, apply the criteria you used in analyzing the difficulty level of the texts included above. In order to avoid Watson-Reekie's criticism of the artificiality of simplified texts, try to include some sentence variety and cohesive devices, even on the lowest level.

VERSION A
    Silicon chips are the brains of computers. In many ways, they are similar to human brains. They can do a lot of work in a very small space. A chip that is the size of a dime can remember the contents of an entire book. Chips look like a map of a city. The "streets" are the circuits which carry electronic messages in a way comparable to the nerves in our brains.
    There are also obvious differences between silicon chips and human brains. Chips can do only what they are programmed to do. They are unable to create new ideas. They can't compose even a simple composition on their own. However, they can remember more, and remember it faster, than our brains can. And they forget only what they are programmed to forget.
    Some people argue that chips are very beneficial because they can do the ordinary work and free our brains to do more creative work.

VERSION B

Silicon chips are the brains of computers. They are like our brains in many ways. They do a lot of work in a small space. One chip is the size of a dime, but it can remember a book. Chips look like a map of a city. The "streets" carry electronic messages. Our nerves are like streets too. They carry electronic messages in our brains.

Chips are different from our brains in many ways. They can do only the things they are made to do. They can't do anything new. For example, they can't write a composition. But chips are faster than our brains. They can remember more, and they don't forget.

Some people say silicon chips are very good for us. They can do the ordinary work, and allow our brains to think in new ways.

VERSION C

Silicon chips are the brains of computers. In many ways, they are comparable to human brains. Like our brains, they are able to do a great deal of work in a very small area. A chip that is less than a square centimeter in size can remember the contents of an entire book. Under a microscope, chips appear similar to a city viewed from miles up. The "streets" are the circuits which carry electronic impulses in a way comparable to the nerves in our brains.

There are also obvious differences between silicon chips and human brains. Chips are only able to do what they have been programmed to do. They are unable to create new ideas. They can't even compose a simple composition on their own. However, chips have larger and faster memories than humans.

Some people contend that chips are very beneficial because they can do ordinary, repetitive tasks, and free our brains for more creative work.

ACTIVITY 2

Background   Literature is extremely rich in being, as Watson-Reekie puts it, "windows onto culture in its widest sense, revealing customs, values, assumptions and attitudes toward the world and man as perceived by speakers of the target language" (page 97). This can be both an advantage and a disadvantage. It is an advantage insofar as students can grow in their understanding of the new culture. It is a disadvantage, however, if the students are unfamiliar with the cultural assumptions in the text and thus misinterpret the text.

Application   Select a piece of literature which you believe would be appropriate for an intermediate-level ESL class. Then point out all the cultural information contained in the text which might not be understood by the students. This might include cultural expectations as to appropriate behavior in a particular situation, historical background, religious mores, or national customs. Finally, discuss what you see as the major advantages and disadvantages of using literature in an ESL composition class.

REFERENCES

Britton, James. 1978. The Composing Processes and the Functions of Writing. In C. Cooper and L. Odell (eds.). *Research on Composing*. Urbana, Illinois, National Council of Teachers of English.

Corder, S. P. 1967. The Significance of Learners' Errors. *IRAL* 5:161–170.

Eschholz, Paul A. 1980. The Prose Models Approach: Using Products in the Process. In T. R. Donovan and B. W. McClelland (eds.). *Eight Approaches to Teaching Composition.* Urbana, Illinois, National Council of Teachers of English.

Kaplan, Robert A. 1966. Cultural Thought Patterns in Intercultural Education. *Language Learning* 16: 1–20.

Krashen, Stephen. 1978. Adult Second Language Acquisition and Learning: A Review of Theory and Practice. In R. Gingras (ed.). *Second Language Acquisition and Foreign Language Teaching.* Washington, D.C., Center for Applied Linguistics.

Murray, Donald M. 1968. *A Writer Teaches Writing.* Boston, Houghton Mifflin Company.

Paulston, Christina B., and Gerald Dykstra. 1973. *Controlled Composition in English as a Second Language.* New York, Regents Publishing Company, Inc.

Raimes, Ann. 1978. *Focus on Composition.* New York, Oxford University Press.

Rivers, Wilga M., and Mary S. Temperley. 1978. *A Practical Guide to the Teaching of English as a Second or Foreign Language.* New York, Oxford University Press.

Taylor, Barry P. 1981. Content and Written Form: A Two-Way Street. *TESOL Quarterly* 15: 5–13.

White, Ronald V. 1980. *Teaching Written English.* In M. Geddes and G. Sturtridge (eds.). *Practical Language Teaching* 3. London, George Allen and Unwin.

7

Teaching Those Missing Links in Writing[1]

Vivian Zamel

Numerous devices exist for connecting ideas in writing. Halliday and Hasan (1976), in their exploration of connecting devices, identified five major categories of cohesive ties. In addition, parallel structure and even tense can signal relationships within written texts. While English language students need to learn to identify and use the whole variety of linking devices, they particularly need careful instruction in the use of *conjuncts*—those connectives more specifically referred to in grammars as coordinating conjunctions, subordinating conjunctions, and conjunctive adverbs or transitions. They need to learn not only the words themselves but the relationships they signal within and between sentences and between larger units of discourse.

Teachers of writing have all seen student compositions in which the meaning or intent has been obscured, either because these conjuncts are missing or because the links used are inappropriate semantically or syntactically. The following, taken from a student paper, is a case in point:

Men and women in the village share the chores equally. Men sometimes take care of the children and women sometimes trade with other tribesmen. *Nevertheless,* the women participate in politics and religious ceremonies.

Here the student probably intended a link that signifies addition, but erroneously chose one that indicates contradiction, thereby confusing the reader who has certain expectations about what can and cannot follow the particular conjunct used. Many examples similar to the one above appear in our students' writing. Unfortunately, we get so distracted by the inappropriateness or total absence of conjunction that students are rarely given credit for attempting to put into practice the devices we have urged them to use.

A BRIEF SURVEY

Cohesive ties are important because they turn separate clauses, sentences, and paragraphs into units of connected prose which refer back and forth to each other. Because these conjuncts signal a "relation between an element in a text and some other element that is crucial to the interpretation of it" (Halliday and Hasan 1976:8), they make obvious and visible the writer's "line of thought" (Broadhead and Berlin 1981:306). Researchers are beginning to point out that these ties are an important property of writing quality (Witte and Faigley 1981:195–197), indeed, that they may be essential for preserving the author's meaning (Raimes 1979). Without conjuncts, it would be extremely difficult to make sense of connections between ideas, for these linking words alert us to the intended relationship, preparing us to anticipate the ideas that follow. It is precisely because of this anticipated relationship that the student example cited above and others like it prove to be so problematical.

Whereas native speakers of English generally learn to use these cohesive elements as they do other aspects of language, English language students seem to have great difficulty in mastering them (Dubin and Olshtain 1980: 356–362). Cohen et al. (1979) found that nonnative speakers of English were particularly troubled by markers of cohesion in their reading. Yet another study, focusing on the ability to use cohesive links in writing, found that conjunction caused many problems (Bacha and Hanania 1980). Furthermore, the researchers hypothesized that these problems may stem "from a restricted knowledge of linking words in the English language and the logical relationship associated with each" (Bacha and Hanania 1980:251) rather than from the differences between the rhetorical systems of the two languages, as Kaplan's well-known theory would have us believe (1967).

TRADITIONAL APPROACHES

It seems that, despite the critical role that conjuncts play in writing, English language students are not always able to take advantage of them. This may be primarily because they have not been taught to identify them during reading instruction or to use them correctly in their writing. What they *have* been offered, if composition texts are any reflection of our teaching strategies, are lists of cohesive devices categorized according to function. The following list, taken from a recent ESL writing text (Bander 1980:8–10) is a representative example:

Transitions that qualify: *but, however, although, though, yet, except for*
1. But the clerk refused to answer.
2. The letter came two days too late, however.
3. We hoped, though, that she would change her mind.
4. Yet there was still a chance that he would win.
5. Except for one girl, all the hikers returned.

Transitions that contrast: *unlike, in contrast, whereas, on the other hand, instead*
1. Unlike the Porsche, the Cadillac is a large car.
2. In contrast, the red fluid does not lose its color.
3. The husband wanted a boy, whereas the wife wanted a girl.
4. On the other hand, a student needs time to relax.
5. Instead, the new law caused many problems.

Transitions that concede: *although, nevertheless, of course, after all, clearly, still, yet*
1. Although she ran after the train, it left without her.
2. He planned, nevertheless, to ask for a promotion.
3. It may rain tomorrow, of course.
4. After all, you learn to cook many foods in this job.
5. Clearly, a garden needs a lot of attention.
6. Still, a winter vacation can be pleasant.

Lists such as this can be misleading, for they fail to recognize that "the most important characteristic of cohesion is the fact that it does not constitute a class of items but rather a set of relations" (Dubin and Olshtain 1980:356). Borkin (1978) points to the absurdity of presenting a list of cohesive ties as if they expressed similar logical relationships, and emphasizes the fact that these connectives *can't* be understood without taking into consideration the discourse contexts in which they appear. Widdowson (1978) makes the same type of criticism of materials and teaching strategies that focus on the conjuncts to be learned rather than on how these links make contextually related ideas clear and logical. Thus, because these lists do not demonstrate how cohesive devices establish the logical relationship between the ideas presented, they are ineffective as an aid in teaching these links. For example, referring to Bander's list, how can students appreciate the meaning of "on the other hand" unless they have been provided with a sentence which *precedes* the one given? Numerous other problems are created for students when they are given such lists. Some transitional markers may have more than one function in English. For example, "since" can be used to signal time clauses (as in "Since we got here last week, the weather has been awful"); or it can signal cause (as in "Since he didn't study, he failed the test"). Added to this complexity is the fact that a marker like "since" can be used to signal either time or cause, depending on one's meaning or interpretation as in "Since you went away, the days grow cold." The same cohesive link can even function in completely opposite contexts: "At the same time," for example, can be used to indicate *either* a concurrent temporal relationship *or* opposition. Yet another serious problem is the fact that devices categorized together are not necessarily interchangeable: "but" and "however" cannot be substituted for "on the contrary" or "on the other hand," although they are often classified together. Even when linking devices in a list *do* serve similar semantic functions, however, the fact that they may carry different grammatical weight causes other difficulties. Thus, if one refers again to Bander's list above, one becomes immediately aware of the problematic nature of categorizing "but" together with "however." If students conclude from consulting such a list that these two words are syntactically equivalent, they may succeed in connecting their ideas but may create sentences that are not acceptable grammatically. It is obvious from all of this that providing students with a knowledge of conjuncts is no easy matter, for students must not only learn the individual meanings of these links and their semantic restrictions, that is, what relationships they express and which ones are appropriate in which contexts; they must also learn their grammatical restrictions, that is, why linking devices that are *lexically* similar cannot be used to perform the same *syntactic* functions.

SUGGESTED TEACHING STRATEGIES

Rather than the typical textbook approach of presenting lists of conjuncts categorized according to meaning, it would be more effective to begin by classifying linking devices according to their grammatical functions. In other words, coordinating conjunctions (e.g., "and," "or," "but"), subordinating conjunctions (e.g., "because," "although," "if"), and conjunctive adverbs (e.g., "on the other hand," "nevertheless") should all be introduced separately. In this way, students could learn how each type of marker works within the sentence and between sentences. They could learn that coordinating conjunctions *connect* independent clauses, that subordinating conjunctions *transform* the independent clauses to which they are appended into subordinate ones, and that conjunctive adverbs have *semantic* weight, but no *grammatical* function. As students learn these necessary distinctions, they can also be taught the appropriate punctuation for each type of connective. Shaughnessy has pointed out that this is the only way to introduce punctuation, for "the study of punctuation ought not to begin with the marks themselves but with the structures that elicit these marks" (1977:29).

It is not enough, however, to teach students the different categories of connectives and how each type operates grammatically; it is this grammatical emphasis that has "narrowed unduly our conception of conjunctive devices" (Holloway 1981:215). They must learn to differentiate the linking devices found within each grammatical category semantically. Explicating Saussure, Sommers points out that "meaning is differential or diacritical, based on differences between terms rather than essential or inherent qualities of terms" (1980:385). Students therefore need to understand what happens, for example, when "but" is used instead of "and" or when "although" is used instead of "because."

Completion Exercises

The following types of exercises are easy to devise and can help students learn how a particular connective indicates a particular relationship between the ideas presented.

1. The following examples lack subordinating conjunctions. Consider the relationship between the two clauses and fill in an appropriate conjunction for each example.
    a. _____ the weather is favorable, we will go to the beach.
    b. _____ the weather is favorable, we will stay home.
    c. _____ the weather is favorable, we can't go to the park.

2. The following examples lack subordinate clauses. Consider the subordinating conjunction used and write an appropriate subordinate clause for each example.
    a. Even though _____, he is not a happy man.
    b. Because _____, he is not a happy man.
    c. He is not a happy man whenever _____.

3. The following examples lack transitional devices. Consider the relationship between the two sentences and fill in an appropriate transition for each example.
    a. China is opening its door to the West. It will probably always remain a traditionally Eastern culture.
    b. China is opening its door to the West. Its traditionally Eastern culture is likely to undergo some change.
    c. China is opening its door to the West. The West is embracing much of the culture of the East.

4. In the following examples consider the transitional devices used and complete the sentences so that they are logically related to the other sentence.
    a. Educators are beginning to conclude that children who watch violent TV programs will act more violently themselves. However, _____.
    b. Educators . . . themselves. As a result, _____.
    c. Educators . . . themselves. In fact, _____.
    d. Educators . . . themselves. Moreover, _____.

Sentence Combining

One could also present students with sentence-combining exercises consisting of pairs of sentences and ask them to use a particular type of conjunct to connect them. For example, students could be instructed to combine the following pair with a subordinating conjunction.

Mr Jones did whatever his wife asked.
She complained and yelled all the time.

Some students might suggest "because"; others might offer "even though." By discussing the difference in meaning depending on the particular expression used, students can begin to see how necessary it is to choose the appropriate one.

Once students have learned both the grammatical and lexical distinctions, they can begin to do sentence-combining exercises that depend on their ability to manipulate the entire repertoire of links they have been taught. These exercises can be signaled (that is, students can be instructed as to which type of link to use, as in 1 below) or they can be unsignaled, leaving students free to choose a connecting device, as in 2.

1. Combine the following pairs of sentences by using the connector indicated.
    a. The men were exhausted. They kept fighting the fire. (transition)
    b. The college is now offering ESL courses. It is offering a course in black studies. (coordinating conjunction)
    c. She studied very hard. She failed. (subordinating conjunction)
    d. She studied very hard. She passed. (transition)
    e. They were late. They missed the dinner. (subordinating conjunction)

2. Combine the following pairs of sentences using any connector you want.
   a. Living in a new culture is difficult. It is a valuable experience.
   b. Old people in America feel isolated. They feel depressed.
   c. Many people are getting divorced. Children are raised by single parents.
   d. He was an illegal resident. He was deported back to his country.
   e. He has to take the entrance exam. He has to complete the application.

Exercise 2, which is less controlled, not only would check on the students' ability to use the various conjuncts correctly but would give rise to discussion. This is likely to happen either when students come up with alternative ways to say the same thing or when they express something quite differently because of the particular connective used. Students could even be challenged to link the same pairs of sentences in as many ways as they could, thus again illustrating the fact that alternative strategies exist for connecting ideas. Such an exercise illustrates what Frank (1981) calls sentence combining based on a notional-functional approach, since students would be learning the different ways that language can express the same semantic function.

Longer Units of Discourse

Exercises, however, should not be limited to sequences of pairs of sentences. Students should learn to work with longer units of discourse. For example, they can be given texts and instructed to identify the linking devices in order to determine the relationships they signal between sections of these texts. They can be presented with passages and asked to supply linking words where appropriate. Similarly, they can be asked to supply cohesive devices in passages from which they have been deleted. These deletions could be random or deliberate, depending on one's teaching purpose. After filling in the texts, students could compare the various options proposed. Furthermore, students could be instructed to reorder lists of scrambled sentences in which the links themselves would provide clues as to how the sentences should be sequenced. One variation on this type of exercise consists of identical sets of scrambled sentences differentiated only by the location of the transitional device used:

Unscramble the sentences and number them according to their order.
1. _____ Some people thought that it was water which came from above the sky through "windows."
   _____ Before the scientific age, however, people had many strange ideas about rain.
   _____ Other people thought that certain gods controlled the rain.
   _____ We now know that rain comes from the clouds.
   _____ One group of people thought that frogs controlled the rain.

2. _____ Some people thought that it was water which came from above the sky through "windows."
   _____ Before the scientific age, people had many strange ideas about rain.
   _____ Other people thought that certain gods controlled the rain.
   _____ We now know, however, that rain comes from the clouds.
   _____ One group of people thought that frogs controlled the rain.

Notice that the resulting sequence for each of these sets of sentences would be different. Of course, sets of scrambled sentences could be stripped entirely of their links, in which case students would not only have to reorder them but also to add the missing connectives. Students would presumably come up with alternative combined passages. Again emphasizing the point that links set up relationships between chunks of discourse, one could provide students with longer passages that lead up to a particular conjunct and ask them to predict the information that is likely to follow. After students have discussed the possibilities, the original passage can be examined and the differences or similarities between the student versions and the actual text can be considered.

CONCLUSION

These exercises are only a few examples of the type that need to be created in order to teach linking words and the relationships they signal. When instruction is based on this kind of approach rather than on the more traditional methods suggested by textbooks, students can be expected to understand what the different conjuncts signify and to learn to use them appropriately in their writing. Teachers need to bear in mind, however, that, important as these links are, learning when *not* to use them is as important as learning when to do so. In other words, students need to be taught that the excessive use of linking devices, one for almost every sentence, can lead to prose that sounds both artificial and mechanical. As Raimes (1979) put it, when the emphasis is placed on these overt markers rather than the ideas communicated, the "glue" rather than the message "stands out."

Conjuncts are not always necessary, because there are other cohesive mechanisms that help weave various parts of the text together. Conjunction is only one of five categories described by Halliday and Hasan (1976), the other four being reference, substitution, ellipsis, and lexical cohesion. As a matter of fact, this last category, lexical cohesion, has been found to be "the predominant means of connecting sentences in discourse" (Witte and Faigley 1981:193). The following paragraph (Bronowski cited in Brostoff 1981:290) illustrates how various types of cohesive devices (such as the repetition of key terms and the use of pronouns, and notably not conjunction) operate together to maintain the logical pattern throughout.

The *process of learning* is essential to our lives. All *higher animals* seek *it* deliberately. *They* are inquisitive and they *experiment*. An *experiment* is a sort of harmless trial run of some action which we shall have to make in the real world; and this, whether it is made in the laboratory by *scientists or by fox cubs* outside their earth. The *scientist experiments and the cub plays;* both are learning to correct their errors of judgement in a setting in which errors are *not fatal*. Perhaps *this* is what gives them both their air of happiness and freedom in these activities.

It is obvious from this passage that the different means through which cohesion is achieved need to be taught in ways similar to those described here for the teaching of conjuncts. For example, students could be asked to locate pronouns, synonyms, and key terms and to identify their antecedents, as is done in the Bronowski text above.

Finally, teachers need to be especially aware of the fact that, while these explicit mechanisms may render a text cohesive, it may nonetheless not be coherent. Widdowson (1978) has pointed to the distinction between cohesion and coherence, indicating that it is the latter that allows writing to function and to be understood as a unit of discourse. And analyses of student compositions have led researchers to conclude that cohesion is but one feature of discourse that accounts for a text's readability (Brostoff 1981; Witte and Faigley 1981). Our teaching of writing must therefore take into account *all* the factors that interact to produce coherent writing. To ignore these crucial discourse considerations, which should form the basis of all writing instruction—the writer's purpose, the audience, the topic—would not only lead to a failure to address composing itself; it would result in writing in which it was no longer important whether the links were missing or not.

EXPLORING THE IDEAS — *Applying Theoretical Concepts*

ACTIVITY 1

Background   As Zamel points out, composition teachers are quite familiar with compositions "in which the meaning or intent has been obscured, either because . . . conjuncts are missing or because the links used are inappropriate semantically or syntactically" (page 110). The following sentences illustrate inappropriate use of various conjuncts.

1. John waited for the bus unless his father didn't pick him up.
2. Ann did not see anyone to meet her in the airport so that she waited for a bus.
3. Even if my roommate studied all night, she flunked her test.
4. In spite of we arrived at school in time for the opening of the semester, we couldn't add the English class.

Application   For each of the sentences listed above, explain in what way the conjunct has been used inappropriately either semantically or syntactically. Then list all the examples you can find of conjuncts that are used inappropriately in the student essays included under the Kaplan article.

ACTIVITY 2

Background   The first strategy Zamel describes for teaching linking devices is completion exercises (pages 113–114). However, exercises such as 1 and 3 presuppose that students have already been introduced to various subordinating conjunctions and transitional devices and thus they can select an appropriate item. One way to introduce linking devices is to present students with two linking devices which they might confuse. The following exercise illustrates this type of presentation. As Zamel suggests, the introductory material of the exercise explains important semantic distinctions and punctuation rules.

Subordinating conjunctions are used to connect dependent clauses with independent clauses or sentences. When the dependent clause precedes the independent clause, a comma is used to separate the two clauses. If the dependent clause follows the independent clause, no comma is used. *Although* introduces a dependent clause that indicates contrast or concession to the idea expressed in the main clause.
Example: He went to bed although he wasn't sleepy.
        Although he wasn't sleepy, he went to bed.
Because introduces a fact or explanation in the dependent clause that supports the idea expressed in the main clause.
Example: He went to bed because he was sleepy.
        Because he was sleepy, he went to bed.
Fill in the blanks with the appropriate conjunction, because or although.
1. _____ the driver was careless, he crashed the car.
2. _____ the driver was careful, he crashed the car.
3. I lent her the money _____ she didn't need it.
4. I lent her the money _____ she needed it.

Application   Design two completion exercises, one dealing with subordinating conjunctions and the other dealing with transitional devices. As in the example above, limit each exercise to two items, and include introductory material which explains important semantic distinctions and punctuation rules.

ACTIVITY 3

Background   Another strategy for teaching linking devices described by Zamel is sentence combining. As she points out, these exercises can be signaled or unsignaled. One type of unsignaled exercise is an open exercise such as the following.

Directions: Combine the following sentences. Write each group as one sentence; then combine the sentences into paragraph form.
THE TELEVISION STAR
1.   a. She is a television performer.
     b. She is extraordinary.
2.   a. Many people watch her program.
     b. The program is a musical.
     c. The program is on TV every week.
3.   a. She is not really beautiful.
     b. She is not particularly talented.
     c. Her face is famous.
     d. Her body is famous.
     e. Her voice is famous.
4.   a. People like the freshness of her show.
     b. People like the humor of her show.
     c. People like the variety of her show.

5. a. She sings at the opening of the program.
    b. She sings at the closing of the program.
6. a. She always wears a dress.
    b. The dress is stylish.
7. a. She speaks to the audience.
    b. Her voice is soft.
8. a. This young woman is a daughter to every father and mother.
    b. This young woman is a sister to every woman.
    c. This young woman is a lover to every young man.
9. a. Each person sees her differently.
    b. To all, she is a star.

Application   First complete the exercise above and discuss what you see as the strengths and weaknesses of this technique. Then design your own open exercise. In addition, include several follow-up activities for the exercise. For example, with the exercise listed above, students could be asked to discuss various television stars who fit the description, or they could be given a cloze-type version of the same exercise (e.g., She is a _____. She is _____.) Another strategy would be to give each student in the class one of the clusters of sentences to combine, and the class could then order the combined sentences into a paragraph.

ACTIVITY 4

Background   The last strategy for teaching linking devices that Zamel presents deals with larger units of discourse. She describes several techniques such as modified cloze exercises and scrambled sentences.

Application   Design an exercise for teaching linking devices which involves one or more paragraphs. You can use one of the techniques suggested by Zamel or create your own type of exercise.

Composition Evaluation

ACTIVITY 1

Background   As Zamel points out, conjuncts are only one type of cohesive device. Another common cohesive device is reference; reference occurs when one item in a text points to another element in the text for its meaning. There are three major types of reference ties: pronominals, demonstratives and definite articles, and comparatives. Witte and Faigley (1981:191) provide the following examples of reference cohesion:

Reference Cohesion, Pronominal
At home, my father is himself.
He relaxes and acts in *his* normal manner.
Reference Cohesion, Demonstrative
We question why they tell us to do things.
This is part of growing up.
Reference Cohesion, Definite Articles

Humans have many needs, both physical and intangible.
It is easy to see *the* physical needs such as shelter.
Reference Cohesion, Comparative
The older generation is often quick to condemn college students for being carefree and irresponsible. But those who remember their own youth do so *less* quickly.

In all the examples, the meaning of the italicized word presupposes information that is stated earlier in the text.

Application   The following student essay makes frequent use of reference cohesion. Begin by underlining all of the examples of reference cohesion in the text. Then circle any instances in which the referent for the item is unclear. Finally, describe how you might help the student correct any errors he has made.

MY NEIGHBORHOOD
   This was a neighborhood I could never forget. It was in my own hometown village in Lebanon. That poor old man living in a huge old place right across the street from us, was so lonely. He enjoyed every minute he spent with us. The only smile you could see on his face was when he passed by our house to greet us good morning. He even considered us his family.
   Just down the street lived the happiest family. It was consisting of three energetic boys, a tall and cheerful father and their sweet and loving mother. From the first moment of dawn you could hear the roar of the car engine warming up. Cooking was one of his wife's favorite jobs during the early morning. The aroma would sometimes escape through our window. It was one of our favorite ways of waking up or it was the voices of their boys. They would wake up just after breakfast was prepared. With their pyjamas on, they would come outside and sing as loud as they could. It was so cute to catch a peak at them from my window.
   And last but not least, the oldest couple that lived down the alley. They weren't that friendly type. Without children of their own, they had this habit of killing time by critisizing each other. Neither one of them ever said a right thing about each other, but if you intended to watch a battlefield, they produced the best one.

NOTE

   1. This article is based on a paper presented at the 1981 MATSOL Conference in Boston, Massachusetts.

REFERENCES

Bacha, N. S., and E. A. S. Hanania. 1980. Difficulty in Learning and Effectiveness of Teaching Transitional Words: A Study on Arabic-Speaking University Students. *TESOL Quarterly* 14/2:251–254.
Bander, R. G. 1980. *From Sentence to Paragraph*. New York, Holt, Rinehart and Winston.
Borkin, A. 1978. On Some Conjuncts Signalling Dissonance in Written Expository English. Paper presented at Twelfth Annual TESOL Convention, Mexico City, 1978.
Broadhead, G. J., and J. A. Berlin. 1981. Twelve Steps to Using Generative Sentences and Sentence Combining in the Composition Classroom. *College Composition and Communication* 32/3: 295–307.
Brostoff, Anita. 1981. Coherence: Next to Is Not Connected "to." *College Composition and Communication* 32/3:278–294.

Cohen, A., et al. 1979. Reading English for Specialized Purposes: Discourse Analysis and the Use of Student Informants. *TESOL Quarterly* 13/4:551–564.

Dubin, F., and E. Olshtain. 1980. The Interface of Writing and Reading. *TESOL Quarterly* 14/3:353–363.

Frank, M. 1981. Sentence Combining That Integrates Notional Relationships, Usage, Style. Paper presented at Fifteenth Annual TESOL Convention, Detroit, Michigan, 1981.

Halliday, M. A. K., and R. Hasan. 1976. *Cohesion in English*. London, Longman.

Holloway, D. W. 1981. Semantic Grammars: How They Can Help Us Teach Writing. *College Composition and Communication* 32/2:205–218.

Kaplan, R. B. 1967. Contrastive Rhetoric and the Teaching of Composition. *TESOL Quarterly* 1/4:10–16.

Raimes, A. 1979. A Grammar for Composition: The Grammar of Cohesion. Paper presented at Thirteenth Annual TESOL Convention, Boston, Massachusetts, 1979.

Shaughnessy, M. 1977. *Errors and Expectations*. New York, Oxford University Press.

Sommers, N. 1980. Revision Strategies of Student Writers and Experienced Adult Writers. *College Composition and Communication* 31/4:378–388.

Widdowson, H. G. 1978. *Teaching Language as Communication*. London, Oxford University Press.

Witte, S. P., and L. Faigley. 1981. Coherence, Cohesion and Writing Quality. *College Composition and Communication* 32/2:189–204.

8

Strategies for Teaching the Rhetoric of Written English for Science and Technology

Robert Weissberg and Suzanne Buker

Recent analyses of the grammar and rhetoric of scientific English have yielded valuable information to the EFL teacher. Yet so far the results of this research have been applied primarily in the area of reading. A parallel though often neglected need is the teaching of technical writing, since many EFL students have developed proficiency in reading technical English, particularly in their fields of specialization, but lack equally well developed writing skills. Such students are not fully prepared for university programs at English-speaking institutions.

This chapter describes teaching strategies employed in a technical writing course for Latin American students at New Mexico State University. This course, which incorporated current knowledge of correspondences between grammatical form and rhetorical function in EST, treats linguistic forms not as ends in themselves but as integral features of written communicative acts. Students learn to perform these acts through contextualized guided writing activities designed to help them identify each rhetorical function in the context of published technical bulletins, analyze its principal linguistic features, and practice it extensively. Contextualized practice of relevant linguistics items is provided through cloze exercises based on published bulletins; carefully selected charts, tables, and diagrams are used as writing stimuli.

Much teaching material has become available recently in the field of English for science and technology for the nonnative student. Yet most of this material is geared primarily toward the teaching of reading comprehension, with writing handled as an adjunct activity. Our experience with foreign students at the master's level has led us to believe the greatest strength of many EFL students is in reading technical English, particularly in their field of specialization, whereas their writing skills are seldom as well developed. The ability to write acceptable scientific English becomes a major concern for those students who must successfully complete a thesis as part of their degree requirements. Thus we have developed a writing program based on recent research in EST in an effort to help our students prepare for the final stage in their degree programs. The purposes of this paper, then, are are (1) to identify that part of the literature we found most applicable to classroom use; (2) to indicate the steps we took to translate research findings into a course syllabus; and (3) to describe the resulting teaching materials.

GENERAL APPROACH

Widdowson (1977) identifies three approaches to the analysis of scientific discourse: text, textualization, and discourse. Of the three, textualization seemed to us the most easily adaptable to instructional use. Textualization is concerned with establishing correspondences between linguistic form and rhetorical function in written language. In a more restricted sense it can be defined as the process of describing how grammatical structures match up with meaning, or in Widdowson's words, "how they express elements of discourse." This approach has served as the basis for much of the analyses of EST rhetoric done by Lackstrom, Selinker, and Trimble (1970, 1973), and by the latter two authors in collaboration with Robert Vroman (1974). Their findings have provided us in turn with the orientation and, in some cases, the specific teaching points for our course syllabus.

Lackstrom et al. (1973) (Figure 1) constructed a rhetorical-grammatical process chart for EST which consists of a hierarchy of descending levels of organization. The chart clearly presents the progression of choices available to both the technical writer and the EST materials developer. A choice of rhetorical function at any level on the chart determines the kinds of choices available at the next lower level and also determines grammatical choice. A writing text for EST could be organized around one or a combination of any of these choices. Since most of our students are preparing to write research reports in the form of master's theses, we have chosen the functional units of level B (i.e., reporting past research, stating the problem, describing apparatus, etc.) as the framework for our syllabus. The examples listed under this level serve in part as the teaching units in our program.

Examples of Units	Grammatical Choice
Reporting Past Research	Most
Discussing Theory	Tenses
Stating Purpose	in
Describing Apparatus	EST
Explaining an Illustration	
Stating the Problem	Article

Figure 1.   Functional units of rhetoric (level B from rhetorical-grammatical process chart for EST in Lackstrom/Selinker/Trimble 1973)

DEVELOPING A SYLLABUS

As the basic stylistic model for our course we have chosen the technical writing published in agricultural research reports. Our choice was determined by the fact that a majority of the students in the Spanish-speaking master's program are working in the fields of animal science, range science, agronomy, and agricultural economics. Originally we expected merely to draw on the rhetorical-grammatical analyses presented by Lackstrom et al., matching them with contextual models from the publications. Often we were able to do just that, but in some instances we found ourselves vainly poring through published reports in search of a particular grammatical form. In such cases we ultimately chose to alter the rhetorical-grammatical correspondences posited by Lackstrom et al. to reflect our specialized corpus. Once we had that approach, we found ourselves developing new generalizations, which we incorporated into our teaching materials. In addition, we have amplified the list of examples under level B of the hierarchy in order to provide a series of teaching units that cover all major subdivisions of a research report (see Figure 2).

In spite of our modifications, the basic assumption underlying Lackstrom's hierarchy, i.e., that rhetorical function determines grammatical choice, remains central to our approach. This means that we try to teach our students the grammatical features of EST not as ends in themselves but rather as necessary consequences of a predetermined sequence of rhetorical acts. The sequence varies from writer to writer, and the units may be expanded or compressed at one point or another, but the components outlined above appear to be the major conventions in a highly stylized form of writing. As such they lend themselves well to use as teaching units and in fact form the major subdivisions of our course, with two to three weeks teaching time during the semester allotted to each. Each unit focuses on one or two grammatical choices and on lexical items and collocations that typically occur in a given rhetorical category, regardless of research topic. Thus technical writing is presented as an integrated whole composed of overall rhetorical form, vocabulary, and grammar.

Rhetorical Unit	Grammatical Choices and Lexicon
A. Introduction	
1. Providing background (setting the problem situation)	Generic use of articles
2. Reviewing the literature	Tenses, verbs of report, citation conventions
3. Stating objectives and value of study	Hypothetical (modals, verbs, adverbs) tenses
B. Methods and Materials	
1. Describing an apparatus	Tenses, statives
2. Describing a procedure	Passive/active voice, verbs of procedure
C. Results and Discussion	Tenses, comparative/superlative
D. Summary and Conclusions	Hypothetical forms

Figure 2.   Rhetorical teaching units (Lackstrom/Selinker/Trimble's level B as adapted for an intermediate-advanced level ESL writing course in scientific and technical English)

MATERIALS

We introduce each rhetorical subunit by using transparencies of research reports to analyze the attendant linguistic forms and to identify lexical collocations (see Figure 3). The class then moves on to intensive writing practice.

Chile Fertilizer Trials at the
Espanola Valley Branch Station

Apple orchards are the most common farm enterprise in the Espanola Valley, but chile is also an important cash crop. In recent years, the apple crop has been lost frequently to late spring freezes. When an apple crop is lost, farmers increase their chile plantings to help compensate for the loss. Chile has been grown in this area for several hundred years. The common practice for many years was to use the plentiful supply of barnyard manure as the source of fertilizer. However, the practice of keeping various kinds of livestock on the farm has dwindled so that the manure supply is no longer ample nor readily available, even for the small chile farmers. The expense of transport makes the use of manure on commercial chile fields prohibitive. Green manure crops are used only to a limited extent. Most farmers have turned to chemical fertilizers to supplant the manure.

The amounts of nitrogen, phosphorous, and potassium now applied to chile vary according to the producer's experience with these nutrients on other crops. Research on fertilizer requirements for chile in the Espanola Valley has not been conducted, and recommendations as to the chemical fertilizer requirements of this crop have been ambiguous. It was, therefore, important to the economy of the area to ascertain the response of chile crops to various application rates of nitrogen, phosphorous, and potassium fertilizers, alone and in combination. Consequently, chile fertilizer trials were conducted at the Espanola Valley Branch Station from 1964 to 1968.

Figure 3. Lecture presentation: materials include copies of appropriate sections from published research reports and bulletins (the sample was used in teaching the rhetorical unit *Introduction: Background Information* and its corresponding linguistic feature *Generic Noun Phrases*) (Trujillo and Gledhill 1971)

Initial writing exercises, focusing on the rhetorical-grammatical corre-spondences, are progressively decontrolled in design (Weissberg 1978). A new selection from another research report, chosen for its general clarity and accessibility, is used as the basis for a series of three deletion exercises. The first of these, called *identification*, requires the student to read through the original text, identifying and underlining all instances of the target feature. The purpose of this exercise is to call upon students to transfer recognition of what they have learned to a new context. As soon as they have finished, they check their responses (see Figure 4).

Once the students complete the identification exercises, they proceed to a *fill-in* exercise. This exercise makes use of the same text, but with blanks replacing the target features. The students read through the selection and fill in an appropriate form for each blank. No lexical cues are provided, since it is

A Portable Rainfall Simulator and Runoff Sampler
J. U. Anderson, A. E. Stewart, P. C. Gregory

Field research on the interactions between soil and water commonly depends on natural rainfall or on some form of simulated rainfall. Dependence on natural rainfall limits research because neither the timing nor the characteristics of a rain are known until it is over. This is a particularly serious problem in semiarid and arid areas where precipitation is infrequent and erratic. With a rainfall simulator, an investigator can control the frequency, rates, and intensities of the rainfall in his studies.

Figure 4. Identification exercise (introduction: background information—generics). Directions: Identify all examples of *generic noun phrases* in the selection by underlining them.

presumed that the students are sufficiently familiar with the topic from having already worked with the text (see Figure 5). Furthermore, the absence of cues forces the students to make contextually meaningful choices, rather than mechanically patterning the forms. Once again we provide answers to the exercise as soon as it is completed. Alternative lexical items considered appropriate are acceptable since the purpose of the exercise is not to memorize the original text but to complete the rhetorical unit.

A third exercise, a *completion* exercise, is again based on the original text, but this time larger word groups encompassing the key features are deleted. Again the students are called upon to replace the missing information in their own words, this time providing not only key features but also their broader contextual environment (see Figure 6). Thus, the students' central concern becomes that of attending to the content of the passage, a process more closely resembling the actual priorities involved in writing, while nevertheless making deliberate choices related to the linguistic items. The students correct the exercise immediately upon completion.

This process of progressively decontrolled practice, involving identification, fill-in, and completion activities, enables the students to gain control of

---

A Portable Rainfall Simulator and Runoff Sampler
J. U. Anderson, A. E. Stewart, P. C. Gregory

_____ field research _____ on the interactions between _____ soil _____ and _____ water _____ commonly depends either on _____ natural rainfall _____ or on some form of _____ simulated rainfall _____ . Dependence on _____ natural rainfall _____ limits _____ research because neither _____ timing _____ nor _____ characteristic _____ of _____ rain _____ are known until it is over. This is a particularly serious problem in _____ semiarid and arid area _____ where _____ precipitation _____ is infrequent and erratic. With _____ rainfall simulator _____ , _____ investigator _____ can control _____ frequency, rates, and intensities of _____ rainfall _____ in his studies.

Figure 5. Fill-in exercise (introduction: background information—generics). Directions; Fill in the blanks with the plural -*s* or the articles *a, an,* or *the* where necessary.

A Portable Rainfall Simulator and Runoff Sampler
J. U. Anderson, A. E. Steward, P. C. Gregory

Field research on the interactions _____ commonly depends either on _____ . Dependence on _____ limits research because neither the timing nor the characteristics of _____ it is over. This is a particularly serious problem in _____ _____ where _____ and erratic. With _____ can control the frequency, rates, and intensities _____ in his studies.

Figure 6. Completion exercise (introduction: background information—generics). Directions: Complete the missing clauses and phrases that have been omitted from the selection to the best of your memory. Exact wording from the original text is not necessary.

the target features through gradually larger units of self-generated writing. They are then ready for a practice phase requiring more extensive writing.

The first practice activities in the new phase are application exercises. In these exercises we use a variety of stimuli to present the students with the information they need to write a particular report unit with its targeted linguistic features. One stimulus is to provide a topic outline of the relevant content from a published text, which the students use to write their own versions. Another is to present carefully selected graphics (diagrams, tables, charts, etc.) taken from a variety of scientific sources. As stimuli for exercises on methods/materials and results/discussion, graphics serve to prompt the students to write up the depicted information in a form appropriate to the particular rhetorical unit under study. They are ideal stimuli, since they provide the greatest opportunity for entirely student-generated text organization and language uses (see Figure 7).

Still another approach, this time as an aid in writing a literature review section, is to provide students with a set of note cards indicating the contributions of various investigators to a topic, along with a set of bibliography cards. The students first alphabetize the bibliography cards in order to assign citation numbers to the investigators. Then they organize the information contained on the note cards in logical order. Finally, using the cards as guides, they write the literature review section. The steps in this exercise are particularly valid in that they closely correspond to the actual process of organizing and adapting library sources for use in a literature survey.

An application strategy we find especially well suited to practicing the first subunits of an introduction is to provide students with the full text of a short research report *minus* the first one or two paragraphs (up to, perhaps, the beginning of the literature review section). Students must induce the generalizations upon which the report is based from the specifics provided, and expand these into connected discourse to replace the missing paragraphs.

Once all the rhetorical subunits making up a section of an actual research report are taught and practiced, students are given an *integration* exercise. These are similar in design to those in the application phase (i.e., making use of outlines and graphics) except that they include a larger number of rhetorical subunits and corresponding linguistic forms. For example, once the class has covered all four subunits making up a typical introduction, students are asked to write a complete introduction in which they appropriately incorporate all of the relevant items. We use the integration activity first for practice and later for testing the student's control of this phase of instruction.

The final practice phase of our EST program is a *consolidation* exercise, consisting of a week-long project in which students write the text of an entire, original research report. We give them the raw data along with some background source material, but they are entirely responsible for organizing and writing the report. It is essential that the report be based on some general, though technical, topic which all can understand clearly. Our students, for example, are given data on pre- and post-test scores of former students in the intensive English

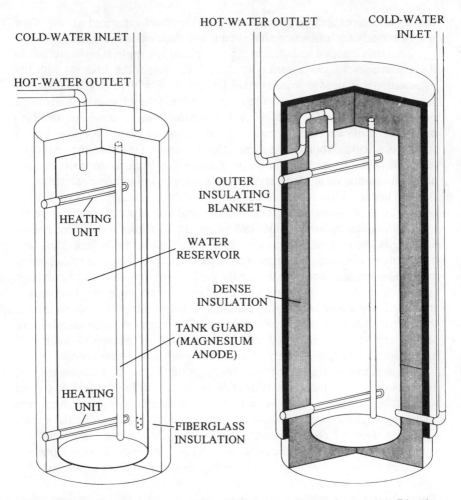

HOT-WATER OUTLET

COLD-WATER INLET

HOT-WATER OUTLET

COLD-WATER INLET

HEATING UNIT

OUTER INSULATING BLANKET

WATER RESERVOIR

DENSE INSULATION

TANK GUARD (MAGNESIUM ANODE)

HEATING UNIT

FIBERGLASS INSULATION

Figure 7. Application exercise (methods and materials: present and past tense). Directions: Assume that you are writing the methods and materials section for a research report. Your report is about an improved electric water heater which you have designed to conserve energy. Study the graphic and make note of the information provided; then write the text for your report. (*From Scientific American, December 1977.*)

component of the Spanish-speaking master's program on a standardized test of English language proficiency. They are asked to write a report examining the possible use of entrance scores as predictors of improvement in proficiencies. They are told that the study is a replication of previous research done in a similar program, and are provided with copies of relevant journal articles for use in the literature review section. Since the students in our program take two semesters of statistics concurrently with their English, they are also asked to treat the statistical data for inclusion in their report. The topic is one with which they readily identify, making the activity a meaningful process of drawing together all that they have learned and practiced in technical writing.

CONCLUSION

The consolidation exercise is our most successful step so far in contextualizing EST writing practice for our students, creating as it does an ideal opportunity to utilize the rhetorical units and linguistic forms learned over the semester and to apply them to a research topic of direct personal relevance. Our present goal is to expand the application phase in each unit of the syllabus to include more exercises of an individual nature, asking students, for example, to provide data, sources, and general topics taken from their own fields of study as the basis for class exercise. Our ultimate objective, after all, is that of all second language instruction: to provide learners with the forms and conventions needed to express their own ideas.

EXPLORING THE IDEAS — *Theoretical Discussion*

QUESTION 1

Background   Some of the rhetorical units which Weissberg and Buker mention are stating the problem, reviewing the literature, stating objectives, and describing a procedure. Meyer in her article delineates five major plans: antecedent/consequent, comparison, description, response, and time order.

Discussion   Do you find any rhetorical functions described by Weissberg and Buker which do not fit into one of Meyer's five plans? Do you see any distinctions between what Weissberg and Buker call rhetorical units and what Meyer calls plans?

QUESTION 2

Background   Weissberg and Buker point out that on occasion they had to modify the rhetorical-grammatical correspondence posited by Lackstrom to reflect the technical literature of agriculture.

Discussion   Given the fact that rhetorical-grammatical correspondence seems to vary from field to field, what do you see as the advantages and disadvantages of linking rhetorical units and grammatical features in the ESL curriculum? Do you see any way of avoiding the problems which arise from linking the two dimensions in the curriculum?

Application of Theoretical Concepts

ACTIVITY 1

Background   Weissberg and Buker provide a list of common rhetorical units in EST, along with related grammatical choices and lexicon (Figure 2, page 124). They also include an example from an agricultural journal of one of the rhetorical subunits, *Introduction: Background Information*, along with its corresponding linguistic feature, *Generic Noun Phrases* (Figure 3, page 125).

Application   Select one of the rhetorical subunits listed in Figure 2 (page 124) and find a specific example of this subunit in some field of EST. Then underline any example of the grammatical structures and lexicon that are included by Weissberg and Buker for this rhetorical unit. For example, if you select describing a procedure, find an example of such a text in a scientific journal and underline all the instances of the use of the passive voice and verbs of procedure in the text. It is possible that you will find no examples of the grammatical structure or lexicon which are listed by Weissberg and Buker in your particular text. If this is the case, select another salient grammatical feature in the text and underline all its occurrences.

Teaching Strategies

ACTIVITY 1

Background   Weissberg and Buker provide examples of a series of progressively decontrolled exercises involving identification, fill-in, and completion activities. The purpose of these activities is to familiarize students with the target grammatical feature.

Application   Select one of the rhetorical subunits listed in Figure 2 (page 124) and find a specific example of this subunit from any area of EST. Then identify a target grammatical structure for the unit. (It can be one of those listed in the Weissberg and Buker chart or another, if that is more salient in the text.) Then design three exercises to accompany the text—one identification, one fill-in, and one completion. In your directions, be certain to make it clear to the students what you expect them to do with the text. One way to do this would be to give them a specific example of the grammatical feature or features you expect them to identify.

ACTIVITY 2

Background   Weissberg and Buker provide an example of how a visual could be used as a stimulus for giving students practice in writing on a particular rhetorical subunit (pages 127 and 128).

Application   Select a graphic (a diagram, chart, table, etc.) from some scientific source. Then design a writing assignment for an EST class on a particular rhetorical subunit to accompany the visual.

ACTIVITY 3

Background   The final phase in the EST program designed by Weissberg and Buker is a *consolidation* exercise (pages 127 and 128) in which students are given the raw data with which to write a report.

Application   Design a consolidation exercise for an intermediate-level EST class. Consult some scientific source or make up your own raw data to include in the assignment. In your directions, be certain to make it clear to the students how you expect them to analyze the data and what they should include in their report.

REFERENCES

Anderson, J. U., A. E. Stewart, and P. C. Gregory. 1968. *A Portable Rainfall Simulator and Runoff Sampler.* Las Cruces, New Mexico State University Agricultural Experiment Station (Research Report 143).

Lackstrom, John, Larry Selinker, and Louis P. Trimble. 1970. Grammar and Technical English. *English as a Second Language: Current Issues,* R. C. Lugton (ed.). Philadelphia, The Center for Curriculum Development.

Lackstrom, John, Larry Selinker, and Louis P. Trimble. 1973. Technical Rhetorical Principles and Grammatical Choice. *TESOL Quarterly* II:127–133.

Selinker, Larry, Louis Trimble, and Robert Vroman. 1974. *Working Papers in English for Science and Technology.* Seattle, College of Engineering, University of Washington.

Trujillo, P., and V. H. Gledhill. 1971. *Chile Fertilizer Trials at the Espanola Valley Branch Station.* Las Cruces, New Mexico State University Agricultural Experiment Station (Research Report 575).

Weissberg, R. 1978. Progressive Decontrol through Deletion. *TESL Reporter* II, 2:1–4, 14.

Widdowson, H. G. 1977. The Description of Scientific Language. *Le Francais Dans Le Monde.*

3 EVALUATING

Composition teachers often commiserate over the task of correcting papers. As Robinett points out (1972. On the Horns of a Dilemma: Correcting Compositions. In J. Alatis (ed.). *Studies in Honor of Albert H. Markwardt.* Washington, D.C., TESOL: 143), "correcting or grading compositions often presents a dilemma to both teacher and student: the teacher finds it a bothersome chore, and the student finds the 'red-pencilled' papers a source of frustration and discouragement." What is even more frustrating for both the teacher and the student is the question of whether or not the correcting process is doing any good to help students develop their writing proficiency.

As composition teachers, before we correct papers we need to clarify our standards for evaluating them. A well-written essay demonstrates quality on various levels including such things as knowledge of the subject, awareness of the audience, clarity of organization, richness of details, vividness of language, and accuracy of grammatical rules. While all these should in principle be evaluated, it is the last area which has often been the major concern of much of the literature, research, and materials in ESL composition. Perhaps the focus has been on grammatical competency because this is the area that is easiest to deal with. Grammatical errors can usually be readily identified and students can be referred to a particular regularity in the language to remedy the situation. Other aspects of writing such as unfamiliarity with a topic, lack of specificity, and poor organization do not offer such clear solutions.

A second reason for the focus on the grammatical level is likely the nature of our students. Students who are writing in their second language will invariably have more grammatical errors than native speakers. It is important to remember, however, that errors are a factor of trying to use the language and learn its grammatical rules. The literature on error analysis clearly demonstrates that making errors is a natural part of learning a language. What we as composition teachers want to do is to become aware of students' reasons for making a particular error and to help them avoid it in the future.

One danger of devoting a good deal of attention to grammatical errors is that teachers may minimize the importance of the other elements of good writing. Good writing involves many elements beyond grammatical accuracy; it involves not only the use of a variety of cohesive devices, but also the fit of a particular text to its context. While grammatical errors are certainly one area of concern for ESL composition teachers, hopefully the articles and activities which follow will help you explore other important aspects of quality in writing.

9

Error Analysis and the Teaching of Composition

Barry M. Kroll and John C. Schafer

Teachers of basic writing skills have perenially been concerned with "error." There is a familiar caricature of the composition teacher as a revenge-thirsty monster wielding pen and red ink to bloody a stunned freshman's paper. While this caricature is more fiction than fact, many composition teachers have tended to view errors in solely negative terms. Over the last several years, we have tried to approach our students' errors from a different point of view. We have begun to view errors as exceptionally interesting clues about what is going on in our students' minds, as clues to the linguistic and cognitive processes that function unobserved.

Our view of errors has been shaped by a particular aspect of our experience. Although we now teach composition, we have both taught English as a second language (hereafter ESL)—one of us in Europe, the other in Asia and Africa. While teaching English to nonnative speakers, we listened to what a number of teachers and applied linguists were saying about how they approached the problem of error in language learning. We would like to present insights from the current ESL approach to error because we believe that teachers of native speakers can gain a new perspective by considering the matter of error from the second-language point of view.

Although there have been several influential approaches to error in the ESL field, there has been a general movement from approaches emphasizing the *product* (the error itself) to approaches focusing on the underlying *process* (why the error was made). At the product end of the spectrum, many teachers simply corrected individual errors as they occurred, with little attempt to see patterns of errors or to seek causes in anything other than learner ignorance. With the advent of structural linguistics, ESL teachers were prepared to detect patterns in the errors that emerged when two languages—the student's native language (NL) and the target language (TL)—collided in a language-learning situation. The systematic nature or errors was explained by the 'contrastive analysis hypothesis": students will err in the TL where it differs from their NL. Contrastive analysis discovered systematicity in errors, but there was little tolerance for error in contrastive-analysis pedagogy, primarily because this pedagogy was a marriage of structural linguistics and behaviorism. Influenced by behaviorist learning-theory, teachers worried that if a student repeated a pattern, this wrong pattern might become a habit that would be difficult to extinguish later.

The most recent approach to error in ESL, error analysis, has moved even further toward the *process* side of the spectrum.[1] Error analysts are cognitivists, not behaviorists, in their psychological orientation. They look upon errors in the speech and writing of foreign students learning English in much the same way that Freud regarded slips of the tongue or that Kenneth Goodman views "miscues" in reading:[2] as clues to inner processes, as windows into the mind. Hence, errors help the teacher identify the cognitive strategies that the learner is using to process information; errors are also good for the learner because, as Heidi Dulay and Marina Burt aptly state, "You can't learn without goofing."[3]

The following chart illustrates, in capsule form, some key issues which divide the product and process approaches to learners' errors—approaches which originated in the ESL field but which seem equally relevant to composition teaching.

APPROACHES TO LEARNERS' ERRORS

Issue	Product Approach	Process Approach
Why should one study errors?	To produce a linguistic taxonomy of *what* errors learners make.	To produce a psycholinguistic explanation of *why* a learner makes an error.
What is the attitude toward error?	Errors are "bad." (Interesting only to the linguistic theorist.)	Errors are "good." (Interesting to the theorist and teacher, and useful to the learner as active tests of his hypotheses.)
What can we hope to discover from learners' errors?	Those items on which the learner or the program failed.	The strategies which led the learner into the error.
How can we account for the fact that a learner makes an error?	It is primarily a failure to learn the correct form (perhaps a case of language interference).	Errors are a natural part of learning a language; they arise from learners' active strategies: overgeneralization, ignorance of rule restrictions, incomplete rule application, hypothesizing false concepts.[4]
What are the emphases and goals of instruction?	A *teaching* perspective: eliminate all errors by establishing correct, automatic habits; mastery of the target language is the goal.	A *learning* perspective: assist the learner in approximating the target language; support his active learning strategies and recognize that not all errors will disappear.

Our point in presenting these contrasts is to suggest that the process approach is a coherent philosophy of error applicable beyond the domain of

ESL. The teacher who adopts an error-analysis perspective accepts a distinctive attitude toward error: instead of viewing errors as pathologies to be eradicated or diseases to be healed, the error analyst views errors as necessary stages in all language learning, as the product of intelligent cognitive strategies and therefore as potentially useful indicators of what processes the student is using. This is not to say that the error analyst does nothing about error; clearly, the error analyst adopts a target form or level of discourse as the goal. However, the error analyst recognizes the many sources of a particular error and the benefit of investigating the reasons for the error before constructing a teaching strategy.

Specifically, the composition teacher as error analyst *investigates* error (to discover how a student arrived at the mistake) and then *applies* these insights (to help the student move further toward the target form). We will first illustrate the investigative role of the error analyst by discussing two errors: the omission of *-s* from verbs and the ambiguous use of *this*. Later we will explain how the teacher can apply the results of his investigation. We have chosen our examples to demonstrate error analysis at two levels: at the morphological level (the *-s* omission error) and the discourse level (ambiguous use of *this*). The former error is commonly made by speakers of other languages or dialects; the latter is a quite prevalent error even among fluent native speakers of English. The error analyst would begin an investigation of both these errors by testing several general hypotheses which seem to account for a variety of language-learning errors. Although errors may vary greatly in form, they may spring from a small set of common strategies. It is this set of general strategies which has received substantial documentation in the ESL literature. We try to demonstrate the utility of the error-analysis framework in our discussion.

Both teachers of ESL and teachers of native speakers (particularly speakers of Black English Vernacular) encounter errors such as the following:

Marsha, ninety pound lighter, is a lifetime Weight Watcher now. Watching television, she no longer eat potato chips.

Notice that the student has left the *-s* off the noun "pound" (but not "chips") as well as omitted the *-s* from the verb "eat." We would like to concentrate on the latter error. The error analyst would agree with a contrastive analyst that omitting the *-s* might be an interference error. (For example, if the student spoke a language such as Vietnamese with no consonant clusters and no inflected verb forms, these disparities between the two languages might account for the error.) The error analyst would not agree with the contrastive analyst, however, that the student is a passive learner, a slave to his or her first language habits, nor would the error analyst stop with a contrastive explanation. If students speak a language or dialect in which verbs are not inflected, they might be actively applying the *wrong* strategy. Deciding to handle TL verbs as they have always handled verbs in their own language (by not inflecting them), they try this approach on English verbs. If this strategy doesn't work, they goof, but they have a strategy. And if their teacher reacts to the error in an appropriate way, the students can discover a new strategy (rather than memorize one new item).

The error analyst would also point out other possible explanations for the -s omission error. One explanation stems not from the learner's language, but rather from the verb system of standard English. There is an *intralingual* explanation (within the TL) as well as an *interlingual* explanation (between the NL and TL). [5] Perhaps noticing that English verbs in the present tense generally are not inflected for the different persons (i.e., I eat, you eat, they eat), the students adopt a strategy of generalization and decide to operate on the hypothesis that no present-tense verb in any person has an inflected ending. The students may even find confirmation for their overgeneralization in constructions such as *Does she eat there often?* where the stem form of the verb occurs next to the third-person singular pronoun. Thus it is not surprising to find students producing such sentences as "She eat the sandwich."

A second intralingual source of confusion arises from the fact that an -s marks verbs as singular, but it marks nouns as plural. If the students employ a logical strategy, they might well confuse these two contradictory uses of -s.

Still another possible explanation for the -s omission error, error analysts point out, may be the student's adoption of a "strategy of communication."[6] Because there is redundant linguistic information in the sentence *She eats potato chips,* they find they can communicate adequately without worrying about the -s at all. The -s as a marker of person is redundant information, because the pronoun *she* has already signaled the third person.

The error might also be a result of the particular strategy that a teacher has used. Error analysts do not overlook the possibility of "teacher-induced" errors.[7] Teachers sometimes lead their students into what Richards calls "hypothesizing false concepts" by presenting oversimplified examples without sufficiently warning students of the numerous exceptions.[8] Students form their own rules based on the language data which the teacher presents; hence, it is imperative to present a rich and representative sample. In the case of the -s ending, teachers, annoyed by the dropping of -s's, may overemphasize the rule that third-person, present, singular verbs must have an -s (without mentioning the kind of exceptions mentioned above). When the students encounter a sentence like *Does she eat there often?* their attempt to make sense of the verb system comes into conflict with the simplified rule their teacher has been stating. This conflict can lead to frustration, a feeling that the language is unsystematic.

Although the stubbornly persistent -s omission error can frustrate teachers and students, we should not exaggerate the severity of the problem. Omitting an -s seldom impairs the intelligibility of a composition. By contrast, the next error we will discuss, a break in coherence, can render an entire paragraph incomprehensible. There is a variety of kinds of breaks in coherence, running the spectrum from unbridgeable gaps to vague (but decipherable) pronoun references. The following paragraph, from a nursing student's paper, illustrates incoherence produced by a *this* which refers to an idea not present in the text:

Baths are not needed so frequently by the older patient because of the decreased sweat secretion. This will help to preserve the major skin areas; however, special attention must be given to the pereneum to prevent skin excoriation.

⌜Why does a student make this kind of error? To ask this question, rather than simply to mark the error in red, is to begin to act as an error analyst.⌟

The error analyst would recognize that the word *this,* like the morpheme *-s,* is a form with many functions. *This* can be used to make references that are both particular and general, limited and extended. Even in conversation, with the assistance of props from the environment, it is not always clear what kind of reference is intended. Suppose a person lifts up a bottle of cola from which she has just drunk and says, "This is good." Does *this* refer to the liquid in that particular bottle, to that brand of cola, to all cola-flavored drinks? In both speaking and writing, it is often unclear how far we are to extend the reference of *this.* M. A. K. Halliday and Ruqaiya Hasan give an example from *Alice's Adventures in Wonderland:*[9]

"Give your evidence," said the King: "and don't be nervous, or I'll have you executed on the spot." This did not seem to encourage the witness at all.

How much of the preceding sentence are we to include as the antecedent of *this*? The error analyst would also be interested in explanations for general coherence problems, particularly if a student exhibited a number of coherence-related errors. One explanation for general coherence problems in writing lies in a difference between reference in spoken and written discourse. Child-language researchers have observed that the conversation of children is full of reference to things physically present in the situation. Therefore children may become quite accustomed to using words like *this, these, he, she,* or *it* without taking much care about their antecedents, since antecedents are often clarified by the situation and appropriate gestures. In written discourse, however, reference is textual, not situational: words like *this, these,* or *it* refer to other words, not to things or events in the situation. Students whose spoken language depends heavily on the physical context may exhibit general coherence problems in writing. With situational props and opportunity for gestures removed, they egocentrically assume that the events or objects present in their minds are also present in the minds of their readers.

Another source of general coherence errors may stem from limited experience in communicating with people who do not share the same cultural experiences. For example, teenage social groups often develop a neighborhood "language" based on shared experiences, goals, and values. In such situations, coherence markers become redundant. When communicating within such a shared context, listeners can make many connections themselves, and a speaker quite naturally learns that adequate communication is possible without worrying about explicit reference. The student may not make reference explicit for the same reason some students omit *-s* in sentence such as *She eat potato chips:*

because the explicit reference or -*s* marker is redundant information. The two errors are quite different, but the strategy leading to the errors might be the same.

Even schooling may unwittingly contribute to coherence problems. It is quite possible that students who have received extensive English instruction involving sentence-based "grammar" exercises (as opposed to text-based exercises) may have learned little that will help them with coherence problems. In fact, drill on exercises which involve manipulation of elements within sentences (but seldom across sentence boundaries) may compound coherence problems by centering the students' attention on sentence-level errors (e.g., focusing on errors in subject-verb agreement but rarely on reference errors). Excessive emphasis on writing sentences or on composing only for the teacher often usurps the attention that should be given to the writer's "sense of audience." There would seem to be an intimate connection between audience sensitivity and coherence, since coherence involves connecting discourse for the benefit of the reader.

We have thus far focused on the teacher's investigative role. However, teachers are rightly concerned with pedagogy, with applying the results of their investigations. On this crucial issue, the error analyst's advice is less specific but still useful. Error analysts caution us that the sources of error can be complex and that simple exercises or explanations will reach only some students. They recommend thinking of teaching as hypothesis testing: trying one technique based on analysis of the error but remaining open to other approaches. Error analysis can be seen as providing insights about the sources of an error but not as dictating any single teaching device. In this view, error analysis helps teachers utilize materials and teaching strategies more effectively by indicating the precise nature of the problem. The teacher uses these insights to match teaching strategies to the error (or perhaps to design new materials based on specific sources of error). Such an approach seems most practical in a learning-center environment, where there is ample opportunity for individualization of instruction.

However, we feel that error analysis can be useful for the classroom composition teacher as well. When teachers understand the paths that lead to particular errors, they can more effectively show their students how they came to make a particular mistake. We have found that explaining the sources of error can be quite effective for some students. When students can make sense of their errors, coming to terms with them as the result of consistent and understandable strategies, they are more likely to try to change (without demolishing their self-concept). In our experience, helping students to understand the source of their errors can produce changes even in errors that resist drill.

The practical requirements for adopting the error-analysis approach are, first, a good system of keeping records of errors. This system is important because analysis involves looking for systematicity and pattern. A well-designed grading form can be useful. Second, error-analysis teaching requires as much individualization of instruction as possible. The best way to show a student the source of his or her errors is in periodic conferences, in which the teacher can present evidence for the error from the student's papers, summarize the conclusions about the possible sources of the error, and start the student working on materials specifically geared to the source of the error. In our view, such conferences are more effective than extensive annotations on papers.

Frequent conferences and individualization may, however, represent unrealizable ideals for many composition teachers. For teachers in this situation error analysis can still be useful. One of the central tenets of error analysis is that the sources of error, while complex, are not infinite: a host of product errors are reducible to common and systematic processes (although, one must admit, the exact nature and number of these processes await further investigation). The lesson here is that teachers can deal with common errors in class. As error analysts, they could present a series of passages illustrating a specific error. Then they would discuss why the writer might make such a mistake—in much the same way that we discussed the coherence error above, tracing the paths that might logically lead to the mistake. The next step would be to have students participate in such a discussion, trying to analyze the sources of particular errors. Ideally, students would begin to investigate their own errors and, consequently, would be more receptive to the teacher's pedagogical suggestions.

We have come, quite recently, to the error-analysis approach through our experiences as teachers of ESL. However, the move from a product- to a process-analytic approach to error has been occurring in the field of composition as well as in ESL. Professor Mina Shaughnessy's recent book, *Errors and Expectations,* is a brilliant case in point. To quote only one of many possible examples, Professor Shaughnessy, in the spirit of error analysis, says,

Note how often the errors students make with verbs, no matter how peculiar they may sound to a teacher, are the result not of carelessness or irrationality but of *thinking*. Part of the task of helping such students master the formal verb system therefore depends upon being able to trace the line of reasoning that has led to erroneous choices rather than upon unloading on the student's memory an indifferent bulk of information about verbs only part of which relates to his difficulties.[10]

Although some scholars and teachers within our discipline have arrived at a process approach to error (by a route apparently independent of work in ESL), we believe that a consideration of the issues involved in the evolution of error analysis in ESL can contribute, both theoretically and methodologically, to our study of the errors students make in written composition. Error-analysis scholars have, for example, developed a sophisticated terminology for discussing error; we might well utilize that terminology. A standard terminology and shared methodology for investigating error would promote the type of interdisciplinary work that we see as crucial to the advancement of composition theory and pedagogy.

EXPLORING THE IDEAS — *Theoretical Discussion*

QUESTION 1

Background   Teachers of ESL and basic writing classes have traditionally been concerned with errors. In some cases the errors made by both groups are similar and thus the two types of students are placed in the same classes even though their reasons for making identical errors may be very different. The fact that these two types of students are often grouped together raises the question of in what ways they are alike and in what ways they are different. David Bartholomae (1980. The Study of Error. *College Composition and Communication* 31, 3:254–255) maintains that basic writers have the following characteristics:

1. Basic writers "are beginning writers, to be sure, but they are not writers who need to learn to use language. They are writers who need to learn to command a particular variety of language—the language of a written, academic discourse—and a particular variety of language use—writing itself."

2. Basic writers "get into trouble by getting in over their heads, not only attempting to do more than they can, but imagining as their target a syntax that is *more* complex than convention requires. The failed sentences, then, could be taken as stages of learning rather than the failure to learn, but also as evidence that these writers are using writing as an occasion to learn."

3. Basic writers "lack control, although it may be more precise to say they lack choice and option, the power to make decisions about the idiosyncracy of their writing."

4. Basic writers "are not performing mechanically or randomly but making choices and forming strategies as they struggle to deal with the varied demands of a task, a language and a rhetoric. The 'systems' such writing exhibits provide evidence that basic writers *are* competent, mature language users. . . . The approximate systems they produce are evidence that they can conceive of and manipulate written language as a structured, systematic code."

Discussion   Which of these characteristics of basic writers do you believe are shared by ESL students? What additional characteristics do you think ESL students have that basic writers often lack?

QUESTION 2

Background   Errors in word choice are common to both basic writers and advanced ESL students. Mina Shaughnessy in *Errors and Expectations* delineates the following types of vocabulary errors made by basic writers (1977. New York, Oxford University Press, pp. 190–192).

1.   Wrong word form resulting in a word which doesn't exist:
     a. I wish my life to be *forfilling* with happiness.
     b. With my capacities of learning brought forth by my education, I can be *subcepticle* to learn a variety of things.

2. Wrong word form resulting from an error in use of a derivational suffix:
    a. He is headed in a *destructional* way.
    b. People are judged by what they *product* on the job.
3. Use of a word that is phonetically similar but semantically unrelated:
    a. The program uses a new *floormat* (format).
    b. They used him as an *escape goat* (scapegoat).
4. Use of words that are semantically similar but inappropriate for the situation:
    a. I will try to *perpetuate* my children in the same track as I am.
    b. They are *eliminating* waste and gas from combining with air.

Discussion   The following sentences were written by nonnative speakers. For each one, indicate the type of error that exists according to Shaughnessy's classification. Do you think the reasons for making any of these errors would be different for ESL students as opposed to native speakers? Consider, for example, the relative proficiency in spoken English between the two groups of students.

1. I am glad to *recall* to your attention that the United States is willing to provide engineers.

2. The country will become less *dependable* on other countries to a certain *extend* if she can develop natural resources of her own.

3. The Immigration and Naturalization service *regulates* that all foreign students with F-1 visas have to be full time students.

4. Students get very upset when their teachers *mark* them with low grades.

5. This fact certainly *experts* a serious influence on medical care.

6. This *acquired* him a considerable amount of experience.

7. He *owns* the qualities of a true American.

8. He will *innovate* different approaches for challenging problems.

QUESTION 3

Background   As Kroll and Schafer point out, "the error analyst recognizes the many sources of a particular error and the benefit of investigating the reasons for the error before constructing a teaching strategy" (page 137).

Discussion   The following grammatical errors appear in Jack Richards's article (A Noncontrastive Approach to Error Analysis. In J. Oller and J. Richards. 1973. *Focus on the Learner.* Rowley, Massachusetts: Newbury House Publishers, pp. 108–109). For each one, discuss why you think the student might have made the error he did.

1. We are live in this hut.
2. He is speaks French.
3. The teacher was told us.
4. He did not found.
5. He born in England.

QUESTION 4

Background   Kroll and Schafer contend that a host of product errors may be reducible to a common and systematic process.

Discussion   Consider the following errors made by a nonnative speaker in the use of the verb *develop*. What generalization could you give to the student to help him use the verb *develop* correctly in the future?

1. Life in Japan has developed a taste for light food.

2. Reading books as a hobby in her childhood developed a talent for writing novels.

3. The dampness of that area developed many kinds of illness.

QUESTION 5

Background   According to Richards, one reason for developmental errors is ignorance of rule restrictions.

Discussion   The following errors in word choice were made by nonnative speakers. For each one, discuss why you think the italicized verb sounds inappropriate for the context. In order to do this, it will help to consider the subject that the student has used with each verb.

1. The families of the couple will not *harmonize* with each other.

2. He is 59 years old which *depicts* that he has a good deal of experience.

3. In my country a person with a high school diploma will be able to *gather* $2900 in one year.

NOTES

1. Three sources offer a more detailed view of the evolution of error analysis in ESL: Jack C. Richards (ed.). *Error Analysis: Perspectives on Second Language Acquisition.* London, Longman Group, 1974; S. Pit Corder, *Introducing Applied Linguistics.* Harmondsworth, England, Penguin, 1973; and S. Pit Corder, Error Analysis, Interlanguage, and Second Language Acquisition, *Language Teaching & Linguistics: Abstracts* 8 (1975), 201–218.

2. Kenneth S. Goodman (ed.). *Miscue Analysis: Applications to Reading Instruction.* Urbana, Ill., NCTE, 1973.

3. Heidi C. Dulay and Marina K. Burt, You Can't Learn without Goofing: An Analysis of Children's Second Language Errors, in Richards, *Error Analysis,* pp. 95–123.

4. Jack C. Richards, A Noncontrastive Approach to Error Analysis, *English Language Teaching* 25 (1971), 204–219 (rpt. in Richards, *Error Analysis,* pp. 172–188).

5. Richards makes this distinction in "A Noncontrastive Approach to Error Analysis."

6. The term is used by Larry Selinker in Interlanguage, *International Review of Applied Linguistics* 10 (1972), 219–231 (rpt. in Richards, *Error Analysis,* pp. 31–54).

7. S. Pit Corder mentions this source of error in Error Analysis, Interlanguage, and Second Language Acquisition, p. 208.

8. Richards uses this phrase in "A Noncontrastive Approach to Error Analysis."

9. M. A. K. Halliday and Ruqaiya Hasan, *Cohesion in English.* London, Longman Group, 1976, p. 67.

10. Mina P. Shaughnessy, *Errors and Expectations: A Guide for the Teacher of Basic Writing.* New York, Oxford, 1977, p. 105.

10

The Treatment of Error in Written Work
James M. Hendrickson

THE ROLE OF CONSTRUCTIVE FEEDBACK

Recent research in second-language acquisition suggests that language learning is a creative process whereby learners produce oral and written utterances based upon the rules of a language system which they have internalized.[1] If a learner understands and uses the rules correctly, he or she will produce utterances that are meaningful, grammatical, and appropriate. If a learner's hypotheses of the language rules are occasionally incorrect, however, some of his or her utterances will contain errors of varying types and frequencies. It is virtually impossible to avoid errors when learning any new skill, particularly when learning a foreign language. It is logical, therefore, to ask a rather critical question: Can error correction benefit language learners?

According to Krashen,[2] children learn their native language as well as foreign languages in a "natural" or subconscious way. Normally, children are more interested in communicating meaningful information than concerned with producing linguistically correct sentences. Krashen believes, therefore, that error correction will not significantly influence the linguistic performance of children. By contrast, adults who learn a foreign language in formal situations such as in classrooms and in self-study courses, are often quite conscious of their errors. For these adults, whom Krashen calls "monitor-users," error correction helps to discover the functions and limitations of the grammatical structures and the lexical forms of the language they are studying. Put another way, error correction in the adult foreign language classroom helps many learners become aware of the exact environment for applying grammatical rules and for discovering the precise semantic range of lexical items.

GUIDELINES FOR CORRECTING COMPOSITION ERRORS

Discovery Learning and Error Correction

Experienced teachers are quite familiar with the various kinds of errors their students produce when speaking spontaneously or writing creatively in a foreign language. Unfortunately, few teacher training programs (in the United States, at least) provide adequate instruction, if any, on how to deal with student errors. The current status of error correction in foreign language teaching remains ambiguous. Research on the subject is both scant and speculative.[4] Indeed, no standards exist on whether, when, which, or how student errors should be corrected or who should correct them.[5] Moreover, little empirical research has been conducted to test the effectiveness of various approaches and techniques that teachers use for correcting students' oral and written errors.

One common technique for correcting composition errors produced by native and foreign language learners is simply to provide the correct forms and structures in students' faulty sentences. Teachers often supplement these corrections with marginal notes that explain why particular errors are incorrect, such as errors in spelling, lack of subject-verb agreement, and inappropriate style. (One might call this procedure "editing" rather than "correcting.") One thing is certain: providing all the correct forms in students' imperfect sentences is a time-consuming ordeal that can also be frustrating to teachers, especially when they see that identical types of errors appear repeatedly on compositions written over a period of time by the same student. Certainly, from the learner's perspective, it is disconcerting to receive a "corrected" composition with many words crossed out, new words added, and an array of marginal comments—all usually written in blood-red ink. Small wonder, indeed, that some students are embarrassed and lose confidence when they receive their written work corrected in this way. Supplying all the correct forms on adult students' written work may actually hinder rather than facilitate the process of second-language acquisition in formal learning situations.

Recently, Dulay and Burt,[6] and Krashen[7] proposed that a selective approach to error correction, tailored to the learner's internal level of linguistic development, might be beneficial to students in both cognitive and affective terms. According to Corder,[8] Gorbet,[9] and Valdman,[10] a discovery approach might also be worthwhile. These three researchers suggest that a discovery approach would help students make inferences and formulate concepts about the target language, and would help them to fix this information in their long-term memories.

Considerations in Error Correction

When deciding which errors to correct and how to correct them, one should consider at least four critical learner factors. First, one needs to be aware of a student's purpose and goals for communicating in writing. For example, does the student need to develop his or her writing skills in the foreign language well enough to compose a class term paper, or to write a master's thesis? Or does the student simply want to be able to write a letter of invitation or a thank-you note to a friend? We might suppose that many readers would be more tolerant of a thank-you note replete with errors than they would be of a master's thesis that contains proportionately fewer errors.

Second, one must take into account students' written proficiency in the target language at any given time. I have found that as students' level of proficiency increases, they become better equipped to correct their own errors. Because beginning and intermediate students have presumably internalized the foreign language system to a lesser degree than have advanced learners, their limited linguistic repertoire is often insufficient to allow them to locate and find solutions to their errors. Consequently, less advanced students need specific clues about their errors. Advanced students, however, are better able to correct their own errors if their teacher indicates where the errors are.

A third critical factor in error correction is the teacher's awareness of error types and frequencies as well as an understanding of how these two aspects relate to students' writing goals. Certainly, errors that impair the intelligibility of sentences merit a higher priority for correction than errors that do not. Similarly, errors that stigmatize the writer from the perspective of native speakers should be among the first corrected. Also, mistakes that occur frequently in students' compositions probably deserve more immediate attention than those that are less frequent.

The fourth and possibly most critical factor in correcting written errors is the students' attitudes about their nature and correction. According to Carroll,[11] willingness to use a foreign language—and to make errors—is one characteristic of a successful language learner. Carroll states that a student's attitude toward learning involves "a kind of self-control and confidence whereby the learner can attempt self-expression without feeling self-conscious or threatened by making errors and being corrected" (p. 6). One implication of this statement is the need for teachers to create a healthy learning environment in which students recognize that making errors is a natural, indeed, a *necessary* phenomenon in language learning. Excessive embarrassment caused by one's errors can be an obstacle to learning from them. A more positive attitude would be to seek information actively on the correctness and appropriateness of one's efforts to communicate. Such an open attitude toward learning from errors can and should be cultivated by the language teacher. Generally speaking, students who manifest low self-confidence in their ability to express themselves in a foreign language need a greater amount of supportive feedback on their errors than do their more confident peers. Teachers can help build student self-confidence by focusing on high-priority errors while tolerating less important ones, particularly when students are not required to rewrite their compositions. Moreover, it may be wiser to give low-confidence students more credit for the *content* of their ideas rather than for the *form* in which they are expressed. As these students gain greater control in using the foreign language, the teacher can shift to other error-correction strategies.

Indirect and Direct Correction Treatments

Recently I have been experimenting with various combinations of indirect and direct treatments for correcting compositions written by students of intermediate Spanish.[12] I require my students to write five picture-story compositions as homework assignments. As they write, the students are encouraged to use self-help resources such as their textbook, dictionaries, and grammar books. The students have several days to complete and turn in a first draft of their picture-story composition.

Indirect correction treatments may indicate either the presence or the specific location of errors. I use such treatments whenever I assume that students will be able to discover an acceptable solution for a given error by reconsidering the error itself or by using the appropriate self-help references mentioned above. Some suggestions for marking errors are as follows:

1. Underlining incorrect orthographic and morphological forms. Examples:[13]

    The woman wont to kook the fich.

    Mon frere parl francais tres bien.

    Gloria priefere un taza de cafe.

    Morgen geh er nicht in die schul.

2. Circling an inappropriate word. Examples:

    They are very happy with their plays. ("games")

    Ma soeur est cinq ans.

    El chico tiene una pelota en el mano.

    Gestern hat meine Mutter nach Hause gekommen.

3. Inserting an arrow (ʌ) to indicate a missing word. Examples:

    The man ʌ saying good-bye to his wife.

    Les marins ʌ parlé avec les jeunes femmes.

    ʌ señor Rojas està trabajando en su oficina.

    Dann fängt sie ʌ die Aufgabe ʌ lesen.

4. Placing a question mark alongside a confusing phrase or structure. Examples:

    Two girls are going that brought other tree. ?

    J'aime retrouver folle des filles. ?

    La mujer corre abajo de las escaleras lo desde. ?

    Das Hotel heisst Krone, dass Herr Meier uns sagte. ?

Direct correction treatments not only indicate the presence or location of errors in a sentence but also provide clues or tips on how students can correct their own errors. I use direct treatments whenever I assume that students will not be able to correct certain errors if I merely identified them; I have found that providing this additional, more specific feedback often leads students to provide solutions to their errors. Here are several suggestions that vary in their degree of directness, beginning with the *least* direct correction treatment:

1. Underlining a word and providing a written tip. Examples:

   She <u>finds</u> her watch inside the drawer.

   Use past tense
   Le chat <u>regarder</u> la petite fille.

   Conjugate
   Dudo que Carlos lo <u>permite</u> entrar.

   Use subjunctive
   Ich <u>können</u> mich mit ihr befreunden.

   Conjugate

2. Bracketing a misplaced word or phrase and indicating its proper place in a sentence. Examples:

   " 'Well, nothing is forever,' told them ⌈their mother⌉."

   J'aime votre jupe ⌈beaucoup⌉.

   Puedo ⌈no⌉ verle muy bien.

   Weil ⌈ist⌉ es gesund, ich ⌈esse⌉ gern Wurst.

3. Crossing out a superfluous word. Examples:

   When the boy was riding his bicycle, a car hit to him.

   J'ai cherché partout pour mon ami.

   Voy a pedirle para cinco dólares.

   Heidi ist bei der Firma Oldsmobile beschäftigt mit.

4. Providing a correct form or structure of an incorrect word or phrase. Examples:

   dug
   They digged around a small tree.

   maison
   Je vais à ma habite.

   salvavidas
   El marinero le echó el anillo de goma.

   ledig
   Der Mann hat keine Frau; er ist single.

I have found that indirect and direct correction treatments can be more effective if they are used together in hybrid fashion. The combined treatments that a teacher uses will vary not only from one learner to the next, but also from one composition to the next. As stated previously, when correcting an individual's written work, the teacher needs to be aware of the learner's writing goals, level of writing proficiency, types and frequencies of errors, and motivation to learn from those errors. The composition in Figure 1 was corrected using a combination of indirect and direct treatments. It was written by an intermediate adult student of English as a second language in a community college, who intends to transfer later to a four-year institution. The types and frequencies of errors in the composition are those that this highly motivated student typically produced.

When I return my students' first drafts, I ask them to rewrite the compositions at home and turn them in at the next class meeting. At that time I

This story is about a man who gott up late
everyday and he often arrived late to his office.
So one day he dicided to buy an alarm o'clock that
can gett ∧ up early by it and ⁵⁰ can arrive to his   ✱ who??
office on time. After he bought it he wanted ∧ try
it, so when he wanted to go ∧ bed he (stringed)✱ ∧up[it].   ✱ wrong verb – Use
Than he slept. In the morning when the alarm   dictionary
o'clock began to ring, he wake up nervousness   ✱ wrong tense
and suddenly shoot out his pillow over the   ✱ use past tense
alarm o'clock. Than the table with ∧ alarm o'clock
and pillow fell down on the (ground)✱. So the   ✱ wrong noun – use
o'clock stopped to ring_ and Mr. Lazy slept again   dictionary
Because he ∧ usued to gett _ up late. So that was
very difficult for him ∧ gett up early.

Figure 1. A Sample composition[14]

collect both their first and second drafts, then supply the correct forms and
structures of any errors remaining on the second draft. I assume that the students
were unable to correct these remaining errors by themselves.[15] A student's
grade is based on a ratio of the number of words in a composition to the number
of errors remaining on the second draft.[16]

It is important to emphasize at this point that the treatments presented and
illustrated above are merely suggestions. Teachers will want to modify and add
to them according to their own teaching style and their students' communicative
and linguistic needs. Nevertheless, students need to be given as many
opportunities as possible to discover solutions to their written errors. This
discovery approach to correction allows students to assume a greater responsibility for their own learning. Also, the approach may well develop students'
abilities to write more clearly and accurately in a foreign language than would be
the case if teachers supplied all the correct forms and structures of students'
errors.

Certainly, many research questions on error correction still remain. For
example, how do students react to different correction treatments? Which
correction techniques are most effective for particular cognitive styles and
personality types? To what extent does error correction actually benefit (or
hinder) language learning? Undoubtedly the answers to these queries will raise
additional questions, but they can also lead to the development of more efficient
and humane ways to correct student errors.

Final Suggestions

It has been stated that using combined indirect and direct treatments to
correct compositions is probably more beneficial to students than providing all

the correct or appropriate solutions to their written errors. Nevertheless, teachers need to reinforce any correction approach or treatment with monitoring and learning activities designed to improve the writing skills of their students. Here are seven such activities, some of which have recently been mentioned elsewhere in the professional literature.

1. Chart and tally written errors in order to diagnose students' individual communicative and linguistic problem areas, and to measure their writing proficiency. In addition, make a master error chart to help you decide which errors should receive high, medium, or low priority for correction.[17]

2. Identify mistakes that occur frequently on individual students' compositions. Ask students to search out and correct their own high-frequency errors before turning in the first draft of each subsequent composition.

3. Discuss the kinds of errors that students produce most often on their compositions. Distribute sentences or short paragraphs containing these common error types; then ask students to locate and correct them. This exercise can be assigned as homework, then discussed at the next class meeting.

4. Try to discover the cause of students' errors by discussing their compositions with them on an individual basis. Understanding why particular errors occurred on one composition is an initial step in helping students to avoid similar errors on future compositions.

5. Record comments concerning written errors on cassette tapes that students supply along with their compositions. This technique provides a highly personalized approach to error correction whenever it is difficult to meet with students individually.[18]

6. Develop and implement communicative drills based on grammatical structures and vocabulary items that are most troublesome for students. These kinds of drills provide valuable practice in using language meaningfully.[19]

7. Instruct students to work in pairs and to correct each other's compositions before submitting them. This procedure allows students to work in a nonthreatening educational setting that helps build their self-confidence and fosters learning by discovery and sharing.[20]

CONCLUSION

While waiting for basic and applied research on second-language learning to provide more information on the issues surrounding error correction in foreign-language teaching, teachers will need to continue experimenting with different feedback strategies in their classrooms. In this paper, I have discussed some general guidelines as well as specific treatments for dealing with written errors in the adult foreign-language classroom. Teachers and researchers should regard these guidelines and treatments as suggestions. Experience suggests that what works effectively for one teacher may not necessarily be equally effective for another. Nevertheless, based on current language-learning theory and research as well as on observation and practical experience, one can indicate a logical direction for error correction to take. The suggestions presented here were built upon that premise—one that awaits the necessary rigor of empirical experimentation and further refinement. ⌡

EXPLORING THE IDEAS — *Theoretical Discussion*

QUESTION 1

Background   Hendrickson points out that the most critical factor in correcting errors is the student's attitude. He states that it might be wise "to give low-confidence students more credit for the *content* of their ideas rather than for the *form* in which they are expressed" (page 147).

Discussion   Do you believe it is important to give credit for content primarily for low-confidence students, or is it important for all students? Refer to the sample composition shown in Figure 1 (page 150). What comments could you add to this paper to give attention to its content and not just its form?

QUESTION 2

Background   Hendrickson points out that "the current status of error correction in foreign language teaching remains ambiguous. Research on the subject is both scant and speculative. Indeed, no standards exist on whether, when, which, or how student errors should be corrected or who should correct them. Moreover, little empirical research has been conducted to test the effectiveness of various approaches and techniques that teachers use for correcting students' oral and written errors" (page 146).

Discussion   Select one of the activities discussed by Hendrickson on page 151 that you believe warrants investigation. Discuss a possible research project which could be undertaken to test the effectiveness of this activity for reducing students' errors.

Composition Evaluation

ACTIVITY 1

Background   Hendrickson contends that the following types of errors merit the most priority: those which impair the intelligibility of sentences, those which stigmatize the writer from the perspective of a native speaker, and those which occur frequently in the student's writing.

Application   Read the following folktale written by a Japanese student and underline any errors which you believe impair intelligibility or stigmatize the writer from a native speaker's perspective. In addition, indicate any type of error that reoccurs in the essay and thus deserves more attention.

WHY PEOPLE SPEAK DIFFERENT LANGUAGES

A long time ago, men used only one language in the world. However, most parents in their families interfered their conversations everytime the children made utterances and found fault with whatever their children spoke. Then the sons and daughters discussed the matter of their parents' over-involvement in their speeches among them and decided to invent a new language so that they can talk freely. Some smart children got together everyday to work up to a creation of a new language. It took them for about two years. After that, the children adopted the new language to communicate each other.

But the parents got angry at their children's use of the new language which the parents did not understand at all. Then the adults vanished them to another territory far away from the home land. The children kept on using the new tongue and enjoyed free conversations. But when they got married and had their own children, they started to give sharp words towards their children, too. Then the children made another new language; as a result, they were sent away to another area.

Then the third generation did the same thing as their grand parents and parents did. So the fourth generation created the fourth language. As the same thing was done from one generation to another over and over again, at present there remain many differnt languages as consequences of children's self-defence against their parents all over the world.

ACTIVITY 2

Background   Hendrickson describes various indirect and direct correction techniques. He believes that a combination of the two is the best correction strategy. However, he points out that in order to effectively use this technique a teacher needs to be aware of the learner's writing goals, level of writing proficiency, typical errors, and motivation.

Application   The following essay was written by a highly motivated advanced ESL Japanese student enrolled in a university class that she had to pass in order to fulfill her literacy requirement. Correct the essay using a combination of direct and indirect techniques.

WHY THERE ARE STARS IN THE SKY

A long time ago, there was a peaceful village, and the daughter of village chief was very beautiful. He was proud of the daughter. He was going to marry her to the strongest man in the world. Many men wanted to marry to the girl so they tried to show how strong they were or to curry favor with the village chief. However, his daughter felt depressed. She didn't want to marry to those men because some men were very stupid although they were strong. On the other hand, some men were just rude.

One day, a stranger came to the village. He was so skinny, and he was in rags but he was very intelligent and kind to everybody. He made some medicine by plants and helped sick people or injured animals. As the girl saw the stranger, she fell in love with him. But the village chief didn't allow their marriage because the stranger was not strong really. The chief ordered a big eagle to take the stranger away into the sky. Since the sky was so cold, he was frozen and became the moon.

Since then, he tried to send some messages to the daughter of the village chief. But the messages were also frozen before they came down to the village, and they became stars in the sky. When he felt lonely, his message became a blue star, and when his message was passionate, a red star appeared. When he cried, his tear drops became white stars. Even though the messages have never get the earth, he has never stop sending them. We sometimes find new stars because he is still sending his message now.

ACTIVITY 3

Background   Another technique for correcting essays is to use a checklist.
This method is described by B. W. Robinett in On the Horns of a Dilemma:
Correcting Compositions (1972. *Studies in Honor of Albert Markwardt*, J.
Alatis (ed.). Washington, D.C., TESOL: 143–151). As Robinett points out, the
advantage of using a checklist is that it helps the teacher ascertain each student's
particular problems and thus provides a basis for assigning individual remedial
work. The following description and checklist are taken from her article (pages
144–145).

   (a) When the student hands in his composition, he also hands in a checklist containing his
name and the title of the composition.
   (b) The instructor begins reading the composition. When he comes to an error, he writes a '1'
above the portion of the composition that is incorrect and a '1' in the blank on the checklist which
best indicates the nature of the error. The second error will be marked '2', the third '3', and so forth,
on both the composition and the checklist.
   (c) If the instructor feels that the composition contains several identical errors, he is free to
mark them with the same number on the composition and with a single number on the checklist. This
can be done, for example, if more than one misspelling of the same word occurs.
   (d) It may be necessary to place more than one number over a single word: for example, if a
word is out of proper order and is also misspelled.
   (e) There is no need to number the errors in perfect sequence. If an incorrect item is numbered
out of sequence on the composition, it makes no difference since numbers do not appear in sequence
on the checklist.
   (f) When the instructor has finished marking the composition and the checklist, he looks over
the checklist to see what kind of errors the student is making and decides whether correction of errors
by the student on the same composition, rewriting, or some other form of further study is necessary.

Application   Below are three essays written by intermediate-level ESL
university students in response to the following question.

   Write a two-paragraph essay developed as follows:
   First paragraph: Describe a particular place in which you feel comfortable. It can be a corner
in your room, a street in your neighborhood, or a place in the country or at the beach. Try to make
each detail of your description contribute to a clear picture of this place.
   Second paragraph: Explain why this place is "comfortable." You may use additional
examples to illustrate your definition.

First, read all three essays and indicate which one you believe best fulfills the
assignment and why. Next, correct all of the essays using the checklist format.
Circle any errors which are difficult to categorize according to the checklist
format. Finally, discuss what you believe are the advantages and disadvantages
of using this system from both a teacher's and a student's point of view.

STUDENT A
Native Language: Burmese
   The place which I feel comfortable is Chinatown Branch Library. The library is quite small. It
has the small room in the back of library which has only one big table, many chairs, many book-
shelves and many books. The room is very bright and quiet.

COMPOSITION GRADING CHECKLIST

Name _____
Composition _____

AGREEMENT
_____ subject and verb do not agree
_____ pronoun and referent do not agree

ARTICLES AND DETERMINERS
Omission   Incorrect Use
_____ a   _____
_____ an   _____
_____ the   _____
_____ others   _____

CAPITALIZATION
_____ omission
_____ incorrect

COMPARISONS
_____ use *like*
_____ use *the same as*
_____ use *different from*
_____ use *-er*
_____ use *more – than* --
_____ use *the -- est*
_____ use *the most* --

CONTENT
_____ incorrect information
_____ awkward: needs rewording
_____ cannot understand your meaning

DOUBLE NEGATIVE
_____ avoid double negatives

FORMAT
_____ improper heading
_____ improper size paper
_____ not written in ink
_____ no title
_____ improper left margin
_____ improper right margin
_____ indent for each paragraph

NOUNS
_____ should be singular
_____ should be plural
_____ improper form
_____ mass noun (should be singular)

PARAGRAPHING
_____ begin new paragraph
_____ no new paragraph

PENMANSHIP (Handwriting)
_____ handwriting interferes with
      communication
_____ avoid non-English symbols

PREPOSITIONS
Omission   Incorrect Use
_____ in   _____
_____ on   _____
_____ at   _____
_____ to   _____
_____ of   _____
_____ others   _____

PUNCTUATION
Omission   Incorrect Use
_____ period .
_____ question mark ?
_____ exclamation point !   _____
_____ comma ,   _____
_____ colon :   _____
_____ semicolon ;   _____
_____ apostrophe '   _____
_____ hyphen -   _____
_____ quotation marks " "   _____
_____ underlining _____   _____
_____ others (dash, parentheses, _____
      etc.)

SENTENCE
_____ incomplete sentence
_____ two sentences run together

SPELLING
_____ incorrectly spelled

VERBS
_____ tense incorrect
_____ form incorrect
_____ do not use *to* after a modal
_____ do not use *-ing* after *to*
_____ use *to* + *verb* form
_____ use plain form
_____ use *-ing* form
_____ incorrect sequence of tenses

VOCABULARY
_____ form incorrect
_____ item incorrect
_____ word(s) omitted
_____ unnecessary word(s)

WORD DIVISION
_____ divide words at syllable boundaries
_____ write as one word
_____ write as two words

WORD ORDER
_____ observe SVO *Place Time* word order
_____ incorrect question word order
_____ incorrect included question word order
_____ change word order as indicated

The small room in the library is comfortable. Because very quiet in there, so I can concentrate on my work. The place is bright because it has many windows which make one very comfortable. The cornor of the small room has a restroom, and a water fountain which make very convenient for a longer period of time. The room has some soft chairs which are very comfortable. The room has many references books which I need for my work. Everybody in there are reading or doing their work which make me do my work, and I have done a lot of work there which specially make me very happy and comfortable.

STUDENT B
Native Language: Spanish
 A particular place where I would feel comfortable would be a peaceful place. A place where I could only hear the birds sing. A place where I could feel the wind blowing my hair. A place that has beautiful green grass, and some of my favorite flowers. for example; red roses, red carnations, and yellow daisies. This place should also have different kinds of miniature fruit trees. for example; an apple tree, a cherry tree, and an orange tree.
 The particular place where I always like to be is in my mother's garden. I feel very comfortable and happy when I'm there. I do my homework there, because I feel I can concentrate more than when I'm inside the house. The garden for me is so special, because I can really notice nature. The smell of the flowers and the growing of the fruits make me go everyday and stay there for at least an hour.

STUDENT C
Native Language: Chinese
 The left corner of my room, just opposite to my bed, is the most comfortable place for me. A brown modern-designed desk, which is placed close to the wall, is matched with an orange armchair. Just above the desk on the wall is hung with a small abstract painting. On the right, between the desk and the window, there is a stand lamp. On the other side of the desk is the brown wooden book-shelves. It stands from the floor up to the ceiling. Piles of books are put in it according to alphabetical order of author.
 This place is comfortable because it is quiet and elegant. Sitting on the chair and looking out through the window, it is the nice backyard which is cultivated with colorful charming flowers. People scarcely go down the backyard, that I can read my books quietly without any border. If I am not reading, I can switch on the casette on my desk and listen to the music. This corner is so lovely that I always spend a whole night in it.

ACTIVITY 4

Background   Another way to evaluate writing is holistically. Charles Cooper defines holistic evaluation as "any procedure which stops short of enumerating linguistic, rhetorical, or informational features of a piece of writing" (1977. Holistic Evaluation of Writing. In Charles Cooper and Lee Odell (eds.) *Evaluating Writing.* Urbana, Illinois, National Council of Teachers of English, p. 4). The aim of the evaluation is to sort or rank the essays under consideration.

Application   Read the following essays, which were written in response to the same question as the previous three essays. Next, rank order the essays, with number one being the highest score, and compare your rating with several other readers. Finally, list the criteria you feel you employed in rank ordering the essays.

STUDENT A
Native Language: Spanish

An island located in the caribean sea is the place, which is very comfortable to me; its name is "Isla Mujeres," in Engllish means "Women island," and it is named like that because it has a shape as a woman's. This island belongs to Mexico.

It is very small, I don't know exactly its area, but to give you an idea how small it is, I will tell you that it can be walked in approximately 8 hours, having some stops during that period.

The beaches around the island are wonderful, the water is warm and it has a baby blue color, and it's so clear that you can see the bottom easily; the sea is not brave, and the sand is white and fine like powder. There are a lot of people who practice skin diving because of the water.

The main production of the island is coconut, there are coconut trees everywhere you go, and you can easily find coconuts fell down in the ground.

This island is very comfortable to me because all qualities I wrote in the first paragraph; in other words for its weather, peacefulness, atmosphere and so forth.

One another reason that is not physic or climatic but sentimental is that I spent part of my honeymoon there.

STUDENT B
Native Language: Chinese

Repulse Bay is the only place in which I would spend my whole life without hesitation. It is located in the southern part of the Hong Kong Island. The beach which is half-moon shape, is deeply covered by fair and smooth sand. The water is blue in color, with unusually good smell of fresh sea water which no other beach can give me. The scenery is picturesque. There are some very extraordinary rocks which eject out from the steep sea-cliffs, forming some natural scruptures. Laying on the golden sand, soothing by the warm sun and soft-breeze, and embracing by the graceful scruptures wash away my worries, miseries, and strains completely.

I enjoy staying in a place where social tension and pollution do not exist. It has to be natural, gigantic and extraordinary. I prefer ocean scene rather than mountain view because the former is always the representation and symbol of softness and motherhood. It should also be quiet and impressive because I enjoy privacy very much. No other place can give me such comfort and fulfillment, but my most favorite beach—Repulse Bay.

STUDENT C
Native Language: Farsi

The place that I would like to stay there and be comfortable, is Stinson Beach.

Stinson Beach, with sandy coast, beautiful views, calm weather, and short ocean's waves is my only favorite place to go. There are a lots of recreation area available for people to B.B.Q.; also there are other facilities for people to be comfortable.

I enjoy looking at the seagulls which are flying over the blue waters; also seeing the people who are hanging around, or laying on the ground with colorful baiding suits, and passage of a beautiful girls with nice bodies in front of my eyes, makes me to forget about everything and to have a good time.

In my opinion, a place which has the same specifications as above, is a comfortable place.

Teaching Strategies

ACTIVITY 1

Background   Robinett points out that in her checklist "little attention has been paid to rhetorical features although categories labelled 'content' and 'paragraphing' point in this direction. Problems which arise in longer discourse are beyond the scope of this checklist" (Robinett, 1972, p. 144).

Application   Expand her checklist so that it includes more attention to rhetorical features such as organization, relevancy of support, and cohesive devices. You might include some of the dimensions of writing that you found to be relevant when you evaluated the papers holistically.

NOTES

1. I wish to thank Gerard L. Ervin (Ohio State University) for his many helpful suggestions and comments concerning this paper. For any errors in its content or form, I assume full responsibility.

2. Stephen D. Krashen, The Monitor Model for Adult Second Language Performance. In Marina Burt, Heidi Dulay, and Mary Finocchiaro (eds.). *Viewpoints on English as a Second Language.* New York, Regents, 1977, pp. 151–156.

3. Stephen D. Krashen and Herbert W. Seliger, The Essential Contributions of Formal Instruction in Adult Second Language Learning. *TESOL Quarterly* 9 (1975), pp. 173–183.

4. James M. Hendrickson, Error Correction in Foreign Language Teaching: Recent Theory, Research, and Practice. *Modern Language Journal* 62 (1978), pp. 387–398.

5. Marina K. Burt, Error Analysis in the Adult EFL Classroom. *TESOL Quarterly* 9 (1975), pp. 53–63.

6. Heidi Dulay and Marina Burt, Remarks on Creativity in Language Acquisition. *Viewpoints on English as a Second Language* (see note 2), pp. 95–126.

7. Krashen (see note 2).

8. S. Pit Corder, The Significance of Learners' Errors. *International Review of Applied Linguistics* 5 (1967), pp. 161–170.

9. Frances Gorbet, Error Analysis: What the Teacher Can Do: A New Perspective. Ottawa, Research Division, Public Service Commission of Canada. November 1974 (EDRS:ED 100 193).

10. Albert Valdman, Learner Systems and Error Analysis. In Gilbert A. Jarvis (ed.). *Perspective: A New Freedom.* Skokie, Ill., National Textbook Co., 1975, pp. 219–258.

11. John B. Carroll, Characteristics of Successful Second Language Learners. In *Viewpoints on English as a Second Language* (see note 2), pp. 1–7.

12. These students complete three 11-week Spanish courses prior to enrolling in this "intermediate" class. This class stresses reading vocabulary improvement, review of grammatical structures, small group conversation, and the development of basic writing skills.

13. The example sentences are based on common errors produced by intermediate adult learners of English as a second language, French, Spanish, and German.

14. This composition was elicited by Picture Story 23 in L. A. Hill's *Picture Composition Book.* London, Longman, 1960.

15. Because approximately 15 students are enrolled per quarter and because their compositions seldom exceed more than 200 words, it is not overly time-consuming to correct the second drafts. For teachers who have many students who write lengthy compositions, however, a modified approach would be advisable. For example, teachers could draw the students' attention only to serious communication errors, highly stigmatized errors, and to mistakes that occur very frequently in their compositions. This procedure focuses on linguistic problems that need greater and more immediate attention than do less important errors.

16. By dividing the number of words in a composition by the number of errors it contains, one can determine such a ratio. The teacher can then develop a *word:error ratio scale* for evaluation purposes. For example, one could assign number or letter grades to particular ranges of *word:error ratios*, thereby making it possible to compare writing accuracy from one composition to another for any individual or, if desired, between two or more students' compositions.

17. James M. Hendrickson, Evaluating Spontaneous Communication through Systematic Error Analysis. *Foreign Language Annals* 12 (1979), pp. 357–364.

18. Maryruth B. Farnsworth, The Cassette Recorder: A Bonus or a Bother in ESL Composition Correction? *TESOL Quarterly* 8 (1974), pp. 285–291.

19. Christina Bratt Paulston, Structural Pattern Drills: A Classification. *Foreign Language Annals* 4 (1970), pp. 187–193.

20. Michael C. Witbeck, Peer Correction Procedures for Intermediate and Advanced ESL Composition Lessons. *TESOL Quarterly* 10 (1976), pp. 321–326.

11

Responding to Student Writing
Nancy Sommers

More than any other enterprise in the teaching of writing, responding to and commenting on student writing consumes the largest proportion of our time. Most teachers estimate that it takes them at least 20 to 40 minutes to comment on an individual student paper, and those 20 to 40 minutes times 20 students per class, times 8 papers, more or less, during the course of a semester add up to an enormous amount of time. With so much time and energy directed to a single activity, it is important for us to understand the nature of the enterprise. For it seems, paradoxically enough, that although commenting on student writing is the most widely used method for responding to student writing, it is the least understood. We do not know in any definitive way what constitutes thoughtful commentary or what effect, if any, our comments have on helping our students become more effective writers.

Theoretically, at least, we know that we comment on our students' writing for the same reasons professional editors comment on the work of professional writers or for the same reasons we ask our colleagues to read and respond to our own writing. As writers we need and want thoughtful commentary to show us when we have communicated our ideas and when not, raising questions from a reader's point of view that may not have occurred to us as writers. We want to know if our writing has communicated our intended meaning and, if not, what questions or discrepancies our reader sees that we, as writers, are blind to.

In commenting on our students' writing, however, we have an additional pedagogical purpose. As teachers, we know that most students find it difficult to imagine a reader's response in advance, and to use such responses as a guide in composing. Thus, we comment on student writing to dramatize the presence of a reader, to help our students to become that questioning reader themselves, because, ultimately, we believe that becoming such a reader will help them to evaluate what they have written and develop control over their writing.

Even more specifically, however, we comment on student writing because we believe that it is necessary for us to offer assistance to student writers when they are in the process of composing a text, rather than after the text has been completed. Comments create the motive for doing something different in the next draft; thoughtful comments create the motive for revising. Without comments from their teachers or from their peers, student writers will revise in a consistently narrow and predictable way. Without comments from readers, students assume that their writing has communicated their meaning and perceive no need for revising the substance of their text.[2]

Yet as much as we as informed professionals believe in the soundness of this approach to responding to student writing, we also realize that we don't know how our theory squares with teachers' actual practice—do teachers comment and students revise as the theory predicts they should? For the past year my colleagues, Lil Brannon, Cyril Knoblach, and I have been researching this problem, attempting to discover not only what messages teachers give their students through their comments but also what determines which of these comments the students choose to use or to ignore when revising. Our research has been entirely focused on comments teachers write to motivate revisions. We have studied the commenting styles of thirty-five teachers at New York University and the University of Oklahoma, studying the comments these teachers wrote on first and second drafts, and interviewing a representative number of these teachers and their students. All teachers also commented on the same set of three student essays. As an additional reference point, one of the student essays was typed into the computer that had been programmed with the "Writer's Workbench," a package of twenty-three programs developed by Bell Laboratories to help computers and writers work together to improve a text rapidly. Within a few minutes, the computer delivered editorial comments on the student's text, identifying all spelling and punctuation errors, isolating problems with wordy or misused phrases, and suggesting alternatives, offering a stylistic analysis of sentence types, sentence beginnings, and sentence lengths, and finally, giving our freshman essay a Kincaid readability score of 8th grade which, as the computer program informed us, "is a low score for this type of document." The sharp contrast between the teachers' comments and those of the computer highlighted how arbitrary and idiosyncratic most of our teachers' comments are. Besides, the calm, reasonable language of the computer provided quite a contrast to the hostility and mean-spiritedness of most of the teachers' comments.

The first finding from our research on styles of commenting is that *teachers' comments can take students' attention away from their own purposes in writing a particular text and focus that attention on the teachers' purpose in commenting.* The teacher appropriates the text from the student by confusing the student's purpose in writing the text with her own purpose in commenting. Students make the changes the teacher wants rather than those that the student perceives are necessary, since the teachers' concerns imposed on the text create the reasons for the subsequent changes. We have all heard our perplexed students say to us when confused by our comments: "I don't understand how you want me to change this" or "Tell me what you want me to do." In the beginning of the process there was the writer, her words, and her desire to communicate her ideas. But after the comments of the teacher are imposed on the first or second draft, the student's attention dramatically shifts from "This is what I want to say" to "This is what you the teacher are asking me to do."

This appropriation of the text by the teacher happens particularly when teachers identify errors in usage, diction, and style in a first draft and ask students to correct these errors when they revise; such comments give the student an impression of the importance of these errors that is all out of proportion to how they should view these errors at this point in the process. The comments create the concern that these "accidents of discourse" need to be attended to before the meaning of the text is attended to.

It would not be so bad if students were only commanded to correct errors, but more often than not, students are given contradictory messages; they are commanded to edit a sentence to avoid an error or to condense a sentence to achieve greater brevity of style, and then told in the margins that the particular paragraph needs to be more specific or to be developed more. An example of this problem can be seen in the following student paragraph:

> *you need to do more research*
>
> *wordy - be precise* *which Sunday?* *comma needed*
>
> Every year [on one Sunday in the middle of January] tens of millions of people
>
> *word choice*
> cancel all events, plans or work to watch the Super Bowl. This audience includes
>
> *wordy* *Be specific - what reasons?*
> [little boys and girls, old people, and housewives and men.] Many reasons have been
>
> *and why* *what spots?*
> given to explain why the Super Bowl has become so popular that commercial (spots
>
> *awkward*
> cost up to $100,000.00. One explanation is that people like to take sides and root for a
>
> *another what?*
> team. Another is that some people like the pageantry and excitement of the event.
>
> *too colloquial*
> These reasons alone, however, do not explain a happening as big as the Super Bowl.
>
> *This paragraph needs to be expanded in order to be more interesting to a reader.*

In commenting on this draft, the teacher has shown the student how to edit the sentences but then commands the student to expand the paragraph in order to make it more interesting to a reader. The interlinear comments and the marginal comments represent two separate tasks for this student; the interlinear comments encourage the student to see the text as a fixed piece, frozen in time, that just needs some editing. The marginal comments, however, suggest that the meaning of the text is not fixed but rather that the student still needs to develop the meaning by doing some more research. Students are commanded to edit and develop at the same time; the remarkable contradiction of developing a paragraph after editing the sentences in it represents the confusion we encountered in our teachers' commenting styles. These different signals given to students, to edit and develop, to condense and elaborate, represent also the failure of teachers' comments to direct genuine revision of the text as a whole.

Moreover, the comments are worded in such a way that it is difficult for students to know what is the most important problem in the text and what problems are of lesser importance. No scale of concerns is offered to a student, with the result that a comment about spelling or a comment about an awkward sentence is given weight equal to a comment about organization or logic. The comment that seemed to represent this problem best was one teacher's command to his student: "Check your commas and semi-colons and think more about what you are thinking about." The language of the comments makes it difficult for a student to sort out and decide what is most important and what is least important.

When the teacher appropriates the text for the student in this way, students are encouraged to see their writing as a series of parts—words, sentences, paragraphs—and not as a whole discourse. The comments encourage students to believe that their first drafts are finished drafts, not invention drafts, and that all they need to do is patch and polish their writing. That is, teachers' comments do not provide their students with an inherent reason for revising the structure and meaning of their texts, since the comments suggest to students that the meaning of their text is already there, finished, produced, and all that is necessary is a better word or phrase. The processes of revising, editing, and proofreading are collapsed and reduced to a single trivial activity, and the students' misunderstanding of the revision process as a rewording activity is reinforced by their teachers' comments.

It is possible, and it quite often happens, that students follow every comment and fix their texts appropriately as requested, but their texts are not improved substantially, or, even worse, their revised drafts are inferior to their previous drafts. Since the teachers' comments take the students' attention away from their own original purposes, students concentrate more, as I have noted, on what the teachers commanded them to do than on what they are trying to say. Sometimes students do not understand the purpose behind their teachers' comments and take these comments very literally. At other times students understand the comments, but the teacher has misread the text and the comments, unfortunately, are not applicable. For instance, we repeatedly saw comments in which teachers commanded students to reduce and condense what was written, when in fact what the text really needed at this stage was to be expanded in conception and scope.

The process of revising always involves a risk. But, too often revision becomes a balancing act for students in which they make the changes that are requested but do not take the risk of changing anything that was not commented on, even if the students sense that other changes are needed. A more effective text does not often evolve from such changes alone, yet the student does not want to take the chance of reducing a finished, albeit inadequate, paragraph to chaos—to fragments—in order to rebuild it, if such changes have not been requested by the teacher.

The second finding from our study is that *most teachers' comments are not text-specific and could be interchanged, rubber-stamped, from text to text.* The comments are not anchored in the particulars of the students' texts but rather are a series of vague directives that are not text-specific. Students are commanded to "Think more about [their] audience, avoid colloquial language, avoid the passive, avoid prepositions at the end of sentences or conjunctions at the beginning of sentences, be clear, be specific, be precise, but above all, think more about what [they] are thinking about." The comments on the following student paragraph illustrate this problem:

Begin by telling your reader
↓ *what you are going to write about*

In the sixties it was drugs, in the seventies it was rock and roll. Now in the

avoid — "one of the"

eighties, one of the most controversial subjects is nuclear power. The United States is

elaborate

in great need of its own source of power. Because of environmentalists, coal is not an

be specific

acceptable source of energy. ⟦ Solar and wind power have not yet received the

avoid — "it seems"

technology necessary to use them. ⟧ It seems that nuclear power is the only feasible

means right now for obtaining self-sufficient power. However, too large a percentage

be precise

of the population are against nuclear power claiming it is unsafe. With as many

problems as the United States is having concerning energy, it seems a shame that the

public is so quick to "can" a very feasible means of power. Nuclear energy should not

be given up on, but rather, more nuclear plants should be built.

Thesis sentence needed

think more about your reader.

One could easily remove all the comments from this paragraph and rubber-stamp them on another student text, and they would make as much or as little sense on the second text as they do here.

We have observed an overwhelming similarity in the generalities and abstract commands given to students. There seems to be among teachers an accepted, albeit unwritten canon for commenting on student texts. This uniform code of commands, requests, and pleadings demonstrates that the teacher holds a license for vagueness while the student is commanded to be specific. The students we interviewed admitted to having great difficulty with these vague directives. The students stated that when a teacher writes in the margins or as an end comment, "choose precise language," or "think more about your audience," revising becomes a guessing game. In effect, the teacher is saying to the student, "Somewhere in this paper is imprecise language or lack of awareness of an audience and you must find it." The problem presented by these vague commands is compounded for the students when they are not offered any strategies for carrying out these commands. Students are told that they have done something wrong and that there is something in their text that needs to be fixed before the text is acceptable. But to tell students that they have done something wrong is not to tell them what to do about it. In order to offer a useful revision strategy to a student, the teacher must anchor that strategy in the specifics of the student's text. For instance, to tell our student, the author of the above paragraph, "to be specific," or "to elaborate," does not show our student what questions the reader has about the meaning of the text, or what breaks in logic exist, that could be resolved if the writer supplied specific information; nor is the student shown how to achieve the desired specificity.

Instead of offering strategies, the teachers offer what is interpreted by students as rules for composing; the comments suggest to students that writing is just a matter of following the rules. Indeed, the teachers seem to impose a series of abstract rules about written products even when some of them are not appropriate for the specific text the student is creating.[3] For instance, the student author of our sample paragraph presented above is commanded to follow the conventional rules for writing a five-paragraph essay—to begin the introductory paragraph by telling his reader what he is going to say and to end the paragraph with a thesis sentence. Somehow these abstract rules about what five-paragraph products should look like do not seem applicable to the problems this student must confront when revising, nor are the rules specific strategies he could use when revising. There are many inchoate ideas ready to be exploited in this paragraph, but the rules do not help the student to take stock of his (or her) ideas and use the opportunity he has, during revision, to develop those ideas.

The problem here is a confusion of process and product; what one has to say about the process is different from what one has to say about the product. Teachers who use this method of commenting are formulating their comments as if these drafts were finished drafts and were not going to be revised. Their commenting vocabularies have not been adapted to revision and they comment on first drafts as if they were justifying a grade or as if the first draft were the final draft.

Our summary finding, therefore, from this research on styles of commenting is that the news from the classroom is not good. For the most part, teachers do not respond to student writing with the kind of thoughtful commentary which will help students to engage with the issues they are writing about or which will help them think about their purposes and goals in writing a specific text. In defense of our teachers, however, they told us that responding to student writing was rarely stressed in their teacher-training or in writing workshops; they had been trained in various prewriting techniques, in constructing assignments, and in evaluating papers for grades, but rarely in the process of reading a student text for meaning or in offering commentary to motivate revision. The problem is that most of us as teachers of writing have been trained to read and interpret literary texts for meaning, but, unfortunately, we have not been trained to act upon the same set of assumptions in reading student texts as we follow in reading literary texts.[4] Thus, we read student texts with biases about what the writer should have said or about what he or she should have written, and our biases determine how we will comprehend the text. We read with our preconceptions and preoccupations, expecting to find errors, and the result is that we find errors and misread our students' texts.[5] We find what we look for; instead of reading and responding to the meaning of a text, we correct our students' writing. We need to reverse this approach. Instead of finding errors or showing students how to patch up parts of their texts, we need to sabotage our students' conviction that the drafts they have written are complete and coherent. Our comments need to offer students revision tasks of a different order of complexity and sophistication from the ones that they themselves identify, by forcing students back into the chaos, back to the point where they are shaping and restructuring their meaning.[6]

For if the content of a student text is lacking in substance and meaning, if the order of the parts must be rearranged significantly in the next draft, if paragraphs must be restructured for logic and clarity, then many sentences are likely to be changed or deleted anyway. There seems to be no point in having students correct usage errors or condense sentences that are likely to disappear before the next draft is completed. In fact, to identify such problems in a text at this early first draft stage, when such problems are likely to abound, can give a student a disproportionate sense of their importance at this stage in the writing process.[7] In responding to our students' writing, we should be guided by the recognition that it is not spelling or usage problems that we as writers first worry about when drafting and revising our texts.

We need to develop an appropriate level of response for commenting on a first draft, and to differentiate that from the level suitable to a second or third draft. Our comments need to be suited to the draft we are reading. In a first or second draft, we need to respond as any reader would, registering questions, reflecting befuddlement, and noting places where we are puzzled about the meaning of the text. Comments should point to breaks in logic, disruptions in meaning, or missing information. Our goal in commenting on early drafts should be to engage students with the issues they are considering and help them clarify their purposes and reasons in writing their specific text.

For instance, the major rhetorical problem of the essay written by the student who wrote the first paragraph (the paragraph on nuclear power) quoted above was that the student had two principal arguments running through his text, each of which brought the other into question. On the one hand, he argued that we must use nuclear power, unpleasant as it is, because we have nothing else to use; though nuclear energy is a problematic source of energy, it is the best of a bad lot. On the other hand, he also argued that nuclear energy is really quite safe and therefore should be our primary resource. Comments on this student's first draft need to point out this break in logic and show the student that if we accept his first argument, then his second argument sounds fishy. But if we accept his second argument, his first argument sounds contradictory. The teacher's comments need to engage this student writer with this basic rhetorical and conceptual problem in his first draft rather than impose a series of abstract commands and rules upon his text.

Written comments need to be viewed not as an end in themselves—a way for teachers to satisfy themselves that they have done their jobs—but rather as a means for helping students to become more effective writers. As a means for helping students, they have limitations; they are, in fact, disembodied remarks—

one absent writer responding to another absent writer. The key to successful commenting is to have what is said in the comments and what is done in the classroom mutually reinforce and enrich each other. Commenting on papers assists the writing course in achieving its purpose; classroom activities and the comments we write to our students need to be connected. Written comments need to be an extension of the teacher's voice—an extension of the teacher as reader. Exercises in such activities as revising a whole text or individual paragraphs together in class, noting how the sense of the whole dictates the smaller changes, looking at options, evaluating actual choices, and then discussing the effect of these changes on revised drafts—such exercises need to be designed to take students through the cycles of revising and to help them overcome their anxiety about revising: that anxiety we all feel at reducing what looks like a finished draft into fragments and chaos.

The challenge we face as teachers is to develop comments which will provide an inherent reason for students to revise; it is a sense of revision as discovery, as a repeated process of beginning again, as starting out new, that our students have not learned. We need to show our students how to seek, in the possibility of revision, the dissonances of discovery—to show them through our comments why new choices would positively change their texts, and thus to show them the potential for development implicit in their own writing.

EXPLORING THE IDEAS — *Theoretical Discussion*

QUESTION 1

Background   Sommers points out that teachers comment on students' essays because " as writers we need and want thoughtful commentary to show us when we have communicated our ideas and when not, raising questions from a reader's point of view that may have not occurred to us as writers" (page 160).

Discussion   This certainly is one very essential reason for commenting on students' papers. What other reasons are there for responding to students' papers? Are there any special reasons for commenting on the writing of nonnative speakers as opposed to native speakers?

QUESTION 2

Background   Sommers comments that students are often asked to edit and develop their writing at the same time; this often requires that the student correct or edit a sentence which eventually needs to be eliminated or completely revised in the context of the total essay. Furthermore, students are given little sense of the relative weight of a teacher's comments, since specific comments about form exist alongside substantive comments about content.

Discussion   What strategies could you employ in correcting papers to give students some indication of the relative weight of your comments? What techniques could you use to help students separate the tasks of developing their ideas and editing specific problems in form?

Composition Evaluation

ACTIVITY 1

Background   As Sommers points out, "Comments create the motive for doing something different in the next draft; thoughtful comments create the motive for revising. . . . Without comments from readers, students assume that their writing has communicated their meaning and perceive no need for revising the substance of their text" (pages 160–161).

Application   Refer to the essay included under the Raimes article entitled My Experience and write comments which you believe would help the student to clarify her meaning and revise her paper.

ACTIVITY 2

Background   Sommers makes a convincing argument that rather than focusing on errors "our comments need to offer students revision tasks of a different order of complexity and sophistication from the ones they themselves identify, by forcing students back into chaos, back to the point where they are shaping and restructuring their meaning" (page 166). Peter Elbow's "center of gravity" response scheme helps a reader to formulate such types of comments. He suggests that a reader read a paper and respond in the following way (1973. *Writing without Teachers*. New York, Oxford University Press, pages 86–87):

a. First tell very quickly what you found to be the main points, main feelings, or centers of gravity. Just sort of say what comes to mind for fifteen seconds, for example, "Let's see, very sad; the death seemed to be the main event; um . . . but the joke she told was very prominent; lots of clothes."
b. Then summarize it into a single sentence.
c. Then choose *one word* from the writing which best summarizes it.
d. Then choose a word that isn't in the writing which best summarizes it.

   Do this informally. Don't plan or think too much about it. The point is to show the writer what things he or she made stand out most in your head, what shape the thing takes in your consciousness. This isn't a test to see whether you got the words right. It's a test to see whether the words got you right. Be sure to use different language from the language of the writing. This ensures that the writer is getting it filtered through your perception and experience—not just parroted.

Application   Refer to the essay included under the Flower article in which the student was asked to define the characteristics of a typical American. First respond to the essay using Elbow's response scheme. Then write several comments and questions which would help the student reshape and restructure the essay to include more of the ideas contained in his protocol.

Applying Theoretical Concepts

ACTIVITY 1

Background   Sommers maintains that the main reason we comment on students' papers is to give writers thoughtful feedback which will help them to revise their work. Ultimately, however, writers need to be able to evaluate their own work. In a recent study, Susan Miller (1982. How Writers Evaluate Their Own Writing. *College Composition and Communication* 33, 2:175–183) investigated what criteria professional writers and students use in evaluating their own writing. One thing she found was that while almost all students thought their good writing was writing that the teacher liked, only 30 percent of the professional writers based the success of their writing on a positive response from their readers. Professional writers, in contrast to students, often based the evaluation of their work on whether or not the finished product matched their own intention of what they had set out to do and on whether or not they learned anything in the process of writing it.

Application   Design a self-evaluation form which you could give to your students to aid them in analyzing their own papers. In the form, pose questions which would help students do such things as identify their purpose in writing, indicate what they had learned in the process of writing, and specify what they see as the paper's strength and weaknesses.

NOTES

1. C. H. Knoblach and Lil Brannon, Teacher Commentary on Student Writing: The State of the Art. *Freshman English News* 10 (fall 1981), 1–3.

2. For an extended discussion of revision strategies of student writers see Nancy Sommers, Revision Strategies of Student Writers and Experienced Adult Writers, *College Composition and Communication* 31 (December 1980), 378–388.

3. Nancy Sommers and Ronald Schleifer, Means and Ends: Some Assumptions of Student Writers. *Composition and Teaching* 2 (December 1980), 69–76.

4. Janet Emig and Robert P. Parker, Jr., Responding to Student Writing: Building a Theory of the Evaluating Process, unpublished paper, Rutgers University.

5. For an extended discussion of this problem see Joseph Williams, The Phenomenology of Error. *College Composition and Communication* 32 (May 1981), 152–168.

6. Ann Berthoff, *The Making of Meaning.* Montclair, N.J., Boynton/Cook Publishers, 1981.

7. W. U. McDonald, The Revising Process and the Marking of Student Papers. *College Composition and Communication* 24 (May 1978), 167–170.